Perspectives on Dodd–Frank and Finance

Perspectives on Dodd–Frank and Finance

edited by Paul H. Schultz

The MIT Press
Cambridge, Massachusetts
London, England

MIT Press books may be purchased at special quantity discounts for business or sales promotional use. For information, please email special_sales@mitpress.mit.edu.

This book was set in PalatinoLTStd by the MIT Press. Printed and bound in the United States of America.

Library of Congress Cataloging-in-Publication Data

Perspectives on Dodd–Frank and finance / edited by Paul H. Schultz.
 pages cm
Conference proceedings.
Includes bibliographical references and index.
ISBN 978-0-262-02803-5 (hardcover : alk. paper)
1. Finance—Government policy—United States. 2. United States. Dodd–Frank Wall Street Reform and Consumer Protection Act. I. Schultz, Paul H., 1956– editor of compilation.
HG181.P395 2014
332.0973—dc23
2014007223

10 9 8 7 6 5 4 3 2 1

To Margie, Emma, and Kate

Contents

Acknowledgments

This book is based on a conference on "Dodd–Frank and the Future of Finance" that was held in Washington, DC, on June 13–14, 2013. It was organized and sponsored by the University of Notre Dame's Center for the Study of Financial Regulation, whose mission is to promote rigorous economic analysis of current and proposed financial regulation. I am grateful to Phil Corporon, Carol Elliot, Margaret Forster, and Roger Huang for their ongoing support of the center and its mission.

This conference was supported by a generous grant from NERA (National Economic Research Associates), and several people from NERA contributed to the discussions as audience members during the conference. Planning a conference is a lot of work, and this one could not have taken place without the efforts of Karma Grundy, Julia Lee, Rob Lee, and Marlene Wasikowski. I owe special debts to James Overdahl and Chester Spatt for their advice as well as their participation in the conference.

Deborah Cantor-Adams and Rosemary Winfield did a wonderful job of editing the book and making all of us sound more articulate in the process. Finally, I am grateful for the suggestions and advice of Jane Macdonald and Emily Taber, which improved the book in many ways.

1 Introduction

Paul H. Schultz

To understand the origins of the Dodd–Frank Wall Street Reform and Consumer Protection Act of 2010, it is helpful to recall the events of September 2008. On September 7, mortgage giants Fannie Mae (the Federal National Mortgage Association) and Freddie Mac (the Federal Home Loan Corporation) were taken over by the government. On Sunday, September 14, Bank of America purchased failing broker and investment banker Merrill Lynch. On the following day, Lehman Brothers, with $639 billion in assets, filed for bankruptcy. It was by far the largest U.S. bankruptcy ever. The next day, September 16, American International Group (AIG) received an $85 billion bailout from the Federal Reserve to remain solvent. On that same day, Reserve Primary Money Fund "broke the buck" when the net asset value of the money market fund shares dropped below $1. On September 17, the Securities and Exchange Commission (SEC) announced a temporary ban on short selling of financial stocks. Four days later, Goldman Sachs and Morgan Stanley became bank holding companies, giving them access to the Federal Reserve discount window and subjecting them to greater regulation by the Fed. On September 25, in the largest bank failure in U.S. history, Washington Mutual Bank was closed, and its assets and branches were sold to JPMorgan Chase.

In September 2008, the collapse of the U.S. financial system seemed a real possibility. Dodd–Frank was written with the events of 2008 in mind. Its primary purpose is to prevent another crisis, and it does this in a number of ways. It creates the Financial Stability Oversight Council (FSOC) to identify and defuse systemic risks, it provides for the enhanced supervision of large financial institutions, it limits the activities of banks through the Volcker Rule, and it mandates centralized clearings of swaps. Dodd–Frank also attempts to make it easier to resolve failing institutions through bankruptcy, if possible, or through the Orderly Liquidation Authority (OLA). Making it easier to resolve failing institutions, it eliminates too-big-to-fail bailouts and restores incentives for market discipline of financial institutions.

Other provisions of Dodd–Frank, however, have nothing to do with systemic risk or the financial crisis. In one of the panel discussions included in this book (chapter 5), Jim Overdahl likens the legislative process that led to Dodd–Frank to a bar fight in an old western movie. Rather than hitting the guy who started the fight, brawlers take a swing at the guy they have been waiting for a chance to hit. Parts of Dodd–Frank are not a response to the financial crisis; they are bits of legislation that proponents have sought to enact for years.

Dodd–Frank also avoids taking up some of the major issues of the financial crisis. Fannie Mae and Freddie Mac were at the center of the crisis and were taken over by the government in September 2008. More than $180 billion has been poured into them, but Fannie Mae and Freddie Mac are ignored in Dodd–Frank.

The Contents of This Book

This book originated in panel discussions and presentations at a June 2013 conference on Dodd–Frank that was sponsored by the Center for the Study of Financial Regulation at the University of Notre Dame. The conference brought together prominent academics in finance, law, and economics with regulators and practitioners.

Dodd–Frank is far too large and regulates far too many aspects of the financial sector to be covered in its entirety in one conference or in this book. There are a number of important parts of Dodd–Frank that we will not discuss. One is Dodd–Frank's new regulations of the credit-rating agencies. Dodd–Frank requires the SEC to write rules requiring credit agencies to issue annual reports on internal controls, to reveal information on their ratings methodologies, and to disclose performance statistics. Dodd–Frank also requires all federal agencies to review existing regulations that require use of credit ratings and to substitute an appropriate standard of credit worthiness. It is not clear what this standard should be.

A part of Title VII that we do not discuss is section 737, which allows the Commodity Futures Trading Commission (CFTC) to impose position limits on futures contracts on twenty-eight physical commodities and on economically equivalent options and swaps. Backers of position limits say that they will prevent market manipulation such as the Hunt brothers' 1979 attempt to corner the silver market. Position limits could also prevent market disruptions that might occur when large positions are liquidated. Critics of position limits say that it will restrict legitimate hedging activities of large traders.

Title IX of Dodd–Frank addresses corporate governance and executive compensation issues. Section 952 requires compensation committees of publicly traded companies to be independent of the company. Section 954 requires companies to put clawback policies into place to prevent executives from being compensated on the basis of false or misleading financial statements. Section 956 prohibits financial companies from using incentive compensation that could lead to financial loss. It is reasonable to ask what executive compensation has to do with the financial crisis. Some have argued that incentive-based compensation of chief executive officers (CEOs) of financial institutions led them to take more risks before the crisis. For the most part, though, these are off-the-shelf provisions that governance activists have sought to enact for many years.

Dodd–Frank also regulates some areas of finance that have been lightly regulated. Title IV requires advisers to hedge funds to register with the SEC and keep records. Similarly, section 975 of the act requires municipal advisers to register with the SEC. These advisers include people who provide advice to states and municipalities on issuance of bonds, the investment of bond proceeds, or the use of swaps

Section 342 of the Dodd–Frank Act requires each of the following federal financial agencies—the Department of the Treasury, Federal Deposit Insurance Corporation (FDIC), Federal Housing Finance Agency (FHFA), Federal Reserve System's Board of Directors, each of the Fed's banks, National Credit Union Administration, Office of the Comptroller of the Currency, Securities and Exchange Commission, and Consumer Financial Protection Bureau (CFPB)—to establish an Office of Minority and Women Inclusion. These offices are required to develop procedures to ensure "the fair inclusion and utilization of minorities in the agency's workforce." Section 342 also authorizes the government to compel financial institutions to use more women and minorities in their workforces. This may be a worthy goal, but it has nothing to do with the financial crisis or making the financial system more stable.

These parts of Dodd–Frank and others that we do not discuss here may prove to be important. But with the possible exception of credit agency regulation, they will play a secondary role, if any, in preventing another financial crisis.

This book focuses on a few important parts of Dodd–Frank that are intended to prevent another financial crisis. These include reform of the banking system, exchange trading and centralized clearing of swaps, liquidation of troubled financial institutions, the Volcker Rule, the Consumer Financial Protection Bureau, and mortgage-backed securities. The Consumer Financial Protection Bureau is covered not only because the new agency is large and powerful but also because many believe that sales of inappropriate mortgages to homebuyers was an important contributor to the financial crisis. We also discuss new disclosure requirements for public companies. These are among the parts of Dodd–Frank that have little to do with systemic risk. We discuss them because they establish the important precedent of using SEC disclosures for purposes other than the protection of investors.

It is impossible to cover Dodd–Frank in its entirety in this book, but it is also difficult to discuss it in isolation. To evaluate whether Dodd–Frank will prevent a new financial crisis, we need to understand what caused the last one, and several chapters address this issue. Political considerations and the nature of the regulatory process limit what Dodd–Frank can do and influence what will make it effective. Several contributors discuss the political process behind the law. Finally, Dodd–Frank needs to be considered in the context of Basel III (the Third Basel Accord) and other regulatory initiatives, and these are also topics of discussion in many parts of the book.

Although many of the same themes and issues appear throughout this book, the chapters are meant to stand by themselves. Readers should be able to jump into the book at any point, read the chapters in any order, or focus only the issues that interest them.

Economic principles should play a primary role in the design of financial regulations, but economic principles are often ignored in the practice of regulation. This is a theme of chapter 2, Economic Principles, Government Policy, and the Market Crisis, where Chester Spatt discusses the actions that government took in response to the financial crisis. Among other things, Spatt talks about the need for rules rather than discretion in government policy and regulation. Discretion leads to uncertainty—which chills investment and financial market participation.

The reader who is interested in the regulation of systemically important financial institutions (SIFIs) will find several chapters of interest. In chapter 3, The Basics of Too Big to Fail, Lawrence J. White discusses the characteristics of financial institutions that make them susceptible to runs. He also describes the financial condition of the largest U.S. financial companies at the end of 2007 and how that contributed to the financial crisis. Finally, he offers policy prescriptions for dealing with TBTF institutions in the future.

Similar issues are discussed in chapter 4, Creating a Responsive, Accountable, Market-Driven Financial System. Here, the FDIC's vice chair, Thomas M. Hoenig, expresses concern about the leverage and complexity of the largest financial institutions. He observes that broker-dealer activities within SIFIs are perceived to receive a large subsidy from implicit government guarantees. He proposes pushing broker-dealer activities out of banks and away from the FDIC's safety net. His suggestions go further than the Volcker Rule: he would like banks to drop market making as well as proprietary trading.

SIFIs are also a subject of chapter 5, Panel Discussion on Banking Reform, a discussion that was moderated by James Overdahl. In this chapter, Anil K Kashyap argues that runs of institutions involved in maturity transformation (that is, financing long-term assets with short-term liabilities) were at the center of the financial crisis. Dodd–Frank, he contends, does little to address this problem. Anjan Thakor notes that high leverage can create systemic risk in subtle ways and questions whether the Financial Stability Oversight Council (FSOC) that was created by Dodd–Frank will be aware of these risks in time to intervene. He proposes a novel form of equity capital that reverts to regulators, not creditors, if a bank is bailed out. This form of equity would keep creditors' incentives to monitor intact with higher equity capital. Finally, John Walsh claims that large financial institutions are in much sounder shape than they were during the crisis. He attributes this to Dodd–Frank, Basel III, and better enforcement of existing regulations. Dodd–Frank is mentioned only briefly in chapters 4 and 5. The issues taken up in these chapters include maturity transformation and the leverage, complexity, and liquidity of financial institutions. But although these issues can be discussed without invoking Dodd–Frank, Dodd–Frank requires the Fed to tackle them under the enhanced prudential-supervision requirements of section 165 and allows the Fed to address them at nonbank financial institutions. Arguably, this is the most important thing that Dodd–Frank does to reduce systemic risk.

Finally, the reader with an interest in the regulation of large banks and other SIFIs will want to read chapter 6, Panel Discussion on Stability, Resolution, and Dodd–Frank," a discussion that was moderated by Arthur Wilmarth. Here, James R. Barth discusses regulatory failure.

Most major financial laws in the United States have been a reaction to a crisis. Still, as Barth argues, problems arise because regulators do not enforce existing laws. He is skeptical that the FSOC will prove effective in identifying and reducing systemic risk. John Dearie argues that the enhanced prudential regulation from Dodd–Frank, along with other factors, has resulted in far stronger financial institutions. David Skeel concludes the panel with a thorough, careful, and illuminating discussion of Dodd–Frank's Title II provisions for resolving insolvent institutions.

Section 612, Restriction on Conversions of Banks (the Volcker Rule), of Dodd–Frank is intended to make banks less risky by keeping them out of the business of proprietary trading. In chapter 7, The Origins and Intent of the Volcker Rule, Priyank Gandhi discusses the rationale behind the rule. He then cites evidence that the correlation between bank's revenues from trading and interest income is negative. The negative correlation implies that prohibiting proprietary trading will make banks riskier, not safer.

Readers who are interested in the Volcker Rule should also read chapter 8, Panel Discussion on the Volker Rule. In a lively exchange of views, Charles W. Calomiris contends that proprietary trading may indeed be a core function of banking. He worries that Dodd–Frank will limit market making and drive financial activities offshore. Matthew Richardson argues that principal trading was a source of systemic risk and is best pushed out of banks. He goes on to say that simple rules are harder to game than complex regulations and suggests that a safe harbor that limits the size of banks' inventories of securities would be preferable to the current form of the Volcker Rule.

Chapter 9, Panel Discussion on the Consumer Financial Protection Bureau," which was moderated by Shane Corwin, examines a new agency that wields enormous power over banks and other financial institutions. This chapter should be read by those with an interest in banking or an interest in consumer protection. In discussing the CFPB, both Jeff Bloch and Todd J. Zywicki are critical of the CFPB's governance structure. Rather than a commission of five appointees (like the SEC, FTC, and CFTC), the CFPB has one director with almost complete power over the agency. He or she cannot be fired without cause, and the agency's budget is not subject to congressional oversight. Bloch goes on to criticize the expensive information requests made by the agency and the costly, adversarial examinations conducted by the CFPB. Zywicki says that the motivation for the CFPB is based on a misinterpretation of the causes of foreclosures during the crisis. He contends that the foreclosures, for the most part, were not a result of the sale of risky and complex mortgages by banks to naive borrowers. Rather, foreclosures occurred because sophisticated borrowers rationally walked away from mortgages on homes that had fallen in value.

This chapter is a bit one-sided in its treatment of the CFPB. Both Jeff Bloch and Todd J. Zywicki are critical of the bureau's governance and policies. The CFPB was invited to participate on the panel, but declined to do so.

AIG was bailed out because it was the counterparty to many financial institutions on an enormous amount of over-the-counter derivatives. Dodd–Frank seeks to eliminate systemic risk from derivatives by forcing swap trading onto exchanges and by requiring centralized clearing. This is covered in chapter 10, Panel Discussion on Derivatives Reform. Swaps and other derivatives trade all over the world, and in this session Amy K. Edwards and Raymond P. H. Fishe discuss some of the complications of regulating derivatives that can be traded abroad by U.S. institutions or in the United States by foreign institutions. Robert McDonald and Craig Pirrong discuss the possibility that a central clearinghouse may increase rather than decrease systemic risk. Clearinghouses tend to have cut-and-dried rules, while the flexibility of the over-the-counter market may make it better able to handle crises. Most observers agree that the decline in home prices and the subsequent defaults on mortgage-backed securities were the catalyst for the financial crisis. So Dodd–Frank includes provisions that will have a big effect on the real estate market. The reader who is interested in how Dodd–Frank tackles mortgage-backed securities will find two chapters of particular interest. In chapter 11, Mortgage Reform under the Dodd–Frank Act, Mark A. Calabria discusses Dodd–Frank's qualified residential mortgage requirements and their potential effects on mortgage availability. Readers who are interested in the CFPB will also want to read this chapter because Calabria discusses the CFPB's determination of qualified mortgage standards. In chapter 12, The Dodd–Frank Act and the Regulation of Risk Retention in Mortgage-Backed Securities, Cem Demiroglu and Christopher M. James examine the incentive effects of securitization on originators' incentives to gather soft information and the ways that securitization is likely to be affected by Dodd–Frank's requirement that originators retain some of the risk of securitized mortgages.

In chapter 13, The Controversial New Disclosure Requirements in Dodd–Frank, I discuss the "conflict minerals" rule and the "internal pay equity" rule. These are among the parts of Dodd–Frank that have little or nothing to do with preventing a crisis or reducing systemic risk. Section 1502, Conflict Minerals, requires companies to report whether gold, tantalum, tin, and tungsten that are used in a company's products come from the Democratic Republic of the Congo or surrounding countries. If they do, the company needs to report whether the minerals are conflict free. Subsection b of section 953, Executive Compensation Disclosures, requires companies to report the ratio of the median employee pay to the CEO's compensation. These parts of Dodd–Frank are controversial but probably relatively unimportant by themselves. I believe, however, that they establish an important precedent. Investor protection has always been the mission of the SEC. These Dodd–Frank provisions require SEC disclosure as a means to end the armed conflict in the Congo and to reduce differences in compensation—objectives that have nothing to do with investor protection.

Chapter 14 concludes the book. In this chapter, I discuss the implementation of Dodd–Frank. More than three years after the law was passed, fewer than half of the rules that Dodd–Frank mandates have been completed. I discuss the complexity of the required rules, the difficulty of getting agencies to work together, and other reasons for the slow implementation of the law. Finally, I summarize what the contributors to this book say about whether Dodd–Frank is likely to prevent another crisis.

Readers of this book will discover that the contributors disagree on many things. There are differences in opinion on the Volcker Rule, the level of equity capital needed by banks, and the causes of the 2008 financial crisis. In this light, it is clear that this volume is not the final word on Dodd–Frank. It is a guide to some of the issues and questions that we will face in the coming months and years as Dodd–Frank rules are written, challenged in the courts, and implemented.

2 Economic Principles, Government Policy, and the Market Crisis

Chester Spatt

Much can be learned from economic principles and policies about the challenges that the economy faced during the financial crisis that began in 2007. As they reacted to dramatic challenges and unprecedented concerns, policymakers found it easy to avoid internalizing some crucial implications of economic principles for the new and challenging contexts that they confronted. Financial economics has much to contribute to policy discussions. From a research perspective, these debates suggest interesting issues for financial theory and financial economics, much of which is potentially relevant to the implementation of the Dodd–Frank Wall Street Reform and Consumer Protection Act of 2010. The nominal goal of Dodd–Frank was to eliminate future crises and thereby avoid the need to address the types of policy issues that arose during the financial crisis and are the focus of much of this chapter.

The implications of a number of concepts including—(a) utility maximization and market clearing, (b) resource constraints, (c) the costliness of policy uncertainty and benefits to predictability, and (d) the forward-looking nature of economic incentives—are important for evaluating policy. These concepts are relevant for understanding deleveraging, changes in the availability of credit (and its counterpart, the adequacy of bank capital), changes in the provision of public goods, predictability and government policy, as well as information and capital injections, systemic risk, and bank supervision. I do not explicitly discuss adverse selection and moral hazard here because those themes have received relatively more attention in the crisis and, despite my prior service as the chief economist at the Securities and Exchange Commission (SEC), the much maligned and misunderstood repeal of uptick restrictions on short sales.[1]

Deleveraging and the Availability of Credit

Deleveraging and the closely related contraction of credit are central to the evolution of our economy in the financial crisis, which has indirectly emphasized the recapitalization of financial institutions and the role played by bank capital (equity). In this section, I address how events affected the supply of and demand for loans and loan pricing. As a byproduct of declining housing values and elevated expected housing loan losses, valuation declines for these loans were even larger than the expected loan losses due to liquidity and risk-aversion-induced state-price declines.[2] Without weighing in on the extensive debate about "mark to market accounting," the economic relevance of the valuation of loans can be appreciated by pointing to the fundamental maturity mismatch that arose because financial intermediaries' funding was shorter term than its lending, which is central to the role of financial intermediation. In fact, the use of short-term funding increased by firms whose creditworthiness deteriorated during the crisis. Funding risk and confidence highlight the relevance of interim valuations. Systematic default states reflect changes in discount rates as well as cash flows.[3]

The attention to deleveraging raises the question of what the optimal leverage for such intermediaries is. Although I do not develop an explicit theory for this (with frictions that lead to departures from the Modigliani–Miller theorem's capital structure irrelevance propositions), it is reasonable to presume that many financial institutions were leveraged excessively. This is reflected by the (unexpectedly) large observed costs of financial distress, especially given the common aggregate component to housing prices and loan valuations and the difficulties that have resulted from debt overhang. In light of the potential for governmental bailouts, which spurs excess risk taking, the social costs of debt financing exceed the private costs.[4] The need to reduce leverage together with dramatic "capital holes" that were created by capital losses threatened the stability of many financial institutions and led to a severe contraction of credit in late 2008. Therefore, federal authorities then moved forward with unprecedented measures to inject capital into the financial system. Although Congress has criticized banks that received Troubled Asset Recovery Program (TARP) funds for not lending more, my presumption is that increased lending would not have been realistic in many situations given the desire to reduce leverage and the capital holes in financial institutions.[5] In fact, this experience calls into question the way in which our economy bears and allocates the correlated risks in mortgage loans, especially for debt contracts with tiny downpayments.[6]

One barrier to the ability of financial institutions to deleverage was preexisting credit lines. In particular, the "breaking of the buck" by Reserve Primary Fund and its related suspension of liquidity led to a half-trillion-dollar run on the money market fund industry, which helped feed a collapse of commercial paper and an aggressive drawing of credit lines. Financial institutions learned that the credit lines that they had issued were not as diversifiable as they thought because in weak states of the economy, the option to draw on existing credit lines is likely to be heavily exercised.[7] My suspicion is that bank pleas to companies not to draw their lines at the peak of the financial crisis were counterproductive and that some companies responded by increasing their draws because of concerns about the bank's liquidity or possible cancellation of the credit line. What are the implications of this for credit lines? Due to the aggregate nature of the risk, I anticipate that lower credit lines will be offered at relatively higher spreads than prior to the financial crisis and that new types of credit lines could arise that would be contingent on aggregate variables, such as offering an option on credit except in particularly problematic aggregate circumstances (so far, I am unaware of evidence of these contingent lines).

The consequences of deleveraging by consumers and the financial crisis for the macroeconomy are important. A dramatic decline in wealth included a more than 50 percent decline in equity values from the prior peak to the trough. Unlike other recessions in recent decades, this decline in equity pricing was accompanied by dramatic reductions in the values of residential and commercial real estate, so the overall permanent wealth effect was much larger than in other recessions. These changes in asset values were so sharp that they jeopardized many lenders and seriously affected the economy. During earlier booms, many felt that the consumer drove much of those booms, so in reverse, the wealth effect substantially reduced consumer demand after the large adverse shock to wealth. Additionally, many consumers learned in 2008 that the rates of return that they were anticipating from asset markets had been far too high and that their savings had been inadequate. Investors now realize that they cannot count on measured savings rates near zero to provide adequate savings, and reduced consumption and increased savings rates have emerged.[8] At the same time, the decline in asset prices in the aftermath of the financial crisis reflects higher required returns, including risk premium.

Although two consequences of the low state of the economy were
reduced demand for lending and reduced supply of available funds
due to limited bank and market capital, the borrowing opportunities
for risky borrowers are likely to continue to be limited as a result of
supply responses. First, suppliers of funds have learned about the riskiness of weak credits.[9] Second, changes in the rules of the game with
respect to high-risk borrowers and potential fears of further changes in
the rules will make lenders particularly reluctant to lend to weak borrowers going forward. This may be an important ongoing cost associated with the Dodd–Frank legislation. Both the relative treatment of
automobile bondholders compared to United Automobile Workers
(UAW) debt claimants and credit card legislation that makes it more
difficult to raise rates on delinquent borrowers illustrate this theme.
More recently, the potential treatment of Detroit's general obligation
creditors as unsecured creditors also illustrates this point. The limited
response by Michigan to the situation helped restrict access by other
Michigan municipalities to the bond market due to the lack of state
enforcement.[10] This highlights actions by the government that are
adverse to investors and increases in political and regulatory risk, particularly for funding high-risk and politically sensitive borrowers,
which will affect their access to private investor capital.[11] These risks
need to be understood much better. Indeed, many observers have
noted that the District of Columbia is now at the center of U.S. capital
markets.

Public Goods, Fiscal Policy, and Resource Constraints

Considerable attention has focused on the federal government's use of
fiscal stimulus to offset some of the economic contraction induced by
the extraordinary financial shocks. However, wealth effects raise interesting issues about the composition of the stimulus. To explore this, I
suggest a simple static model. Suppose that there are n identical consumers whose utility function has as arguments private goods and
public goods.[12] As in the tradition in public finance, assume that the
public goods are not excludible so that the same units of the public
goods are being consumed by all. The consumers consume distinct
units of the private goods. Consider the effect of an increase in wealth
across consumers for the demand for the public goods as well as the
private goods. In the neoclassical consumer model, a standard assumption is that the demand for private goods is normal—that is, demand

for each good increases in wealth, so we extend that to the public goods. In the face of reduced wealth, we would optimally allocate fewer resources (compared to the prior optimal) to the public goods that are normal goods as well as to the private goods.[13] However, increased purchases of public goods (that is, government spending) in the immediate aftermath of the financial crisis distorted the allocation of the public goods in the opposite direction.

This raises interesting issues about the composition of fiscal stimulus and the use of tax cuts or government spending to offset the liquidity shocks and wealth effects that arise in "bad" states. The traditional perspectives on this issue highlight that tax cuts are saved as well as consumed (the Keynesian argument in favor of increased government spending rather than tax cuts) and that tax cuts have desirable incentive effects (an argument against increased government spending). My argument above in isolation suggests that given the significant reduction in wealth experienced, we should decrease the supply and equilibrium quantity of the public goods, along with the private goods themselves that are naturally adjusting and for which the tax cuts offset to only a limited degree.[14] This effect was potentially much stronger in the great recession than typical recessions because of the very large wealth effects that reduced indirect utility.[15]

There is an interesting analogy to this in corporate finance. One choice that is open to firms with excess resources is to pay dividends rather than undertake new projects that were not previously viewed as optimal. In the corporate finance context, the firm should not undertake projects that fail the net present value test. After we recognize that in the policy context of the great recession, not all additional government spending increased utility compared to the alternatives, it is helpful to focus stimulus on the specific projects that will benefit consumers and the economy over time because of their short-term stimulus or long-term utility benefits, such as those public goods that are inferior (that is, have demand declining in wealth). For example, with public goods, this latter point suggests that in the low-wealth states, there should be relatively more spending on goods (such as job retraining and health insurance for children) that are at least arguably inferior goods compared to those whose demand increases in wealth (such as new highways and other infrastructure improvements).[16]

During the great recession, we witnessed the role played by budget and resource constraints.[17] Many have expressed concern about the projected explosion in the ratio of debt to gross domestic product

(GDP), which is not simply a consequence of the great recession. Observers have pointed to a long-term Medicare spending crisis, the importance of keeping resources available for future emergencies (such as September 11, hurricane Katrina, and the financial meltdown), the limits that some European countries faced in offering fiscal stimulus, negative outlooks on sovereign debt, and China's huge investment in U.S. Treasury securities. Somewhat related to this, the active and aggressive intervention of the Federal Reserve System in long-term fixed-income markets leads to interesting signal extraction problems that are associated with the informational content of prices in markets that may be manipulated by the central bank by its asset purchases and for which policy uncertainty is considerable.[18]

A related context illustrates the importance of resource issues. Pension plans have long been substantially underfunded because they discount liabilities at an expected return that improperly adjusts for risk.[19] This is one aspect of the financial crisis that I did appreciate in advance. In a speech that I made while serving as the SEC's chief economist, I pointed to the inevitability of underfunding of pension plans with fixed liabilities and substantial equity holdings and the problematic aspect of essentially projecting asset returns at too high a level.[20] Although asset values have recovered to well above precrisis levels, resource constraints continue to be severe in the pension context as reflected by dramatically lower bond yields, which has potential systemic consequences.

Predictability and Government Policy

An important theme to explore with respect to government policy is the central role that is played by predictable policies and clear rules of the game. Unambiguous contractual arrangements facilitate coordination and precommitment. A huge cost of policies that are unpredictable is the discouraging of valuable ex ante investments and participation. Such unpredictable policies discourage investments by those who are concerned about policy risk—because of risk aversion and concerns about being exploited by subsequent government decisions. In their 1977 article for the *Journal of Political Economy*, Finn E. Kydland and Edward C. Prescott highlight closely related fundamental insights about "rules rather than discretion." Although the relevance of this for monetary policy has been broadly recognized, it is important for a broad array of policy concerns. Because it is not completely surprising that decision making in crises can be inconsistent, it is crucial for policymakers to formulate ex ante contingency plans for addressing financial crises.[21]

Consider the nature of federal interventions with respect to key capital market players. There has been much discussion about the connection between the Bear Stearns intervention (where the bondholders did well) and Lehman Brothers (where bondholders fared poorly). Many wonder whether the handling of Bear Stearns made it difficult for the private market to forecast the handling of Lehman—thereby not pushing Lehman to seek capital aggressively enough.[22] Perhaps a more interesting example is the U.S. Department of the Treasury's handling of the Federal National Mortgage Association (Fannie Mae) and the Federal Home Loan Mortgage Corporation (Freddie Mac) in summer 2008. When the Treasury was questioned about how it would intervene, it told Congress that it needed to be flexible rather than commit to a level in the capital structure where it would intervene. But one of the central tenets of Kydland and Prescott (1977) is that flexibility can be useful in a game against nature but is a false virtue in a game against active participants. When the Treasury said that it needed a "Big Bazooka" in seeking a huge funding authorization to intervene, intervention became very likely, and any ability to obtain further private funding disappeared because of the lack of clarity about which financial claims would be protected. For example, how would subordinated debt be treated relative to new federal claims? The answer would have been crucial to the ability to obtain private funding at that level.

A different type of example that illustrates the effect of a lack of predictability was the Treasury's decision to not proceed with the original formulation of the Troubled Asset Recovery Program (TARP) after enactment of the TARP. This was originally marketed to Congress as an attempt to remove troubled assets from the banks, akin to a "good bank/bad bank" solution. A key aspect of that program that never was resolved was the "pricing" and selection of assets. In that sense, the program's effective cancellation was arguably not unexpected. Yet when the Treasury announced in November 2008 that it would not move forward with the plan, the market declined by about 5 percent, and financial services firms declined more sharply. It is interesting to reflect on potential causes of this large decline, and so I suggest several: (1) the market thought that the plan would be effective and was disappointed when the plan was abandoned; (2) the market concluded that the Treasury was intellectually disorganized, although some thought that was already apparent; and (3) financial institutions had responded to the "head fake" from the Treasury and rather than selling had been accumulating (and ex post overpaying for) the "toxic assets" that they had anticipated later selling to the Treasury. There was a similar price decline when the current Treasury did not deliver on a plan in February 2009 that the new president had publicly declared ready.[23] As with the prior Treasury, this plan did not obtain much traction.[24]

The issue of changes in the rules of the game has emerged in a variety of contexts. For example, Congress debated "cram-down," the possibility of altering bankruptcy rules on primary residences to allow bankruptcy judges to reduce the obligation on mortgages for primary residences, although the proposal was defeated by the Senate after passage by the House of Representatives. The current rules prevent a judge from doing so, making it easier for prospective homeowners to obtain financing. These rules might not be the best bankruptcy standards for future loans, but the House addressed only past loans because some in Congress feared the negative effect on future borrowing opportunities for homeowners. The sanctity of contract and the rules of the game need to be respected: if the rules are changed, the changes should focus on future rather than past contracts, the opposite of the House action. Even so, approving a change for the past would not eliminate concerns of future lenders since they could reasonably forecast similar actions in the future. The issue of rules of the game is an important theme in the aftermath of the financial crisis, including extraordinary (and even questionable) pressure on AIG traders from the Congress and the New York attorney general to return compensation, the treatment of automobile bondholders relative to UAW claimants in bankruptcy, and unexpected rules about compensation and personnel restrictions for TARP recipients. Many TARP recipients concluded that there were large tangible indirect costs to having received such funds, unlike discount window support by the Federal Reserve or issuance of FDIC-backed debt in 2008 and 2009.[25] This provided a strong incentive to repay, which may have been desirable but also illustrates the types of strings that can be associated with the government as a silent partner. This would be disadvantageous to the extent that the government feels that participation in the TARP is crucial to how it hopes to manage systemic risk.

Capital Injections, Bank Supervision, and Systemic Risk

Traditionally, secured borrowing by banks at the Federal Reserve's discount bank as lender of last resort has been treated as private to avoid creating stigma for the borrowing institution.[26] In contrast, borrowing under the TARP program was public information. In fall 2008, institutions did not have a strong incentive to keep the information private because they felt that participating in the TARP was positive news in that the Treasury considered them strong enough to loan them money.[27] The applications for TARP funds from weak institutions were rejected to force them to merge or close because the private debt markets were essentially closed.[28] In effect, there was "reverse stigma" associated with receiving TARP funds.

But when the rules for recipients of TARP funds changed, relatively strong institutions were anxious to withdraw from TARP, and many went to the private markets to signal their access to funds, creating stigma or adverse selection for those who could not. In spring 2009, the Treasury and the Fed were reluctant to specify guidelines for repayment, but that should have been reflected in the ex ante design. Although some felt that allowing repayment might create stigma for others, the situations of many of the institutions had become much clearer. The Treasury strongly discouraged the original nine TARP recipients from declining, and they faced threats of supervisory actions if they did so.

There has been much discussion about stress tests that were performed by the federal supervisors. A nice feature of the stress tests is that there was a greater effort to achieve uniformity than previously, providing a significant enhancement of the traditional supervision model. One curious aspect is that it was not decided up front whether the results should be public, yet this would seem to be a fundamental aspect of an ex ante design. Traditional supervisory reports are typically not made public, but unlike the stress tests, their timing is not announced in advance by senior policymakers. It was not viable to hide the stress test results in light of the public announcement of upcoming tests, the focus on having financial institutions add new capital, and even the structure of securities disclosure rules. Furthermore, the underlying economics highlighted the value of separating "good" banks rather than permitting adverse selection to infect all institutions. The rollout of the stress results also was striking in light of the variety of leaks of partial results. For other corporate events, such as earnings announcements, this surely would have triggered investigations of stock price manipulation. Surprisingly, stress tests had not previously been undertaken by the bank supervisors although it would appear to be central to supervision, but the distinction between solvency and stress analyses is somewhat limited because optimal capitalization should be determined by stress scenarios. It is striking that there was not more skepticism about the outcome of the stress test because of the Fed's vested interest in the outcome, whether or not the underlying stress scenario was substantially adverse and the lack of a clearly defined disclosure policy. Finally, if the goal for the stress tests was to spur lending, it is not obvious that one should tell lenders that they are subject to new tests and that the new tests could be harder in the future. These could encourage contraction of lending by the banks for a given state of the economy. Arguably, portions of Dodd–Frank may have similar effects. The introduction of new regulatory standards can create new uncertainties about future regulatory action, which can retard current activity and transactions.

The 2009 stress tests, in fact, laid the foundation for the inclusion of annual stress testing in Dodd–Frank and helped the Federal Reserve hit the ground running with respect to this aspect of Dodd–Frank implementation. For example, the earlier stress testing helped raise the comfort and experience of the Federal Reserve with respect to the necessary modeling and the disclosure of stress test results. The management of stress tests also illustrates the potential for conflict in goals between trying to reduce systemic risk and refereeing the system. Another example of conflict in those goals is tied to the Bank of America's acquisition of Merrill, in which supervisory preferences about the merger from a systemic-risk perspective may have at least indirectly encouraged violations of our disclosure framework.[29] This is another context in which there could be value to designing the system so that precommitment is achieved. The conflicting goals of different regulators also highlight that the meaning of "more regulation" and the calls for greater regulation (whether through broad legislation or other approaches) need not be sharply defined.

In a financial market crisis, policymakers are inclined to view moral hazard as an issue for another day. Although policymakers were undoubtedly busy then, that is still a misguided perspective. The option value from excess risk-taking is especially high when the value of an enterprise is low or its fundamental riskiness is high. Japan's "zombie" institutions in the 1990s are an interesting example, which points to the relevance of the corporate finance "debt overhang" problem and the potential usefulness of a "good bank/bad bank" solution.

Although regulators have emphasized during the financial crisis that some institutions are too big or interconnected to fail, regulators did not focus directly on the ex ante costs that are associated with systemic risks and have been reluctant to limit the ex ante risk-taking costs associated with the government's safety-net policies and subsidies, including restricting bank size.[30] An interesting related example is how the takeover of Merrill Lynch by Bank of America, which had been viewed by the authorities as one of the strongest institutions until summer 2008, nearly brought down Bank of America. This merger, encouraged by the federal authorities with only a modest time frame for due diligence, also illustrates that the distinction between ex ante and ex post consequences is not a sharp one. Yesterday's ex post decisions are ex ante ones that set the stage for the future. Because Dodd–Frank creates systemic-risk regulation for nonbank financial institutions, it is interesting to reflect on the effectiveness of past supervision. For example, the Federal Reserve had been Citigroup's consolidated supervisor, and yet Citigroup essentially collapsed and required a $300 billion federal guarantee (excluding a deductible and 10 percent coinsurance). Designating systemically important financial institutions (SIFIs) as too important to fail could add to systemic risk by reducing market discipline. In my view, an important step forward could be the development of plans for the resolution and unwinding of significant institutions, if it encouraged the unwinding of institutions that failed financially (also see note 21), but this seems to be challenging and perhaps even infeasible given the complexity of global players.

Concluding Comments

I would like to conclude by pointing to some of the challenges that our economy faces and to which the research of financial economists can contribute considerably. Answers to the following questions could help create more effective and focused financial regulation:

• How can we design mortgage instruments and allocate risk-bearing in light of the value of loans modifications and the commonality in housing values?[31]
• How can we limit the adverse consequences for future lending of

unanticipated litigation related to past mortgages?
- How can we enhance the predictability of regulatory policy?
- How can we make progress on restoring market discipline and allowing failure?
- How can we reduce systemic risk, including the portion that is a consequence of government guarantees? How can we limit the moral hazard costs associated with the potential bailouts of debt holders?
- How can we define bank capital standards so that financial institutions will internalize the costs of the risks that they create?
- Can insolvency resolution be improved? Should we be comfortable with relatively more ad hoc handling of bankruptcies? When should resolution by bankruptcy be avoided?
- How do we distinguish liquidity from solvency challenges given the central role of short-term finance? Is there any meaningful economic distinction?
- How can the structure of compensation arrangements be enhanced to avoid artificial risk-taking incentives?
- How should regulatory shopping be limited when the diversity of contexts suggests the value of different types of regulation?[32]
- How can we mitigate adverse selection about counterparty risk among financial institutions and adverse selection and moral hazard problems in the loan origination process?
- How do we adjust to limited societal resources?

Notes

This chapter is based on remarks on the immediate policy responses to the 2008 financial crisis that were prepared for presentation as the distinguished speaker at the Western Finance Association meetings in San Diego on June 19, 2009. I would like to thank participants at presentations at the Federal Reserve Bank of Chicago, the Western Finance Association, the Institute for Financial Research (SIFR) conference on The Governance of Financial Intermediaries, the University of Oklahoma, and Claremont McKenna College for helpful comments, and Campbell Harvey, Paul Schultz, and Duane Seppi for feedback on earlier drafts.

1. In the aftermath of the financial crisis, the SEC's attention to a limited reinstatement of pricing restrictions on short sales illustrates the increasing politicization of financial regulation (e.g., see Sirri 2010 and Shadow Financial Regulatory Committee 2009). Many aspects of Dodd–Frank also illustrate this.

2. This is explored in J. Heaton, D. Lucas, and R. McDonald (2010).

3. The dynamics of valuations and therefore the precise states in which default is optimal reflect the joint evolution of discount rates and payoffs.

4. Reflecting this view, I was a cosigner of a letter to the editor of the *Financial Times* ("Healthy Bank System Is the Goal, Not Profitable Banks," 2010), which called for

substantially higher bank capital (equity) requirements. Surprisingly, this issue was not a key focus within Dodd–Frank.

5. Additionally, D. Diamond and R. Rajan (2011) point out that high anticipated future opportunities during the crisis would have deferred lending. However, the Treasury had emphasized the lending theme to Congress in its marketing of the TARP prior to enactment in fall 2008.

6. A recent study by J. Cotter, S. Gabriel, and R. Roll (2012) documents the considerable extent of integration in housing markets.

7. Some related empirical evidence concerning the exercise of credit lines and tightening of commercial paper is provided in P. Gao and H. Yun (2009). Not surprisingly, the reduction in commercial paper and exercise of credit lines was particularly pronounced in the fall of 2008 among lower-quality credits. Analogously, the supply of bank funding for lower-quality credits may have been squeezed out by the need of larger, higher-quality credits to substitute their funding sources. M. Campello, J. Graham, and C. Harvey (2010) documents a run on credit lines. Bank lending during the crisis is examined by V. Ivashina and D. Scharfstein (2010).

8. The standard theoretical argument is that the effect of changes in returns on saving is ambiguous because of the combination of income and substitution effects. For example, higher perceived returns would increase savings due to a substitution (price) effect but decrease savings due to an income (wealth) effect that increases current consumption.

9. This could reflect learning about both expected payoffs and systematic risk.

10. D. Epple and C. Spatt (1986) argue that state enforcement (facilitated by local debt ceilings) plays an important role in encouraging local general obligation debt.

11. The concern about the automobile bondholders does not require that there was an abuse of the formal bankruptcy process but follows when future bondholders anticipate that political sensitivities will play a new adverse role in their legal protection. Consequently, the coupon rate for such funding will be higher because of risk premium, and so investment will be diminished. The legal handling of these bankruptcies is discussed by M. Roe and D. Skeel (2010).

12. Because we assume that the consumers are identical, we abstract from any redistributive consequences.

13. The benchmark is to the "prior optimal" rather than to the quantity of public goods previously purchased, if these differ.

14. This effect focuses on the composition of consumption. The decrease in government spending that is implicit suggests the possibility of tax cuts to address any adverse Keynesian effects.

15. As in the traditional theory of the consumer with private goods, we define an indirect utility function over prices and wealth that is equal to the direct utility from the optimal allocation of goods, given prices and wealth. As in the traditional theory, a reduction in wealth would reduce indirect utility.

16. This argument focuses on the demand for goods. Advocates of expansion of government-supplied public goods also suggest that the costs of some decline in a downturn (expansion in supply).

17. At a tactical level, budgetary issues are also important to the form of the federal response. After the initial AIG congressional hearings, it became clear that Congress

would not approve additional appropriations for the Troubled Asset Recovery Program (TARP) or other financial rescues. The Obama administration's focus for subsequent rescue initiatives shifted to tactical uses of guarantees from, for example, the Federal Deposit Insurance Corporation (FDIC) that would not require up-front appropriations but were economically equivalent to direct lending, as well as use of resources of the Federal Reserve, which is outside the congressional appropriation process. Although fair value and concerns about off-balance-sheet accounting have dominated much of the discussion about the health of our financial institutions, the federal government itself is not subject to fair-value accounting and does not consolidate its accounts. This is not a call for consolidation of all federal accounts, however. Even absent consolidation, many observers have expressed concern about threats to the independence of the Federal Reserve.

18. Analogously, such concerns also arise with respect to efforts to influence foreign-exchange pricing by central banks. The theoretical analysis of such problems in asset markets began with the pioneering study by S. Grossman and J. Stiglitz (1980).

19. A dramatic example of this is my home city of Pittsburgh, in which the municipal pension liabilities have been underfunded by as much as 75 percent. A broader discussion of public pension promises and liabilities in the public pension context is given by R. Novy-Marx and J. Rauh (2011).

20. See C. Spatt (2005).

21. One can view this as analogous to defense preparedness planning and planning for natural disasters. Although the focus here is on developing contingency plans for policymakers, it also is analogous to the Dodd–Frank requirement that systemically important institutions should develop contingency plans for their own resolution ("living wills").

22. In the aftermath of its collapse, the leadership of Lehman Brothers has been strongly criticized for not being sufficiently aggressive in seeking capital. The Federal Reserve has suggested that it did not have legal authority to intervene for Lehman Brothers, but it aggressively used its section 13(3) emergency authority with respect to Bear Stearns and AIG.

23. Some of that price decline might also be attributable to the Treasury's simultaneous announcement that it would undertake stress tests, which was initially not well received by the market because of concerns about potential dilution. The market later reversed course when it viewed the stress test results as potentially capping the degree of dilution and new funding that would be required by the government.

24. Although the public-private investment program (PPIP) plan for purchasing toxic assets was central to the administration's proposal, interest in the plan declined for a variety of reasons, despite the extensive resources that the administration planned to devote to the program by providing liquidity and nonrecourse financing to the purchasers. This raised questions about how the purchases might be treated in the context of fair-value accounting because the pricing would be artificial in that what was offered to purchasers (funding and unusual guarantees) would be more valuable than the "plain vanilla" sale of the underlying assets. The relative success of the stress tests reduced the inclination of financial institutions to sell assets that they view as artificially depressed (see section 5), while potential buyers became concerned about ex post recriminations if they profited substantially from the purchases.

25. These include scolding by Congress, restrictions on events and activities, and retroactive restrictions on compensation and the ability to obtain H1-b visas (for example, for

graduates of American programs of higher education). These personnel aspects suggest significant competitive issues because many of the relevant business competitors were not TARP recipients (including foreign institutions). Because these costs are discontinuous (a firm is either a TARP recipient or it is not), the repayments of TARP funds tended to be all or none.

26. O. Armantier, E. Ghysels, A. Sarkar, and J. Shrader (2011) highlight the magnitude and economic effects of stigma from discount window borrowing during the financial crisis by examining the use of the Term Auction Facility (TAF) rather than the discount window.

27. Seemingly less costly terms were charged by TARP than by private markets. To see this, compare the TARP terms to those in Warren Buffet's loan to Goldman Sachs. This reflected, in part, differences in the bid-ask spread: Goldman contacted Buffet, whereas the Treasury wanted to loan to a broad group of nine institutions at uniform terms. Buffet was a patient buyer, and the Treasury was an impatient one. Another reason that Buffet could have been able to obtain advantageous terms is because of the certification that he provided solely to Goldman.

28. An example along such lines was the rejection of National City's request for TARP funds and the approval of PNC Bank's request to facilitate its purchase of National City.

29. The differences in the goals of the Securities and Exchange Commission and the Federal Reserve Bank and the import of these differences for disclosure involving Bank of America's acquisition of Merrill Lynch are discussed in C. Spatt (2010).

30. Systemic risk reflects important externalities. As with other externalities such as pollution, fees and taxes should be used to discourage its production.

31. Perhaps the earliest paper on optimal loan modification, although cast in the context of prepayment rather than default, is K. Dunn and C. Spatt (1985).

32. For example, regulatory shopping in the context of credit-rating shopping is explored by F. Sangiorgi, J. Sokobin, and C. Spatt (2009) and F. Sangiorgi and C. Spatt (2013).

References

Armantier, O., E. Ghysels, A. Sarkar, and J. Shrader. 2011. Stigma in Financial Markets: Evidence from Liquidity Auctions and Discount Window Borrowing during the Crises. Federal Reserve Bank of New York Staff Report No. 483, January.

Campello, M., J. Graham, and C. Harvey. 2010. The Real Effects of Financial Constraints: Evidence from a Financial Crisis. *Journal of Financial Economics* 97:470–487.

Cotter, J., S. Gabriel, and R. Roll. 2012. Can Metropolitan Housing Risk Be Diversified? A Cautionary Tale from the Recent Boom and Bust. Manuscript.

Diamond, D., and R. Rajan. 2011. Fear of Fire Sales, Illiquidity Seeking, and Credit Freezes. *Quarterly Journal of Economics* 126:557–591.

Dunn, K., and C. Spatt. 1985. An Analysis of Mortgage Contracting, Prepayments, and the Due-on-Sale Clause. *Journal of Finance* 40:293–308.

Epple, D., and C. Spatt. 1986. State Restrictions on Local Debt: Their Role in Preventing Default. *Journal of Public Economics* 29:199–221.

Gao, P., and H. Yun. 2009. Commercial Paper, Lines of Credit, and the Real Effects of the Financial Crisis of 2008: Firm-Level Evidence from the Manufacturing Industry. June. SSRN: http://ssrn.com/abstract=1421908.

Grossman, S., and J. Stiglitz. 1980. On the Impossibility of Informationally Efficient Markets. *American Economic Review* 70:393–408.

Healthy Bank System Is the Goal, Not Profitable Banks. 2010. *Financial Times*, Letter to the Editor, November 9.

Heaton, J., D. Lucas, and R. McDonald. 2010. Is Mark-to-Market Accounting Destabilizing? Analysis and Implications for Policy. *Journal of Monetary Economics* 57:64–75.

Ivashina, V., and D. Scharfstein. 2010. Bank Lending during the Financial Crisis of 2008. *Journal of Financial Economics* 97:319–338.

Kydland, F., and E. Prescott. 1977. Rules Rather Than Discretion: The Inconsistency of Optimal Plans. *Journal of Political Economy* 85:473–490.

Novy-Marx, R., and J. Rauh. 2011. Public Pension Promises: How Big Are They and What Are They Worth? *Journal of Finance* 66:1211–1249.

Roe, M., and D. Skeel. 2010. Assessing the Chrysler Bankruptcy. *University of Michigan Law Review* 108:727–772.

Sangiorgi, F., J. Sokobin, and C. Spatt. 2009. Credit-Rating Shopping, Selection, and the Equilibrium Structure of Ratings. Manuscript.

Sangiorgi, F., and C. Spatt. 2013. Opacity, Credit Rating Shopping and Bias. Manuscript.

Shadow Financial Regulatory Committee. 2009. Regulatory Initiatives of the Securities and Exchange Commission. Statement No. 276, September 14.

Sirri, E. 2010. Regulatory Politics and Short Selling. *University of Pittsburgh Law Review* 71:517–544.

Spatt, C. 2005. Why Private Pensions Matter to the Public Capital Markets. Executive Policy Seminar organized by the Capital Markets Research Center of the McDonough School of Business, Georgetown University, Washington, DC, November 16. http://www.sec.gov/news/speech/spch111605cs.htm.

Spatt, C. 2010. Regulatory Conflict: Market Integrity vs. Financial Stability. *University of Pittsburgh Law Review* 71:625–639.

3 The Basics of Too Big to Fail

Lawrence J. White

It's only when the tide goes out that you learn who's been swimming naked.

—Warren Buffet

The financial crisis of 2008 brought to political and regulatory prominence the concept of financial institutions that are "too big to fail" (TBTF). TBTF financial institutions were at the heart of the crisis. TBTF institutions were the first recipients of bailouts from the U.S. government through the Troubled Asset Relief Program (TARP) and other federal measures to forestall their reneging on their debt obligations (and in that sense, failing).[1]

The severity of the financial crisis and the Great Recession that followed plus the unpopularity of the apparent bailouts[2] and the TARP program made financial reform legislation inevitable. The Dodd–Frank Wall Street Reform and Consumer Protection Act of 2010 was that inevitable legislation, and Titles I and II were designed to address TBTF issues. The act used the term *systemically important financial institution* (SIFI) to refer to TBTF institutions. This chapter attempts to explain the TBTF concept and the reasons that it was (and potentially continues to be) a problem for the U.S. financial system and U.S. financial regulation.

What Is TBTF?

For the purposes of this chapter, TBTF starts with a relatively large financial institution[3] that holds primarily financial instruments (such as stocks, bonds, loans, and derivatives) as assets on its balance sheet. This category of company includes commercial banks and other depositories, bank holding companies (BHCs), modern investment banks,[4] insurance companies (and their holding companies), pension funds, finance companies, hedge funds, and mutual funds.[5]

Next, the liability side of the TBTF financial institution's balance sheet has comparatively little equity (which, for financial institutions, is the overwhelming component of their capital) and is thus largely fixed-obligation debt; equivalently, these institutions are thinly capitalized and are thus highly leveraged. This condition eliminates most mutual funds because the claimants of mutual funds own shares that fluctuate in value with the value of the fund's assets and thus do not represent the fixed obligation that is associated with debt.[6]

Next, the assets of the TBTF financial institution tend to be relatively opaque and illiquid, with thin markets.[7] Because the assets are opaque, they are hard for outsiders to value; and because the assets are relatively illiquid, they cannot be sold quickly except through substantial price discounts from whatever quotes existed in their (thin) markets.

Further, the TBTF institution's assets tend to be longer-term than its debt liabilities; in particular, a significant fraction of its debt liabilities are quite short-term. For banks, these are generally deposits. For other financial institutions, these short-term liabilities could be commercial paper or repurchase agreements (repos).

These short-term liabilities mean that the institution is "runable": the liability holders (creditors) can either withdraw their funds (in the case of bank deposits) or refuse to roll over their existing (short-term) loans. Although runs by bank depositors have been a well-known phenomenon for over a century, the institution of federal deposit insurance in the United States in 1933 has made bank runs virtually an historical relic.

By contrast, in 2008 for the first time ever, the U.S. financial system saw runs on nine TBTF financial institutions by their short-term creditors (who were not depositors). These nine included five large investment banks, two government-sponsored enterprises (GSEs), a large bank holding company, and a large insurance holding company. These creditors were not covered by deposit insurance and were not wholly confident that the federal government would keep them whole.

Why might a run on a financial institution arise? Due to the limited liability of owner-shareholders of a corporation (including financial institutions), if the company's assets are inadequate to cover the claims of its creditors (if it is insolvent), then the owners are generally not liable for the shortfall.[8] Consequently, if short-term creditors fear that the financial institution is likely to become (if it is not already) insolvent,[9] they will want to run to withdraw their deposits (or not roll over their short-term loans) before some form of resolution process (such as bank-ruptcy or receivership) delays their ability to claim their funds or requires them to accept less than "100 cents on the dollar."[10] Further, because these financial institutions' assets are relatively illiquid, even a solvent institution (if it does not have access to a lender of last resort) may be subject to runs. If some short-term liability holders fear that other short-term liability holders may be worried about the insolvency—or even just the illiquidity—of the institution (and might run), then the initial group would want to run first so that the second group's run does not interfere with the initial group's ability to claim their funds.[11]

A run reduces value in multiple dimensions: the short-term liability holders incur transactions costs during the run, and they have to find other places/institutions for their funds. The short-term liability holders who are too late lose immediate access to their funds and are exposed to possible losses of initial amounts. Further, to try to meet the claims of its "running" creditors, the financial institution has to liqui-date loans and other investments that it had expected to hold for a longer term. If the institution is subsequently liquidated, the brand name and specific human capital that was associated with that organi-zation is likely to be destroyed.

Finally, an insolvency (or a run that could lead to an insolvency) at one institution is likely to have negative consequences for other parties, either through a cascade or through contagion, and thereby lead to more widespread runs. To the extent that other financial institutions are claimants (short-term creditors) on the insolvent institution and have their claims (which they consider as assets) impaired, then the claimants on those financial institutions may have their claims impaired, and a cascade may form (and runs may develop in fearful anticipation of the cascade). Alternatively, if short-term (and imperfectly informed) claimants on a financial institution that is roughly similar to the first (troubled) institution see that institution become insolvent (or see a run develop that could lead to that institution's insolvency), then they may become fearful about their own institution's solvency (or become fearful about other creditors' fears) and thus begin a run on their own institution. This latter phenomenon is usually described as contagion.

Again, if the relevant financial institutions are large, then the conse-quences for the financial system and the larger economy of these runs and insolvencies can be substantial. Last-minute decisions by policy-makers to try to avoid those consequences—by providing bailout financial support to the institutions (or, really, to their creditors)—are understandable in this context. But such last-minute actions also create the moral hazard expectations by the institutions' owners and managers, as well as by their creditors, that similar bailouts are likely in the future. Much better would be ex ante prophylactic measures that would lessen the problems and the need for the last-minute decisions.

TBTF in Practice: The Crisis of 2008

Table 3.1 lists the assets and net worth percentages of the fifteen largest financial institutions in the United States as of December 31, 2007—just before the crisis. The net worth percentages are especially relevant because a financial institution's capital is essentially its net worth. For comparison purposes, table 3.2 lists the assets and net worth percentages of the fifteen largest nonfinancial companies in the United States, also as of December 31, 2007.

A few comparisons are immediately worth noting. First, the smallest of the fifteen largest financial institutions was substantially—over 40 percent—larger than the largest of the nonfinancial companies. Second, none of the financial companies had net worth ratios above 10 percent, while (with the exception of the two struggling auto companies) none of the nonfinancial companies had net worth ratios that were below 20 percent. Especially noteworthy are the net worth ratios of the five large investment banks in table 3.1: none of them exceeded 4 percent.

There are a few things that are not fully conveyed by table 3.1. First, Citigroup is best understood as a (roughly) $1.2 trillion depository institution, on top of which was a (roughly) $1 trillion holding company (including its nondepository subsidiaries). The holding company's net worth was smaller than the depository's net worth.[12] In essence, if the net worth of the depository (that is, the capital of the depository, which also counted as an asset for the holding company) was ignored, the holding company was insolvent.[13] The liabilities of the holding company were not deposits and thus were not covered by deposit insurance; the holding company had access to the Federal Reserve (as a lender of last resort) only through its depository subsidiary; and although the Citi holding company was prudentially regulated (albeit, poorly) by the Federal Reserve, there was no resolution process except for bankruptcy in the event that the Citi holding company was found to be unable to satisfy the claims of its creditors.

Second, the assets and net worth data for the American International Group (AIG) neglect the fact that AIG's holding company had a financial products subsidiary that, primarily from its London office, had engaged in major financial activities. These included large investments

Table 3.1
The fifteen largest financial institutions in the United States (by asset size, December 31, 2007)

Rank	Financial institution	Category	Assets ($ billion)	Equity as % of assets
1	Citigroup	Commercial bank	$2,182	5.2%
2	Bank of America	Commercial bank	1,716	8.6
3	JPMorgan Chase	Commercial bank	1,562	7.9
4	Goldman Sachs	Investment bank	1,120	3.8
5	American International Group	Insurance conglomerate	1,061	9.0
6	Morgan Stanley	Investment bank	1,045	3.0
7	Merrill Lynch	Investment bank	1,020	3.1
8	Fannie Mae	Government-sponsored enterprise	883	5.0
9	Freddie Mac	Government-sponsored enterprise	794	3.4
10	Wachovia	Commercial bank	783	9.8
11	Lehman Brothers	Investment bank	691	3.3
12	Wells Fargo	Commercial bank	575	8.3
13	MetLife	Insurance	559	6.3
14	Prudential	Insurance	486	4.8
15	Bear Stearns	Investment bank	395	3.0

Note: The Federal Home Loan Bank System ($1,272 billion) and TIAA-CREF ($420 billion) have been excluded from this list; if GE Capital were a standalone finance company, its asset size ($650 billion) would place it at 12.

Source: Fortune 500, May 5, 2008.

in residential mortgage-backed securities (MBSs), derivatives trading, and the selling of hundreds of billions of dollars of credit default swaps (CDSs), much of it on residential MBSs. CDSs are essentially insurance contracts that protect the CDS purchaser against default (that is, non-repayment) by the borrower of the underlying bonds. However, the financial products unit had not maintained sufficient capital against the possibility that its investments might yield losses, had not set aside sufficient reserves against the possibility that the bonds underlying its CDS sales would default and that AIG would consequently have to make payouts on the contracts, and had not set aside sufficient collateral that would be required by its CDS counterparties if the underlying bonds fell in value (but had not yet defaulted).

Table 3.2
The fifteen largest nonfinancial companies in the United States (by asset size, December 31, 2007)

Rank	Company	Assets ($ billion)	Equity as a % of assets
1	Ford	$279.3	2.0%
2	AT&T	275.6	41.9
3	Exxon Mobil	242.1	50.3
4	Verizon	187.0	27.1
5	ConocoPhillips	177.8	50.1
6	Wal-Mart	163.5	39.5
7	General Motors	148.9	-24.9
8	Chevron	148.8	51.8
9	Proctor & Gamble	138.0	48.4
10	Time Warner	133.8	43.7
11	International Business Machines (IBM)	120.4	23.6
12	Pfizer	115.3	56.4
13	Comcast	113.4	36.4
14	Hewlett-Packard	88.7	43.4
15	Johnson & Johnson	81.0	53.5

Note: Without Ford Credit, Ford would have $118 billion in assets, which would place it at 11. General Electric has been excluded from this list; without GE Capital, General Electric would have $145 billion in assets, which would place it at 9.

Source: Fortune 500, May 5, 2008.

Third, the data for the Federal National Mortgage Association (Fannie Mae) and the Federal Home Loan Mortgage Corporation (Freddie Mac) (the GSEs) neglect the fact that together they also had issued approximately $3.5 trillion in MBSs that carried their guarantees, which protected the MBS investors against defaults by the underlying mortgage borrowers. Because net worth is the buffer that protects a company's debt claimants against losses, the effective net worth ratios (as a protection against the losses that could arise from losses in the value of assets or losses on MBSs) were only a third of the levels shown for the two companies.

Fourth, the data in table 3.1 do not indicate that all of the financial institutions—to greater or lesser extents—had invested in residential MBSs and thus were potentially exposed to losses on those MBSs.

Fifth, the data in table 3.1 do not indicate that, with the exceptions of MetLife and Prudential, all of the financial institutions in the table relied significantly on short-term funding and thus were potentially runable (although the commercial banks had the protection of deposit insurance).

The Crisis

The story of the financial crisis of 2008 is essentially the story of nine of the fifteen financial institutions in table 3.1—the five large investment banks (Goldman Sachs, Morgan Stanley, Merrill Lynch, Lehman Brothers, and Bear Stearns), the two GSEs (Fannie Mae and Freddie Mac), the ($1 billion in assets) Citi holding company, and the AIG holding company. The nine financial institutions shared a number of crucial characteristics. They were large; they were interconnected with each other and with other financial institutions as lenders/borrowers and as counterparties in various types of financial transactions; they were thinly capitalized; they were subject to weak prudential regulation; they relied to a significant extent on short-term funding, so that they were potentially exposed to creditor runs; none of them had deposit insurance or direct access to the Federal Reserve in its role as lender of last resort; and, except for the GSEs, bankruptcy was the only means by which severe financial difficulties could be resolved.[14]

As background to the crisis, from the late 1990s through the middle of 2006, the United States experienced a major housing boom—which is now recognized to have been a bubble. Between 1997 and 2006, the S&P/Case-Shiller Index of home prices rose by approximately 125 percent, whereas the U.S. Consumer Price Index rose by only 28 percent. National housing prices peaked in mid-2006 (as measured by the Case-Shiller Index) and subsequently declined by about 35 percent over the next six years. During the approximately eight years of extraordinary increases in housing prices, a mentality that "housing prices will always increase" seemed to envelop most individuals in and around the housing and housing finance sectors.

Among the consequences of this mentality was a substantial loosening of mortgage underwriting and lending standards. After all, if housing prices would always increase, then the standard indicia of creditworthiness (Did the borrower have a good track record in handling credit obligations in the past? Could the borrower provide a 20 percent down payment? Did the borrower have sufficient income to afford the monthly payments? Were monthly payments important?)

would be irrelevant. Even if borrowers could not directly make the required payments on a mortgage loan, they could always sell the house at a profit (since housing prices would always increase) and thereby pay off the mortgage—or the lender could declare a default, foreclose, take title to the house, and sell it for more than the value of the mortgage.

Further, after tentative starts in the 1980s and 1990s, "private label" securitization of residential mortgages (that is, securitization that was not being done by the GSEs or by Ginnie Mae)[15] finally found traction by settling on a senior/junior tranching structure for residential MBSs that appeared to provide sufficient security to the investors in the senior tranches. Because the mentality of "housing prices will always increase" had spread to residential mortgage securitization, the participants in that process (the mortgage originators, the securitizers, the credit-rating agencies that rated the tranches, and the MBS investors) seemed not to notice or care that mortgage underwriting standards had deteriorated. After all, if mortgages would not be a problem, then the MBSs that were formed from those mortgages also would not be a problem.

After housing prices peaked in mid-2006 and began to decline, mortgage defaults began to rise. By the summer of 2007, it was clear that many residential MBS issuances were experiencing financial difficulties (because of the defaults by the underlying mortgage borrowers), and the three major credit-rating agencies began massive downgrades of (their initially overly optimistic) ratings on hundreds of billions of residential MBSs. The market values of the relevant MBSs were already falling, and the rating downgrades reinforced the process. By the fall of 2007, the financial markets were clearly worried about the consequences of the falling values of MBS for the solvency of many of the TBTF financial institutions listed in table 3.1.

In the early months of 2008, Bear Stearns began experiencing difficulties in refinancing its short-term borrowings as its creditors' worries about its solvency deepened. In March 2008, Bear Stearns's refinancing difficulties became severe; in essence, it was experiencing a run by its creditors. The Federal Reserve concluded that Bear Stearns was too large (with almost $400 billion in assets) and too interconnected to be allowed to enter into bankruptcy and thereby force its creditors to accept delayed and reduced payments (which might then create both a cascade and a contagion). Instead, the Federal Reserve engineered the absorption of Bear Stearns into JPMorgan Chase by providing guarantees to the latter firm against losses that might be experienced on the assets of the former.[16]

During the summer of 2008, it was clear that housing prices were continuing to fall and that mortgage delinquency/default problems were continuing to rise, with concomitant consequences for residential MBSs. Fannie Mae and Freddie Mac had experienced operating losses in 2007. (For Freddie Mac, this was its first annual loss ever; for Fannie Mae, this was its first annual loss since the early 1980s.) Losses for both GSEs continued in the first half of 2008, and by the summer, their creditors were becoming nervous that the two might become insolvent. The capital markets had always assumed that, because of the GSEs' special ties to the federal government, in the event of financial difficulties the two GSEs would be backed by the U.S. Treasury and their creditors would be kept whole; but this was only an implicit guarantee, and the Treasury had always declined the opportunity to make it explicit.

In August 2008, the GSEs' refinancing difficulties became severe as their short-term creditors became increasingly worried that the Treasury might not support the GSEs after all. Again, in essence, this was a run by their short-term creditors. In early September, it was clear that the GSEs had become insolvent and that their financing problems had become too great. On September 6, their prudential regulator—the Federal Housing Finance Agency (FHFA)[17]—placed both of them into conservatorships, and the Treasury announced that it would take a 79.9 percent ownership position and provide the necessary funds to prevent the GSEs from becoming insolvent and thereby honor all of the GSEs' debt obligations. The Treasury had decided that the two GSEs were too big (with over $1.6 trillion in combined assets and another $3.5 trillion in outstanding guaranteed MBS) and their debt and MBSs too widely held to allow their creditors to experience delayed and reduced repayments—especially at a time that the capital markets generally were nervous about the continuing consequences of residential mortgage and MBS defaults. In the end, the capital market's original belief that the Treasury would likely support the GSEs' creditors proved to be correct.

At the same time that the capital markets were growing nervous with respect to the GSEs' financial difficulties, they were also growing nervous with respect to the solvency of Lehman Brothers and with respect to the ability of AIG to honor its CDS commitments, including the posting of adequate collateral against the declining value of the underlying MBS. Lehman experienced difficulties in rolling over its short-term debt obligations in late August and early September 2008. The Treasury and the Federal Reserve announced loudly that they would not or could not rescue Lehman or AIG or aid in the absorption of either company by some other financial institution. After a weekend of frenzied efforts by the senior management of Lehman to find an acquirer, Lehman (with almost $700 billion in assets) declared bankruptcy on Monday, September 15, 2008. The bankruptcy filing meant that all of Lehman's unsecured debt obligations were frozen and could only be subsequently sorted out by a bankruptcy judge.

During the summer, the capital markets had also become nervous with respect to Merrill Lynch's solvency. During the same weekend when Lehman sought but failed to find an acquisition partner, Merrill succeeded (with encouragement from the Federal Reserve and the Treasury) in getting Bank of America to agree to acquire it, thus taking Merrill out of financial danger (although the transaction did not close until early 2009).

In the few days immediately after Lehman's bankruptcy filing, the credit markets froze as institutional lenders became extremely nervous about the safety of lending to any other institution. By Tuesday afternoon, the Treasury and the Federal Reserve changed course and announced that they would support AIG after all. On the same day, a large money market mutual fund (MMMF)—the Reserve Fund—declared that its holdings of short-term Lehman debt were large enough and that the expected value of what it would receive from the bankruptcy resolution was sufficiently uncertain that it would have to "break the buck": it could no longer honor its obligation to redeem its shares at the traditional $1.00 value that was the standard among MMMFs. Although the reduction in share value was relatively small (to $0.97), the shock was large. There was immediately a shareholders' run on a number of other large MMMFs, which was halted only when the Treasury announced at the end of the week a short-run plan for guaranteeing MMMF share values at $1.00.

Although Goldman Sachs and Morgan Stanley were not seen as financially endangered as the other three large investment banks, they were nevertheless not immune to the events of the week of September 15, and they started experiencing their own difficulties in rolling over their short-term debt obligations. During the following weekend, both declared their intentions to become BHCs—primarily so that they could reassure nervous creditors that their investment banks were now under the prudential regulatory authority of the Federal Reserve (and would presumably not be allowed to fail).[18]

Before the end of the week of September 15, the chair of the Federal Reserve (Ben Bernanke) and the secretary of the Department of the Treasury (Henry Paulson) agreed that they needed to seek congressional legislation that would appropriate funds to provide the financial support that the financial sector clearly required. That legislation, the Emergency Economic Stabilization Act of 2008, was passed (after one false start) on October 3 and was signed by President George W. Bush on the same day. The legislation authorized the TARP expenditures. Although the original vision of the TARP was to purchase troubled mortgage securities from the major banks, it quickly morphed into a program whereby the Treasury would invest funds in banks and receive preferred stock in return. The first such investments were made dramatically in nine of the largest TBTF financial institutions in the United States.[19] Their chief executive officers were summarily called into Secretary Paulson's office on Monday, October 13, and told that they must accept TARP funds regardless of whether they felt that they needed the funds. All nine acceded.

In sum, TBTF became a reality for the U.S. financial system in 2008, as manifested by the Federal Reserve's assistance to JPMorgan Chase in March to help it absorb Bear Stearns; the Treasury's support for all of the debt obligations of the two GSEs in early September; the widespread realization of the traumatic effects that Lehman's bankruptcy had on the financial markets in mid-September; the Federal Reserve's decision to support AIG within a day after the Lehman bankruptcy; the Federal Reserve's decision to welcome Goldman Sachs and Morgan Stanley as BHCs a few days later (as well as its earlier encouragement of Merrill Lynch's absorption by Bank of America); and the Treasury's decision in mid-October to spend the first TARP funds on nine of the largest financial institutions in the country.

Appropriate Policies for Dealing with TBTF Financial Institutions

Given the severity of the financial crisis of 2008 and the central role played by TBTF financial institutions, improved policies to address TBTF issues were clearly warranted. The Dodd–Frank Act tried to provide these policies.

To understand the logic of policies that would address the TBTF problem, it is useful to start with the system of prudential regulation that applies to commercial banks (and other depository institutions).

The Prudential Regulation of Commercial Banks

It is worth recalling why prudential regulation of commercial banks is important. Essentially, because a large fraction of a bank's liabilities are short-term deposits, banks are runable. Further, bank assets tend to be illiquid and opaque (and most depositors would be unlikely to have the financial sophistication to be able to assess the solvency of their bank). And the runability of banks and the poor or imperfect information by depositors about their own bank's solvency make banks potentially prone to contagion and cascades.[20]

Prudential regulation is best considered as regulators' efforts to keep a financial institution solvent so that the value of the institution's assets exceeds the value of its debt liabilities.[21] The debt liability holders (for banks, primarily depositors) will thereby remain whole and (in principle) should not feel the need to run on their institution.

At the center of any bank prudential regulatory arrangement is a minimum capital requirement that is commensurate with the risks that are undertaken by the bank.[22] Capital acts as a risk-absorbing buffer to protect the liability holders directly against losses in the value of the bank's assets. Capital also serves to discourage risk-taking on the part of the bank's owners because they have more to lose. Because capital is calculated primarily as the net of the simple subtraction of the value of the debt liabilities from the value of the assets, it is essential that the assets (and any off-balance-sheet obligations) be valued on a market-value basis (although too often this is not the case).[23] Although net worth is (and should be) the primary component of capital, the inclusion of a component of long-term bail-in-able debt (whether it is described as subordinated debt or contingent capital or some other label) can also be useful. It may provide an additional market signal that can be useful to help the regulators monitor the activities of the bank, and it may also bring into the picture a set of knowledgeable stakeholders whose interests are closely aligned with those of the regulator. And the regulator must have the power of "prompt corrective action": as a bank's capital level becomes thinner, the regulator must tighten its restrictions on the bank's activities to tighten restrictions on risk-taking.[24]

Next, prudential regulation must involve restrictions of the activities of the bank. The bank must be limited to activities that the regulator can understand well enough so that an appropriate capital requirement can be set and so that the regulator can monitor the activity and judge whether it is being well managed by the bank. If an activity is not understood sufficiently by the regulator so that the regulator can set an appropriate capital requirement and make judgments as to how well the activity is being managed, how can this activity be appropriate for a bank?

Third, there must be competency and character requirements for the bank's senior management. At the limit, bumblers and felons ought not to be allowed to operate prudentially regulated banks.

Fourth, the financial flows between the bank and its owners (and the friends and associates of its owners) must be tightly monitored because it is too easy to drain a bank (through favorable loans or other concessional transactions) to benefit the owners at the expense of the depositors. All such transactions must be on arm's-length terms.

Fifth, there must be adequate numbers of well-trained and well-paid examiners and supervisors to administer and enforce the regulation.

Sixth, the prudential regulator must have the power of receivership (with clearly specified rules for that receivership) to be able to conduct a prompt and orderly disposal of the bank's assets and liabilities in the event of an insolvency. As the Lehman bankruptcy made clear, a bankruptcy process for a financial institution—especially a large financial institution—creates far too much delay and uncertainty. Further, in the receivership process, there should be a strong presumption that the previous owners and senior management are removed and have no remaining stake in the bank because they are the ones who ran it into the ground.

Seventh, there needs to be a liquidity requirement to allow the bank to satisfy unexpected depositor withdrawals. It would seem that banks' access to the central bank, as the lender-of-last-resort, would obviate the need for a direct liquidity requirement. However, because the lender-of-last-resort will want appropriate collateral, which usually means liquid assets, a liquidity requirement is still needed.

Finally, deposit insurance is a useful (and now near-universal) supplement to prudential regulation, as a backstop against runs (and the contagion and cascades that might further develop) in the event that prudential regulation fails to achieve its goal of keeping a bank solvent.[25]

The Lessons for Dealing with TBTF Financial Institutions

Because the failure—or fears of failure and the consequent short-term creditor runs—of TBTF financial institutions is the central problem, a prudential regulatory regime is necessary. Title I of the Dodd–Frank Act designates the Federal Reserve as the prudential regulator for TBTF institutions that are not otherwise covered by a robust prudential regulatory regime. Banks, BHCs, and insurance companies are already covered by prudential regulation, so the candidate institutions would seem to be large finance companies (such as GE Capital), any new large investment banks (there currently are none, since the remaining four large investment banks are now each a part of four separate BHCs that are regulated by the Federal Reserve), large hedge funds, large insurance holding companies (such as AIG), and large securities clearing organizations.

As is true for bank regulation, minimum capital requirements that are commensurate with the risks of the TBTF institution must be at the heart of the prudential regulation of TBTF institutions. Again, market-value accounting of the institutions assets and off-balance-sheet obligations is essential, and so is a regime of prompt corrective action.

Similarly, there have to be activities limitations because only activities that the regulator can understand well enough to be able set capital requirements and to be able to assess competent management should be allowed within the prudentially regulated institution. Also, financial transactions between the institution and its owners must be tightly monitored, for (again like banks) it is too easy to drain the institution to favor its owners at the expense of the institution's debt claimants.

Because the TBTF financial institutions typically do not have access to the Federal Reserve as the lender of last resort, adequate liquidity requirements are especially important. Further, because the creditors to the TBTF institutions are not covered by deposit insurance (or its equivalent), some other back-up mechanism is necessary to forestall short-term creditor and counterparty runs in the event that prudential regulation fails and the TBTF institution becomes (or is feared to become) insolvent. Here, the role of additional bail-in-able (that is, loss-absorbing) long-term debt is crucial. It is often the case that the valuations of troubled financial institutions' assets are sufficiently murky that the institution can claim that it is still solvent (that is, has positive net worth), while closer examination indicates insolvency. This murkiness causes otherwise unprotected short-term creditors to be nervous and to start to run. To the extent that the institution also has a substantial amount of bail-in-able debt, this creates an extra margin of reassurance for those short-term creditors and should lessen the chances of runs.

Finally, as is true for banks, the prudential regulator (or its designee) needs to have the power of receivership to deal with insolvent TBTF financial institutions. Again, as the Lehman bankruptcy demonstrated, bankruptcy is not a good resolution process for insolvent TBTF financial institutions. Dodd–Frank designates the Federal Deposit Insurance Corporation (FDIC), which is the receiver for insolvent banks, to be the receiver for TBTF financial institutions as the Orderly Liquidation Authority (OLA).[26] The FDIC appears to understand that resolving an insolvent TBTF institution would be substantially more complicated than the resolution of the typical small insolvent bank with which the FDIC periodically has to deal. Among other things, a TBTF institution is likely to have a much more complicated corporate structure, with multiple subsidiaries that have multiple financing sources. Further, many TBTF institutions may have extensive foreign operations, which will require coordination with the relevant prudential regulators overseas.

How well all of this will work in the event of a new crisis (whether the provisions of the Dodd–Frank Act will function well enough so that the large financial institutions in the U.S. economy are no longer TBTF) remains unknown. To the extent that we have not (yet?) had a new crisis, this is good news; to the extent that nevertheless we do not know how well it will work, this is not so good news.[27]

Conclusion

The problem of TBTF financial institutions is real. Nine large TBTF financial institutions were at the center of the financial crisis of 2008.

This chapter has laid out the basics of the TBTF phenomenon—what it means, why it is a problem, how the TBTF problems played out in the crisis of 2008, and why better prudential regulation of TBTF financial institutions than existed prior to 2008 is essential for the future.

Much has been learned since 2008, and some of that learning has been embodied in the Dodd–Frank Act. Whether enough has been learned—and will be remembered—may be difficult to determine. If the United States never experiences another financial crisis that is comparable to the 2008 crisis, perhaps this will be an indication that the lessons have been learned and retained. Or if the beginnings of a crisis develop but then are forestalled without the last-minute maneuverings of 2008, perhaps that will be the appropriate indication. The alternative—that policymakers could forget the lessons and that the United States could experience another crisis of the magnitude of 2008—is one that is not pleasant to contemplate.

Notes

1. As is made clear in this chapter, TBTF is in many ways a misnomer. "Too big to be put through a resolution process that would cause creditors and counterparties not to be paid promptly and fully" would be a more accurate description. But the latter phrase cannot be captured in a simple acronym and is unlikely to attract journalistic, political, or popular attention, so this chapter uses TBTF.

2. As subsequently became clear, the primary beneficiaries of the bailouts were the creditors to the targeted financial institutions.

3. I leave to others the determination of whether a large industrial corporation, such as General Motors, should be considered to be TBTF as well.

4. Until the 1990s, investment banks were primarily financial facilitators in the sense that they were brokers, dealers, market makers, and advisers but had relatively small balance sheets and thus were not primarily holders of financial assets.

5. If real estate is included as a financial asset, then real estate investment trusts (REITs) would also be included as potential TBTF institutions.

6. Money market mutual funds (MMMFs) are the primary exception because they customarily maintain their share values at $1.00 and there is a strong presumption on the part of their shareholders that the MMMFs are committed to maintaining that $1.00 value. As is discussed below, when one MMMF "broke the buck" in September 2008, this sparked a run on other MMMFs.

7. Again, this eliminates most mutual funds.

8. Even if corporate owners were liable for the insolvent corporation's obligations, the limits of personal bankruptcy could effectively limit their liability.

9. The values of the assets are opaque, so the outside liability holders are likely to have difficulties in determining those values and thus determining the solvency of the institution.

10. Again, federal deposit insurance has largely cured this problem for banks.

11. This creates a "prisoner's dilemma" type of problem.

12. The depository's net worth was $143.6 billion; the holding company's net worth was only $113.6 billion.

13. This is ironic because the Federal Reserve, which prudentially regulates BHCs, has for many decades maintained that holding companies are supposed to be a "source of strength" for their depository subsidiaries.

14. For the GSEs, bankruptcy was not an option because their charters had been created through congressional legislation, and it appeared that they could be resolved only by subsequent congressional action. There was some question as to whether the two GSEs could be placed into a conservatorship by their prudential regulator, the Office of Federal Housing Enterprise Oversight (OFHEO), but it was clear that OFHEO did not have the power to place the GSEs into a receivership.

15. Ginnie Mae is a federal agency that is lodged within the U.S. Department of Housing and Urban Development (HUD) and that securitizes residential mortgages that have been guaranteed by the Federal Housing Administration (FHA), the U.S. Department of Veterans Affairs (VA), or the U.S. Department of Agriculture (USDA).

16. After the Bear Stearns transaction, the Federal Reserve greatly eased the ability of primary dealers in U.S. Treasury obligations (which included the remaining four large investment banks and the Citi holding company but not the AIG holding company) to access the Federal Reserve as lender of last resort.

17. The Housing and Economic Recovery Act of 2008, enacted in July, eliminated the GSEs' former prudential regulator (OFHEO) and replaced it with a new prudential regulator (FHFA) and provided the latter with stronger prudential regulatory powers, including the power to declare a receivership. However, for strategic reasons (including the ability to keep the GSEs' $1.5 trillion in straight debt and $3.5 trillion in MBS guarantees off the federal government's books), the Treasury and FHFA decided to put the GSEs into conservatorships in early September 2008.

18. There was a deep irony in their seeking to become BHCs. Although the Gramm-Leach-Bliley Act of 1999 erased many of the boundaries between investment banking and commercial banking, the large investment banks (prior to September 2008) steadfastly resisted becoming BHCs—because they feared that the Federal Reserve's prudential regulatory oversight would inhibit their activities. The events of September 2008 reversed their thinking.

19. They were Citigroup, Bank of America, JPMorgan Chase, Goldman Sachs, Morgan Stanley, Merrill Lynch, Wells Fargo, Bank of New York Mellon, and State Street Bank. Of the fifteen financial institutions that are listed in table 3.1 and that were not in this list of the top nine, AIG was already being helped by the Federal Reserve (although it would subsequently need TARP funds as well); the two GSEs were in conservatorships and receiving Treasury infusions; Wachovia had been acquired by Wells Fargo in early October; Lehman had declared bankruptcy; the two insurance companies were not considered in any serious short-run financial difficulties and had few short-term liabilities that would have made them run-able; and Bear Stearns had already been absorbed by JPMorgan Chase.

20. Prudential regulation in the United States also applies to insurance companies (the regulators are the fifty states) and corporate defined-benefit pension funds (the regulator is the federal Pension Benefit Guarantee Corporation). Although runability is less of a problem for either kind of institution, the limited ability of beneficiaries to protect themselves provides a reasonable justification for the prudential regulation of these categories of financial institution.

21. In an important sense, prudential regulation can be considered the public-sector counterpart to the covenants that banks (as lenders to companies) routinely include in their lending agreements and that are routinely included in bond indentures. The public sector is needed because the liability holders of the regulated financial institution are generally not in a good position to protect their own interests.

22. Recall that for a financial institution, capital is essentially net worth. Risks should be evaluated in a portfolio context.

23. Where markets are thin, some combination of market information and modeling may be necessary.

24. Again, such provisions are standard in the covenants in bank lending agreements and in bond indentures.

25. After deposit insurance is in place, prudential regulation can be also interpreted as the analogy to the set of rules that any insurer puts in place for its insureds to protect itself against the moral hazard and adverse selection problems that generally accompany

the provision of insurance. For example, in this context, the minimum capital requirement can be seen to be analogous to a deductible in a property/casualty insurance policy. As was noted above, there are parallels between the prudential regulation of banks and of insurance companies and corporate defined-benefit pension funds. Deposit insurance extends the similarities because all of the states maintain guarantee funds that make good on some or all of an insured's claim in the event that an insurance company cannot satisfy all claims, and the PBGC has a guarantee fund that makes good on some or all of a pensioner's claim if the original pension fund's assets are inadequate.

26. Although BHCs have been and continue to be prudentially regulated by the Federal Reserve, prior to the passage of the Dodd–Frank Act they could be resolved only through a bankruptcy process. The designation of the FDIC as the receiver for TBTF institutions should make the resolution of a large BHC more feasible.

27. This chapter has not addressed the issue of whether TBTF financial institutions should simply be broken into smaller institutions as the way to deal with the TBTF problem. Although that is a topic for a wholly different essay, one important point can be made here. To the extent that size itself is seen (*ceteris paribus*) as the problem, then it is a negative externality problem; and as economists have known since at least the 1920s, the best way to deal with a negative externality problem is to put an appropriately structured tax on the negative externality. In the present case, this would mean a tax (or in the current tax-phobic milieu of Washington, a more appropriate word may be *fee*) on size. Then the TBTF institutions themselves could decide whether their large size provides sufficient efficiencies that the maintenance of that size (while paying the tax/fee to society to compensate for the negative externalities) is worthwhile or whether reducing their size would make sense for them and, if so, what the least costly way of achieving those size reductions would be.

4 Creating a Responsive, Accountable, Market-Driven Financial System

Thomas M. Hoenig

Narrowing the safety net so that we have a more responsive, accountable, market-driven financial system is of great importance to the long-run economic stability and financial growth of the United States. It is something that I have devoted a significant amount of attention and research to over the past several years as we have experienced the consequences of the crisis of 2008 and its relationship with financial institutions that are considered too big to fail.

The current configuration of the financial system remains a risk to the public and an impediment to the competitive vitality and strength of the U.S. economy. Coming out of the crisis, the financial system is more concentrated, and under current policies, this trend almost certainly will continue. These conglomerates will become yet more complex, and their financial position will define financial stability for the broader economy.

The largest financial holding company in this country has about $2.5 trillion of assets, without counting its off-balance-sheet exposures. That is 16 percent of gross domestic product (GDP) in one company. When the off-balance-sheet exposures are included, it is another trillion and a half dollars, or $4 trillion of assets. That is nearly a quarter of our gross domestic product. The eight largest financial institutions in the United States today have $10 trillion of assets reported on their balance sheets under generally accepted accounting principles—the equivalent of two-thirds of U.S. GDP. If their derivatives and other off-balance-sheet items are included, their assets are $16 trillion, which is the equivalent of 100 percent of GDP. If these institutions get into trouble today, their large size ensures that they will have a dramatic effect on U.S. financial and economic systems.

The largest institutions are a concern because of both their size and their complexity. Over time, the government safety net of deposit insurance, Federal Reserve lending, and direct taxpayer investment has been expanded beyond where it is needed. The government now protects more types of businesses and activities that are outside commercial banking and do not require the backstop to function.

The Financial Services Modernization Act of 1999 (the Gramm-Leach-Bliley Act) expanded the ability of commercial banks to engage in broker-dealer activities, including proprietary trading, market making, swaps, and other risky activities (gambling activities, if you will) with the safety net protecting them. To compete, broker-dealers that were not affiliated with a commercial bank and thus did not receive the same government protections were forced to become acquisition candidates for these institutions or become more like commercial banks. Over time, the broker-dealers that did not join a commercial bank began to engage in activities that were essentially intermediating short-term funds into long-term assets through money markets and repurchase agreements (repos). They were therefore able to "leverage up" their balance sheets like commercial banks and in some cases lever to an even greater extent than banks. The market began to assume that they were as protected as commercial banks. In other words, the market assumed that they had the safety net behind them, at least in an implied fashion, and thus charged them less for funding, which further encouraged the greater use of debt over equity on their balance sheets.

With broker-dealer activities inside the banking organization and thus inside the safety net, the perception persists that, despite the enactment of the Dodd–Frank Wall Street Reform and Consumer Protection Act of 2010, the government will likely support these dominant and highly complex firms because of their outsized effects on the broader economy. This support translates into an enormous subsidy for these institutions. This subsidy has been documented in several independent studies by academics and others who do not have a vested interest in the findings. The value of the subsidy varies across studies, but in all of them, it is in the billions of dollars. Today these institutions still carry these subsidies because of uncertainties about whether they would be allowed to fail when they have such broad effects on the economy. The subsidy brings with it many advantages and therefore is an issue that will continue to confront us. How we address the structure of the financial system that brings about the subsidy will do much to shape the economic landscape for decades ahead.

A Proposal to Narrow the Safety Net

My proposal, which was detailed in a May 2011 paper coauthored with Chuck Morris and titled "Restructuring the Banking System to Improve Safety and Soundness," is to narrow the safety net and confine it to commercial banking activities as intended when it was implemented with the Federal Reserve Act of 1913 and the Banking Act of 1933. Commercial banking organizations that are afforded access to the safety net should be limited to conducting the following activities—commercial banking, securities underwriting and advisory services, and asset and wealth management. Most of these latter services are primarily fee-based and do not disproportionately place a firm's capital at risk. They are similar to the trust services that have long been a part of banking.

Allowing the safety net to continue to cover broker-dealer activities is unnecessary and unwise. Although trading and investment activities are important parts of the financial system, they operate more efficiently and safely without government protections. Keeping them inside the safety net exposes the Federal Deposit Insurance Corporation's (FDIC) Deposit Insurance Fund (DIF) and the taxpayer to loss. Therefore, activities that should be placed outside the safety net and thus subject to market forces are most derivative activities, proprietary trading, and trading for customer accounts (or market making). Allowing customer trading makes it easy to game the system by concealing proprietary trading as part of it. Also, prime brokerage services require the ability to trade and essentially allow companies to finance their activities with highly unstable, uninsured, wholesale "deposits" that come with implied protection. This combination of factors, as has recently been seen, leads to unstable markets and government bailouts.

These actions alone would provide limited benefits if the newly restricted activities migrate to shadow banks—broker-dealers, for example. That sector also must be returned to the market's discipline. To do so, we must address potential disruptions coming from money market funding of shadow banks that fund long-term assets. Money market mutual funds and other investments that are currently allowed to maintain a fixed net asset value of $1 should be required to have floating net asset values. Shadow banks' reliance on this source of short-term funding would be greatly reduced by requiring share values to float with their market values.

Additionally, we must change bankruptcy laws to eliminate the automatic stay exemption for mortgage-related repurchase agreement collateral. This exemption, introduced in 2005, resulted in a proliferation in the use of repos based on mortgage-related collateral. This preferential treatment made it possible for complicated and often risky long-term mortgage securities to be used as collateral when the volume of securities was growing rapidly just prior to the bursting of the housing price bubble. One of the sources of instability during the recent financial crisis was repo runs, particularly on repo borrowers using subprime mortgage-related assets as collateral. Essentially, these borrowers funded long-term assets of relatively low quality with very short-term liabilities.

The reforms specified in the proposal that I propose would not—and are not intended to—eliminate natural market-driven risk in the financial system. They do address the misaligned incentives that have caused many of the extreme risks stemming from the safety net's coverage of nonbank activities, both within the financial conglomerates and in shadow banks. The result would be a return to a system of free enterprise where broker-dealer-related activities are subject to greater market discipline, and only the essential intermediation function of commercial banks is protected by the government safety net.

Dodd–Frank and Restrictions on the Safety Net

The Dodd–Frank Act was enacted, in part, to address this issue of financial institutions that are too big to fail. It has many components that attempt the difficult task of containing the safety net and preventing it from being extended. The Volcker Rule restricts proprietary trading activities, and Title I and Title II are designed to ensure that the taxpayer does not bail out these institutions. Title I is the preferred method and would put these institutions into bankruptcy should they fail or have a liquidity crisis. But many complications arise from the viability of bankruptcy for these largest financial institutions. One is that in a crisis, funds run from these institutions regardless of the circumstances because of uncertainty. That creates an issue with debtor-in-possession financing. In an industrial company, debtor-in-possession financing can be done readily. In a financial institution, when people are grabbing their funds, it is much more difficult. So we have a lot of work yet to do to address the debtor-in-possession financing with the liquidity dimensions of Title I.

A second issue is cross-border challenges. When you have a crisis in a financial institution that operates globally, the tendency of the domestic or the host country is to ring-fence (that is, to protect its own citizens no matter what), which makes the liquidity crisis even more difficult. Although the FDIC and others are working to come to agreement with other countries, it is a difficult process and has not yet been solved.

Because Congress recognized that these issues under Title I would be substantial, lawmakers included Title II in the Dodd–Frank Act. Title II allows the FDIC to take these institutions into orderly liquidation, provide debtor-in-possession financing, and work with other countries to resolve cross-border issues. This provides that the government may provide liquidity and a resolution regimen to ensure that certain depositors and creditors of the failed institution receive uninterrupted access to funds and that essential operations continue. It remains questionable whether Title II represents a truly private-sector solution or whether it is a government solution and bailout to some.

Pushing broker-dealer activities outside the safety net would do much to drive that sector of the economy back to the discipline of the market and away from the explicit and implied guarantees of the federal government. It would also go a long way toward simplifying the system and would make bankruptcy a more viable option for these firms if they should fail. Commercial bank holding companies could more easily be put into receivership. Broker-dealers that have been spun out could more easily be put through bankruptcy. Thus, both types of firms could fail with far fewer negative effects on the U.S. and world economies, as was the case with Drexel Burnham and Salomon Brothers.

Objections to the Proposal

One objection to this proposal is that it would impede the ability of U.S. firms to compete internationally. I think that is an unjustified objection. First, it is based on the premise that you need excessively large banks to realize economies of scale. The studies that I have seen suggest that economies of scale are realized at amounts far less than the $2.5 trillion of the largest institutions in this country and even far less than the $300 billion firms (Gambacorta and Van Rixtel 2013). There is no justification for using economies of scale or scope to try to support the assertion that we would not be able compete internationally. Additionally, the public should not accept the premise that it must subsidize highly risky financial activities to compete for international dominance. It is a serious error to presume that if these activities were not subsidized at U.S. commercial banks, they would cease to be offered by other nonsubsidized U.S. firms. Under the proposal, the largest financial firms would remain large and would be more competitive. Our dynamic markets would continue to provide these services via independent broker-dealers but in a more competitive manner where the taxpayer is not part of the transaction.

The incentives that encourage excessive leverage remain. These institutions were allowed to lever far more than the market would allow if they did not have a too-big-to-fail advantage. When their derivatives are brought onto the balance sheet, as done under international accounting standards, it is apparent that most of these institutions, both U.S. and foreign, have capital ratios (leverage ratios) that are extremely low. Most are in the 3 to 4 percent range. Institutions that are not too big to fail—that is, not large enough to be considered systemically important financial institutions (SIFIs)—have capital ratios that are above 8 percent. The capital ratios of the ten largest nonglobal SIFIs are 8.5 percent. The ten largest institutions that have less than $50 billion of assets operate with almost 8 percent tangible capital, and the ten largest that are worth less than a billion dollars have leverage ratios above 8.5 percent. These are the kinds of capital ratios that should be required for all banking firms. When the safety net is removed, I think that the very largest institutions will have to raise their capital levels, and that will be a much greater service to the public than relying on implied guarantees that are a gift from the taxpayer.

The choices that are made today for the financial system are critical to the future success of the U.S. economy. Rationalizing the structure by making the financial conglomerates more market driven will make the system more stable, more innovative, and more competitive—and will serve to support the largest, most successful economy in the world.

Questions and Answers

Question: Based on what you just said, what would you say that raising the leverage ratio to, say, 9, 10, 15 percent would solve most of the problems with or without Dodd–Frank?

Hoenig: Here is what we know. If you look at the history of tangible capital in the United States, you see that the ratios in the early part of the twentieth century, before we had the safety net of deposit insurance, central bank lending, and ultimately direct taxpayer support, were around 15 percent. Following the Great Depression, they were around 12 to 13 percent. As the safety net expanded to cover financial activities outside of core banking, capital levels systematically came down. We also know from research that has been done on the leverage ratio that higher capital ratios (to as high as 20 percent) reduce the probability of failure significantly. So I have suggested that we look to a 10 percent leverage ratio because it is affordable, it is justified in history, and I think it is very reasonable. A 10 percent ratio does reduce the likelihood of failure. It does not eliminate it, but it reduces the likelihood of failure for these institutions. Remember, no amount of capital will save an institution from incompetent management. Capital is there for competent management that makes mistakes, and we know that 10 percent is a reasonable number to start with, although levels of 5 to 6 percent would be a major step toward improving stability.

Question: Are higher ratios of tangible capital enough, or do you also want to cap the size of the institution?

Hoenig: In our proposal, we do not call for capping the size of an institution. My concern with the largest institutions primarily is their complexity, not their size. Selecting the right size seems arbitrary, and it is usually gamed away. That is why we have proposed separating the gambling side of the balance sheet of financial institutions from commercial banking and letting the market regulate it. The broker-dealer would still be under the SEC, but the market would regulate the capital that is demanded of it. The issue that I think was important in 2008 was that the tangible capital of the ten largest financial institutions in this country was less than 3 percent. They were reporting a risk-based capital ratio of approximately 11 percent at the time, but people do not distinguish between risk-based capital and tangible capital. When you say a capital ratio of 11 percent, most individuals think you mean tangible. But in fact, the tangible capital ratio—the real loss-absorbing level of capital—was less than 3 percent. The margin of error was so slim that it should not surprise anyone that we had a systemic crisis. Many of the major financial institutions had losses of more than 3 percent on their assets, so they ended up being bailed out.

Audience: There is a big difference between GAAP and IFRS [International Financial Reporting Standards] because of the treatment of derivatives. Do you have a view on which one is better?

Hoenig: Yes. I am a strong supporter of the International Financial Reporting Standards because they bring derivatives onto the balance sheet, thus giving us a more accurate picture of a firm's assets and liabilities than we get under GAAP. We were very close in this country to adopting IFRS, but unfortunately, we didn't. First of all, let's make sure we are not booking the notional value of derivatives, which are on the order of $280 trillion. We should be booking the gross fair value that is computed systematically across all institutions and that recognizes that different cash flows can't be netted unless there is a specific contract. Then you can compare across firms in the United States, firms in Europe, and firms in Asia on an apples-to-apples basis. Right now, you can't because GAAP allows gross netting of derivatives. That is like saying, "If I make you a loan and you collateralize it and if I like the collateral, I don't have to report the loan on my books because, of course, it's collateralized." Well, that is what you are doing with these derivatives under GAAP. You have a derivative, and you have a counterparty, but you have netted, so you don't have to put that on your books. That is misleading.

Without derivatives, both GAAP and international accounting standards give you the same result.

Question: You spoke in your talk about the importance of rolling back a safety net in some areas of the financial markets. Title XI of Dodd–Frank has a new provision, however, that allows the Treasury secretary, in times of economic distress, to ask the FDIC and the Fed to vote on whether a liquidity event has happened in the markets. If so, the FDIC can put into place a broad-based guarantee program for solvent banks, bank holding companies, and all their affiliates. Do you have any thoughts about what seems to be a huge potential expansion of the safety net?

Hoenig: Well, that provision in a sense validates what was done in the last crisis because massive guarantees were given to U.S. institutions, and they have had global impact. So it is not something that is new. For lack of a better word, I will call it a safety valve. But we expect that Title I will trigger first and that we will be able to put financial institutions into bankruptcy. Or failing that, Title II will provide for an orderly liquidation. My own experience is that on Friday evenings, secretaries of the Treasury Department do not want to have a bad experience Monday morning, and so there is a tendency to broaden the safety net.

That is what worries me. And that is why I think it is very important to push these high-risk activities away from the bank and away from the safety net. Pushing these activities away from the bank increases the probability that we put these institutions into bankruptcy. I think it is very, very important that we do that.

Question: You propose increasing the amount of capital for banks by a large amount in a relatively short timeframe. You're talking about taking a lot of leverage out of the system. That would be politically difficult even if you phased it in over a long period of time. So how do you think some of these policies could be implemented?

Hoenig: It is true that the political economy is a challenge. But capital matters, and if the largest institutions continue to operate with levels of capital that were proven in 2008 to be unable to absorb downturns and mistakes, eventually we will have another systemic event. I think, for example, that the Basel discussions ought to be focused on what the level of tangible capital should be and what the length of time should be provided to get to the higher level. One of the misleading arguments against this is that lending will contract if we impose higher capital ratios. However, research shows that those institutions that were better capitalized prior to the crisis were able to carry their loans during the crisis much more successfully. They were able to continue to lend or hold existing loans during the crisis. Institutions that were thinly capitalized literally imploded, and credit was constricted to an enormous degree (Kapan and Minoiu 2013).

Question: Are there studies of how much leverage would have to come out of the system and the implications of that deleveraging?

Hoenig: All of these financial institutions are fighting very hard to continue to pay their dividends. Let me tell you some facts. Between 1980 and 2008, these institutions levered up to hit their return on equity (ROE) targets that were absolutely inconsistent with a regulated commercial banking industry. But because of the safety net and their ability to leverage far more than the market otherwise would demand, they leveraged out and the consequences were devastating. So if we want to have long-term, sustainable economic growth, then we ought to have a long-term plan to recapitalize through retained earnings. If they want to grow more quickly, they can raise capital. But to maintain the status quo is to invite the next catastrophe with 8 million people unemployed and no credit available. To me, that is a dire tradeoff. And economists, particularly, should know better than to look only at the short-term effects. It is true that the politics are daunting, but the alternative is worse in the long run.

Question: You mentioned that the problem with bankruptcy is the issue of liquidity with financial institutions. Do you favor creating a new source of liquidity in bankruptcy, and if so, where would the liquidity come from, and what would be the best approach?

Hoenig: Well, that is the issue, and there is a group working pretty diligently on it. You may be familiar with the chapter XIV approach, which is designed to make debtor-in-possession financing more workable in the bankruptcy process for financial holding companies. That would allow these institutions to take certain assets and use them to raise and maintain liquidity in the market. But they have not been able to solve the problem. They have not been able to bring forward the plan that would ensure confidence in the market to provide that liquidity to keep it from freezing up. One of the difficulties right now is lack of confidence that Title I is the solution that we want it to be. Even in Dodd–Frank, bankruptcy is Congress's preferred method of resolution. The problem is liquidity, and we have not solved the problem yet.

The living-will process is a kind of a prepackaged bankruptcy plan. We are working through this now, but it is very difficult to do because of global issues. How do you get the right assets that are not already pledged? How do you redo it? Is there enough debt at the parent company? These questions go on and on with no obvious answer yet.

Question: Would you favor extending chapter XIV to other entities besides commercial banks?

Hoenig: Such an extension would raise the possibility of also extending the safety net to an ever-greater number of firms, which would increase the moral hazard problem by a large factor and put greater pressure on the taxpayer as a bailout source. Or alternatively, we will have to make a decision that these are public utilities that we run like the GSEs—Fannie Mae and Freddie Mac. I do not recommend that because you get worse outcomes. So I think that the better solution is narrowing the safety net to cover only commercial banking and letting the market govern all the other financial activities. If we don't, we eventually will make the largest financial firms into public utilities.

Question: It would seem to me that part of the issue with too big to fail is the market participant's perception that government is willing to assist these institutions and provide the sort of Sunday night assistance we saw during the crisis. So having a toolkit to address these is fine, but if there is no willingness to use that toolkit, it does not seem credible. What can we do to change that part of the equation?

Hoenig: You ask a very good question, and my experience tells me there is not an answer yet. I think that if you take my suggestion and separate broker-dealer activities from commercial banking and the protections that come with it, you will help make it easier to resolve these institutions should they fail. The difficulty is if you have three or four institutions that are 60 percent GDP going down and you are the secretary of the Treasury Department, your incentive is to solve this problem by whatever means necessary. This too often means bailout because we do not want 8 million people out of work and credit to freeze up. To allow the firms to fail without these systemic consequences, you have to simplify their structure by spinning out the broker-dealer functions. Then failing broker-dealers can go into bankruptcy and failing banks through the resolution process, and the creditors in both cases lose. But it is a big challenge to get the structure of our financial system to that point.

Audience: You made a very sensible recommendation to limit tangible rather than risk-based capital. As you know, every investor paid attention to tangible equity ratios and market value. What about your fellow regulators? Are they onboard with you, or are you just a sounding board while they wait to see what other people say?

Hoenig: I can't speak for them, but at this point I have not seen any speeches that are supportive of my position. I think there is a strong view that Basel III is better than Basel II and therefore we are moving forward. My view is that better is not good enough—that we really have to address the fundamental issue of capital. Basel III's denominator, risk assets, still provides real opportunities for the gamesmanship we have seen practiced under Basel II. My proposal takes into account the tangible equity ratio and then uses risk weights as a kind of a backstop measure to the leverage ratio. In my proposal, risk weights indicate whether financial institutions are concentrating too much in one particular area or increasing their risk in a particular asset, but they first face a very strong minimum tangible capital ratio. I agree with you that today, more than ever, investors are looking to tangible capital. They are not paying any attention to risk-based capital and wisely so, wisely so. Hopefully, as more and more evidence comes out that tangible capital is a better indicator—a better predictor of problems—and provides a better margin against mistakes, there will be a wider acceptance of tangible capital as the primary risk measure and risk-weighted capital as a secondary measure.

References

Gambacorta, Leonardo, and Adrian Van Rixtel. 2013. Structural Bank Initiatives: Approaches and Implications. BIS Working Paper No. 412, April.

Hoenig, Thomas, and Charles Morris. 2011. Restructuring the Banking System to Improve Safety and Soundness. Manuscript.

Kapan, Tumar, and Camelia Minoiu. 2013. Balance Sheet Strength and Bank Lending during the Global Financial Crisis. IMF Working Paper.

5   Panel Discussion on Banking Reform

Anil K Kashyap, James Overdahl, Anjan Thakor, and John Walsh

James Overdahl: We will focus on some specific aspects of banking reform—particularly, what has led us to bank reform in the Dodd–Frank Wall Street Reform and Consumer Protection Act of 2010. Gary Gorton's wonderful essay entitled "Slapped in the Face by the Invisible Hand" is one explanation of what happened. It seems to me that what we experienced during the crisis was not a George Bailey problem, although we may have benefitted from having a few more Mr. Potters around. It was not a run on retail deposits like during the Great Depression but an institutional bank run. That is one of the things that we will talk about here.

The legislative process that created the Dodd–Frank Act has been likened to a barroom brawl where participants refrain from hitting the guy who started the fight in favor of hitting the guy that they have been looking for an opportunity to hit. With Dodd–Frank, the legislation failed to address certain key issues that were widely viewed as central causes to the financial crisis of 2007 and 2008, such as the unraveling of systemically important government-sponsored enterprises (GSEs). However, like the aforementioned brawl, Dodd–Frank addressed many issues that were not central to or even remotely related to the crisis but had more to do with settling long-standing grievances. For example, it is hard to construct a plausible path between corporate disclosures regarding conflict minerals, an issue that Dodd–Frank instructed the Securities and Exchange Commission (SEC) to address, and the financial crisis. Likewise, Dodd–Frank instructed the Commodity Futures Trading Commission (CFTC) to adopt federally mandated energy futures market-position limits and to prohibit "disruptive" futures trading. Both issues predated the financial crisis but were included in the legislation.

In this session on the Dodd–Frank Act and banking reform, panelists will address regulations currently being crafted by banking regulators in their efforts to implement the act. The regulatory response to the most recent crisis has produced a banking reform agenda not seen since the New Deal response to the Great Depression. However, unlike the New Deal bank reforms that were aimed at the bank runs on retail deposits that characterized the Great Depression, the financial crisis of 2007 and 2008 has produced reforms aimed at institutional bank runs on repurchase agreement (repo) markets, prime brokerage, collateral, and prime money market mutual funds. Current reforms are also aimed at bolstering the resiliency of banks and other systemically important financial institutions (SIFIs) through regulation of bank capital, bank risk profiles, and the scope of bank activities. Current reforms also address the issue of financial institutions that are judged to be too big to fail or too interconnected to fail. Additional reforms seek to reduce the effects of failed systemically important financial institutions on other institutions by authorizing greater resolution powers to government authorities. As our panelists discuss, considerable controversy exists over whether these contemplated reforms will be effective in preventing another financial crisis or whether they will have the undesirable consequence of planting the seeds for the next financial crisis by merely shifting risk from one set of systemically important financial institutions to other vulnerable parts of the economy.

The Dodd–Frank Act reforms can be implemented only through the rulemaking process at federal regulatory agencies. Dodd–Frank instructed or authorized regulators to write rules to achieve goals articulated in the act but often left the most complex and contentious issues for regulators to deal with. In some cases, the act requires joint rule making by several regulators, further complicating the implementation process. Even though Congress set ambitious timetables for implementation, the complexity of the issues, combined with the obligations of regulators to adhere to the requirements of the Administrative Procedure Act, have slowed the rulemaking pace.

Court challenges to regulations promulgated under Dodd–Frank pose an additional hurdle for implementation. The courts have already invalidated Dodd–Frank rules, such as the SEC's proxy access rules, sending the rules back to regulators for further review on the grounds that regulators have failed to consider the economic consequences of their rules. Court challenges are likely to continue throughout the process requiring that regulators devote the necessary resources to justify the exercise of their regulatory authority. The potential for court challenges will likely further slow the regulatory implementation of Dodd–Frank as regulators must take the time to ensure that no procedural corners are cut, in spite of congressional timetables, so that their rulemaking process will endure judicial scrutiny. Because of the success of court challenges that have turned on the quality of economic analysis considered by regulators, parties likely to be affected by the new Dodd–Frank rules have devoted more attention to the quality of economic arguments they make before regulators. Affected parties hope that their arguments will assist regulators in crafting new rules, but they also hope to lay the groundwork for potential court challenges by creating a record of economic arguments and evidence that can be reviewed by judges.

In addition to instructing regulators to implement new rules and regulations, the Dodd–Frank Act also created new regulatory authorities such as the Financial Stability Oversight Council (FSOC), Consumer Financial Protection Bureau (CFPB), Office of Financial Research, Office of National Insurance, and Office of Credit Rating Agencies. Dodd–Frank also provided regulators with new enforcement tools and authorities, providing another path for the expansion of the boundaries of regulation through path of aggressive enforcement actions. Together, the new regulations and authority at existing regulatory agencies, the new regulatory authorities, and the empowerment of regulators' enforcement divisions mean that banks and other financial institutions face a continually shifting regulatory landscape. It is the job of this panel to help make sense of all this.

John Walsh provides an overview of the regulatory implementation process for Dodd–Frank. Anjan Thakor addresses issues related to bank capital, financial fragility, and banking reform. Finally, Anil Kashyap addresses the issues of run behavior that was displayed at financial institutions during the financial crisis.

John Walsh: I am the nonacademic at this academic conference and have been working at McKinsey and Company for just about nine months, helping financial clients understand what they should be doing to adapt to the new regulatory environment. Ideally, new regulations should be sensible, address actual problems, and develop responses based on sound evidence. We should then implement them with appropriate review to ensure that the solution fits the problem. But this is Washington, D.C., and that is not the way we typically do things.

I have observed through several crises that major financial reforms follow closely on a crisis and tend to be developed in a fever. In the legislative process, reforms are often finalized in marathon all-night sessions in which the participants are deeply sleep deprived. Agreement is reached at, say, 4:30 a.m., and the bill sent off to be prepared as final legislation with results that can be quite chaotic. Legend has it that after the savings and loan crisis, the final bill that went to the White House actually had the name and phone number of a lobbyist in the document sent to the president to be signed. It had to be taken out later in the subsequent technical corrections bill that always follows major legislation.

But politics being what they are these days, a particular and unfortunate feature of this legislation is that partisanship on both sides of the aisle made it difficult to have sensible discussions of how to deal with difficult issues. That same political dynamic has made it difficult to do what normally would be obvious technical corrections and revisions where there are flaws in the legislative language. Inability to act has not stopped the debate, however, so several years after the passage of the all-encompassing Dodd–Frank Act, with many of its implementing rules still to be finalized, there l a debate is still raging over whether the too-big-to-fail problem requires further legislation.

In chapter 4, Thomas M. Hoenig proposes an alternative formulation of the banking system that would look quite different from either the current system or the new framework being put into place. So I am going to set the scene by describing what exactly Dodd–Frank mandates and where we are in implementing it. Then my fellow panelists will examine whether we got any of that right.

Looking back to the Depression era, the laws that changed the financial world at that time were brief documents that stated concisely what should be done. Dodd–Frank, on the other hand, ran to thousands of pages. The implementing rules will be many thousands of pages more. So it is a much more complicated undertaking. Some of that has to do with the evolution of the system over time and the increasing complexity of finance, but it is also true that legislation in the present era is simply much more specific about what institutions will be expected to do.

Alongside the expansion of rules and regulations, regulators have greatly expanded the volume and scope of information that banks and other financial institutions are required to report, including standard reporting like the Call Report, large-bank reporting to the Fed, and transaction-level data on mortgage portfolios, credit card portfolios, and home equity loan portfolios. It is a huge undertaking to keep up with these demands for information and begs the question of how regulators can use that information effectively to evaluate the safety of the system and how institutions are managing risk.

The natural outcome of these new requirements is that CEOs, management, and boards spend a great deal of time dealing with regulation, certainly much more than they did before the financial crisis. Inevitably, they have to understand and implement the new rules that are being put in place and readjust to the new regulatory and business environment.

The Other Regulatory Fronts

This new regulatory environment is not a result of just Dodd–Frank but has emerged on three fronts. First, there is the international response to the crisis. Although one could well argue that the crisis began in the United States, triggered in our subprime sector, the crisis was transmitted to other countries through asset-backed securities and structured financial products and fed by financial leverage. Regardless of where it started, the international character of the crisis brought an international response. The Financial Stability Board, which includes central banks and regulators from twenty of the largest economies, directed a set of international agreements to be put in place. The most prominent among them were agreements developed by the Basel Committee on Banking Supervision as well as by the International Organization of Securities Commissions (IOSCO) and others. The Basel agreement calls for higher capital, greater liquidity, and other changes that are summarized as Basel III.

The second front was national rulemaking that has proceeded country by country, both to implement the international agreements just described and to take such additional regulatory steps as were considered necessary in each country. It can be stated, without fear of contradiction, that the largest of those undertakings is the Dodd–Frank Act in the United States.

The third front, certainly in the United States, is the enforcement process that has resulted in a great deal of specific regulation and changes in business practice, in addition to assessment of penalties. A lot of this involves enforcement of preexisting laws, not new requirements from Dodd–Frank, that deal with fair treatment of customers and proper handling of mortgages, especially in the foreclosure process. Tougher enforcement of laws always follows a crisis, but the response has been particularly marked in this instance. A large portion of the change with which banks are now dealing has emerged from the enforcement process.

Among the least controversial portions of the new regulatory agenda is the internationally agreed program, especially the Basel III framework, which focuses on higher capital and both short-term and longer-term liquidity. Basel III changes capital requirements along several dimensions. First, there is a tighter definition of capital, focused on Tier One common equity. This tighter definition rules out hybrid capital instruments that did not provide a reliable capital cushion in the crisis. Second, the denominator has been expanded to include a wider range of risk-weighted assets. Heavier weights have also been introduced for certain categories of risk. Most important, required capital has been increased in absolute terms. Under the old regime, minimum Tier One common only needed to be about 2 percent of risk-weighted assets, so banks could lever 50 to 1 by this measure, although the market required them to hold more than the minimum. That requirement has now been increased to a base level of 7 percent. For the systemically important financial institutions (SIFIs), an additional 1 to 2.5 percent buffer has been added on top of that.

So this is a substantial change in minimum capital requirements, far more significant than the absolute number would indicate owing to the tightening of definitions and expansion of included assets. One can argue that this set of changes is not enough, but it represents a dramatic change from requirements precrisis. It establishes minimum regulatory capital levels substantially above the capital that was actually held by those banks that came through the crisis without loss of market confidence or capacity.

Although the Basel III agreement enjoys universal support by governments, it is worth noting that the new framework is not fully in effect anywhere yet. The United States has never yet permitted a single bank to operate under the Basel II risk-based capital framework that underlies Basel III for sophisticated institutions. Rather, the annual stress test that the Federal Reserve has been conducting since the crisis—initially known as the Supervisory Capital Assessment Program (SCAP) and now as the Comprehensive Capital Analysis and Review (CCAR)—is the binding capital constraint on U.S. banks. It is a tough test that U.S. banks and certain large foreign banks operating in the United States have to pass to operate free of regulatory constraints or penalties. Other countries are pursuing their own variations on capital and liquidity rules, ring-fencing liquidity, and limiting permissible banking activities. The Swiss, in particular, have pushed up capital levels to levels substantially above those mandated by Basel III.

Although the Basel III agreement has not resulted in consistent national implementation among Basel Committee members, it is noteworthy that its reach has expanded as membership has grown from the G-10 countries to the G-20, an expansion negotiated in response to the financial crisis. There has also been an evolution in the range of banks subject to the rules set in Basel. The original Basel capital rules were developed for large internationally active banks in member countries but were applied and adopted more widely by member and nonmember countries alike over time. They have now become universal standards, effectively applied to all banks in whole or in part, across all countries. So what we now know as the Basel framework has changed in many directions.

Where Dodd–Frank Goes beyond the Basel Framework

Going beyond the Basel framework, Dodd–Frank has introduced reforms of many kinds in the United States. There are basic institutional reforms that include creation of the Financial Stability Oversight Council (FSOC) to monitor risks across the wider financial the system, chaired by the secretary of the Department of the Treasury and including the heads of all of the federal regulatory agencies, state representatives, and others. There is also an expanded and more intensive role for the Fed in bank holding company supervision and increased responsibility for nonbank systemically important institutions designated by FSOC. The Federal Deposit Insurance Corporation (FDIC) has been given an expanded role in orderly liquidations and more involvement in monitoring the largest banks. The former Office of Thrift Supervision has been eliminated and folded into the Office of the Comptroller of the Currency, and a new Consumer Financial Protection Bureau has been created.

In addition to these institutional changes, there are new restrictions and prohibitions on the activities that financial institutions can undertake and their conduct of business. These include the prohibition on proprietary trading and certain fund investments under the Volcker Rule, restrictions on debit fees under the Durbin Amendment, expanded and more intrusive supervision of over-the-counter (OTC) derivatives, systematic reliance on central counterparties for derivatives trades, risk retention for securitized assets, and changes in structure as a result of the living-will process. In addition, the process of devising an international approach to resolve large institutions has resulted in more of a nationally focused approach to supervision with ring-fencing of capital, liquidity, and operations in individual countries. On top of substantially higher capital and liquidity requirements, a range of other costs, including an expanded share of funding for the deposit insurance system and expanded consumer compliance requirements, have affected the large banks.

With all the change that has already occurred, it is worth noting that Dodd–Frank rulemaking is far from complete. About two-thirds of the required rules have been issued in either proposed or final form, so another significant chunk is still to be taken up. Those yet to be written are not the kind of big-ticket items that have been discussed thus far, but during 2013 or early 2014, we expect key pending rules to become final with significant effect on the economics of banking. These include the capital, Volcker, securitization, and derivatives rules. And the first of the new rules have come out of the CFPB for mortgages.

An additional level of complexity for both rulemaking and the supervision and enforcement of those rules arises from the complex U.S. regulatory structure. The Office of the Comptroller of the Currency, the Federal Reserve, and the FDIC are all charged with prudential regulation of banks. The large banks are also subject to direct supervision by the Consumer Financial Protection Bureau, which looks intensively at their retail consumer activities, although the prudential supervisors are not entirely removed from that space. Finally, the state regulators and attorneys general have been active and aggressive, particularly, in the context of mortgage and anti-money laundering activities.

The market regulators—the SEC and the CFTC—also play an important role in rulemaking for banks, and joint rulemakings with them are particularly challenging. If a single agency has to write a rule, it gets to it pretty directly. If the three banking agencies have to write a single rule, it is more complicated, but they all speak the same language and can eventually work out their differences. But some of the Dodd–Frank rules, like securitization, Volcker, and others, are written jointly by the market regulators, the banking regulators, and sometimes the Federal Housing Finance Agency. These agencies have different approaches and need different kinds of rules to inform supervision inside a bank as opposed to setting broad norms for participants in securities and derivatives markets. It is challenging for them to write rules together, which is one of the reasons that some of these rulemakings have taken a long time—even where there are not substantial differences of view about desired outcomes. There can also be an element of regulatory competition or sincere differences of view that complicate matters, which, in the current environment, translates to a battle to see who can be the toughest.

Finally, returning to the effect of enforcement actions, it has been profound. The scandal over foreclosure robo-signing seems like ancient history now, but it was only a few years ago that foreclosures were being filed without proper documentation, and filings were being made in court or before administrative law judges that had been fraudulently prepared—each such action a violation of state law. That resulted in tough mortgage consent orders by the Office of the Comptroller of the Currency (OCC) and Fed against the fourteen largest mortgage servicers and in a settlement by the five largest mortgage services with the state attorneys general for $25 billion in mortgage relief to consumers. So banks face a complex landscape on the enforcement front as well, and that is also changing the ways that banks do business.

What Has Been Accomplished

Let me conclude by posing a few questions that are left to ponder after the crisis and the crisis response that is still being implementing. With the huge changes that have occurred in the way that banks operate and the rules under which they operate, is the system safer than it was before? I believe the answer is categorically yes: the banking system is safer than it was before. Capital and liquidity in the banking system are at much higher levels than before the crisis, and at all the largest banks, they are well above the levels held by similar banks that weathered the crisis without difficulty. The stability both of large individual banks and the overall system has clearly been fortified.

Turning to the continuing debate over the fate of large banks, have we solved the too-big-to-fail problem? Unfortunately, we will not know definitively if we have solved too big to fail until the next time a large bank gets into difficulty and the bank is or is not successfully closed. What we do know is that there are rules in place and institutional arrangements in place to achieve that objective. I believe without a doubt that the authorities will close the next large institution that is on the brink of failure. I see the key question as not whether it is possible to deal with a single institution but what to do about the large financial institutions when you have a widespread market crisis. How do you deal with those institutions in that environment and under those circumstances to prevent runs and a catastrophic meltdown from taking place? Government support will almost certainly be needed—and appropriate.

A third question is whether the system is not just safer as a result of all the new regulation but also sound and capable of providing the appropriate level and range of financial services that the economy needs. I would argue that, with the exception of the capital, liquidity, and risk-management rules, little of the remaining agenda does much to address systemic safety, but significant parts of it challenge the ability of the banks to earn a suitable return on their business. Given all that has gone wrong, we should perhaps not be worried that that new normal of banking will be very different from what went before, but if it is very different, it is important to consider how banks will adapt. They will adapt with difficulty if the result of all the rulemaking is conflicting and overly burdensome rules, and my worry is that regulators are solving every problem two or three different ways—reducing leverage, and increasing capital and liquidity, and requiring more collateral, and restricting specific activities. Coming at the problems from many different directions makes successful pursuit of the business of banking much more challenging.

Finally, are all the regulatory changes setting the right incentives for future financial stability, innovation, customer service, and other policy objectives? There is intense focus and a raging debate at the moment about incentives that government has provided that may encourage bigness in banks. But the government creates all sorts of incentives for the system all the time. Some are virtuous and favor saving, investment, sound banking, and higher capital. But others have been more problematic, placing excessive emphasis on expanding the housing sector and creating fiscal and global imbalances that can create a perverse environment for savings and investment and require massive financial recycling. So although it is appropriate to worry about incentives to excessive size, it is also important to remember that government directly facilitated creation of some of the $2 trillion banks. They did not exist before the crisis and achieved their present size often with the encouragement of government—usually as part of an effort to absorb those that were in weakest condition and protect the overall economy.

Anjan Thakor: I am going to examine financial fragility and banking reform, place Dodd–Frank in a larger context, and address more broadly bank capital.

It is always interesting to me that all discussions of banking reform tend to occur in the aftermath of a crisis. We never seem to discuss banking reform the way that textbooks prescribe, which is in a sensible, calm, rational manner. John C. Coffee, in a 2012 paper called "The Political Economy of Dodd–Frank: Why Financial Reform Tends to Be Frustrated and Systemic Risk Perpetuated," looks at why it is difficult to discuss or legislate any major banking reform unless there is a crisis. The reason is that it is very hard to put together the political coalitions that are needed to make major changes. The popular view (and there is some disagreement) is that this crisis was caused by misaligned incentives—that financial institutions took too much risk because of de jure and de facto safety nets. Regulators were not sufficiently vigilant. They allowed financial institutions to take excessive risks because of a misalignment of incentives between regulators and taxpayers. And politicians did not help, either. Joseph Stiglitz (2010) asserts in his book that many politicians were overly eager to embrace free markets and blocked regulation that would have made a lot of sense. In chapter 2 in this book, Chester Spatt refers to the Financial Crisis Inquiry Commission report that reached a somewhat similar conclusion. It said that regulators saw warning signs of the crisis but deliberately chose to ignore them. The Federal Reserve, in particular, was too supportive of industry growth objectives and failed to put the brakes on risk-taking and growth when it should have.

Not everybody agrees with or endorses this point of view. In an interesting 2012 article in the *Journal of Economic Literature*, Andrew Lo reviews twenty-one books on the financial crisis, roughly half of them written by academics and half by journalists. He says the following:

There are several observations to be made from the number and variety of narratives that the authors in this review have preferred. The most obvious is that there is still significant disagreement as to what the underlying causes of the crisis were and even less agreement as to what to do about it. But what may be more disconcerting for most economists is the fact that we can't even agree on all the facts. Did CEOs take too much risk? Were they acting as they were incentivized to act? Was there too much leverage in the system? Did regulators do their job? Or was forbearance a significant factor? Was the Fed's low interest rate policy responsible for the housing bubble? Or did other factors cause housing prices to skyrocket? Was liquidity the issue with respect to the runs on the repo market, or was it more of a solvency issue among a handful of problem banks? (Lo 2012, 173)

I recently was at a conference meeting at the Federal Reserve Bank of Cleveland, where a paper seemed to suggest very strongly that the unavailability of liquidity that was witnessed during the crisis was more due to bank-specific solvency issues rather than a marketwide liquidity freeze. So there is a lot of disagreement on even the basic facts, such as the widely presumed marketwide liquidity freeze that was used to justify the massive intervention by the Fed that Congress approved during the crisis.

But misaligned incentives, which seems to be the most popular explanation, cannot be the whole story. In a 2013 working paper that is still being revised, I argue that individual agents believe that there is some probability that outcomes for banks are determined by sheer luck and some (higher) probability that they are due to the skills of bankers. The longer things go well, the more confidence we (meaning academics, regulators, bankers, financiers, and rating agencies) develop in the ability of bankers to manage these risks. So if you are a rational, Bayesian updating person, you would do this, which would lead to an increase in risk-taking because it is not punitively priced given the improved ability assessments. As long as banks are experiencing success, risk-taking keeps building, and the financial sector keeps growing as more and more risk gets put on and off the balance sheets of financial institutions. If any events trigger a change from the belief that the ability of banks determines outcomes to the belief that it is largely a matter of luck, liquidity dries up and you get a crisis. And this shift in beliefs could be triggered by a whole host of things including unexpected defaults in certain sectors.

The Dangers of High Leverage

Although I agree with Andrew Lo that there is a lot of disagreement over the causes of the crisis, I think that the emerging research points to a few things that most people can probably agree on. Numerous papers point out that high leverage among financial institutions makes individual financial institutions more risky and more fragile and increases systemic risk. Because it increases systemic risk, it increases the need for bailouts. After financial institutions recognize that the probability of bailouts has gone up, they react rationally and perversely increase leverage and risk-taking. This point has been made in a 2009 paper by Emmanuel Farhi and Jean Tirole (2009). My working paper with Viral Acharya (Acharya and Thakor 2010) makes a somewhat related point. We also argue that if you have more highly leveraged institutions, then the failure of one institution is more likely to trigger the pressure put by creditors on other institutions. This could increase the cost of rollover funding or result in rollover funding being cut off entirely in these institutions. Even though some may view high leverage as a bank-specific issue, it introduces systemic risk through capital-structure-induced contagion. The more highly levered the institutions, the more likely it is that banks' specific problems will be amplified into systemic risk issues. This suggests that the right level of capital for an individual institution involves the risks held by that institution and also the negative spillover effects of that institution's leverage, through this sort of contagion, on other institutions that may hold correlated assets.

One message that emerges from this is that while the FSOC will help improve the tracking of systemic risks, high leverage can create systemic risks in subtle ways, and these risks may not show up in the data in a timely manner that can be tracked usefully. If risks are not reflected in the data that FSOC tracks, then systemic risks may build up silently in the economy, and it may be too late for the Fed to intervene effectively by the time these risks show up in the data. So one message that is coming out of this research is that higher capital requirements are needed. By this I mean equity capital as a percentage of assets and not only risk-weighted assets, to avoid some of the gaming issues with risk weights. This is needed to control both bank-specific risks and systemic risks.

At a recent conference in Europe, my discussant countered that if you look at the top four hundred banks in the United States and the European Union from 1991 to 2004, prior to the crisis, most were above the 4 percent capital threshold, so capital deficiency did not drive the set of events that culminated in the crisis. I think this is highly misleading because it relies on flawed assumptions. One is that we are measuring capital correctly, and the other is that 4 percent is the right capital threshold. There is increasing agreement among a lot of people that 4 percent is far below ideal thresholds. This reminds me of some of the papers that were written before the crisis, with titles like "Why Are Banks Holding So Much Excess Capital?" I have not seen those papers since the crisis.

Increasing Capital Requirements while Maintaining Incentives to Monitor

When higher capital requirements are proposed, one argument (and this argument is more academic than practical) says that if more capital is introduced into banks, then it will increase the safety of banks so much that it also will reduce the incentives of uninsured creditors to monitor these banks, thereby diluting market discipline, making banks more fraud-prone, or making them diminished players in the business of creating liquidity. Market discipline has been an important aspect of bank regulation, and we want to rely on both regulatory discipline and the discipline imposed by markets. The argument is that if you put too much capital into banks, it somehow will reduce those incentives. So in deference to that argument, my 2012 discussion paper, written with Hamid Mehran and Viral Acharya (2012), provides a formal analysis of a proposal to inject more capital into banking without disturbing any incentives for uninsured creditors to impose market discipline on banks. The total capital of the bank can be thought of as consisting of two components—a normal capital account and a special capital account. The normal capital account could be tier-one capital, a leverage ratio, or just equity. The special capital account is equity as a percentage of total assets, which includes both on-balance-sheet and off-balance-sheet assets.

The key innovation is that this special capital account belongs to the banks' shareholders as long as the bank is solvent (for example, it would belong to the acquirer of the bank if the bank is acquired as a solvent entity). But if the bank has to be bailed out, this capital does not accrue to the creditors but belongs to the regulator. As far as the banks' uninsured creditors are concerned, this capital is invisible to them because they can never get it. As long as the bank is solvent, it is being repaid, so the special capital does not matter. When the bank approaches insolvency, this capital is not available to them, so as far as they are concerned, it does not exist. On the other hand, because the shareholders have the possibility of losing this capital, conditional on default, they care very much about it. If we believe that more equity capital in the bank helps attenuate the banks' risk-taking incentives, then this provides the benefits of capital. Shareholders have more at risk, and having additional capital in the bank in the form of special capital lowers the bank's risk-taking incentives. In a sense, it provides the best of both worlds. It provides equity discipline because it puts more of shareholders' money at risk so they have more skin in the game. On the other hand, it does not reduce the skin in the game that the uninsured creditors have, so they have as much incentive to monitor the bank as they would in the absence of the special capital. So the special capital account has positive incentive effects, if that is an important issue, and I believe it is.

There are details to consider in implementing the special capital account. First, how is the special capital account built? How can banks be encouraged to raise equity upfront? I propose that all money that goes into the special capital account should be built up through earnings retentions and dividend restrictions. There can be a phased-in capital requirement rather than a requirement that banks issue equity to meet higher capital requirements. The tier-one capital can be directly invested in anything that is permitted by the bank's charter. It also can be used to leverage the bank's balance sheets so that if the requirement is, say, 10 percent, then every dollar of normal capital is going to allow the bank to add $10 in assets. The special capital account has the same leverage capability as the regular capital account, but it can be invested only in a liquid instrument (for example, Treasuries). This does not address the issue that Chester Spatt has raised about whether Treasuries can be used as collateral when a bank runs out of securities. But this special account can be directly invested only in Treasuries. If the bank's tier-one capital declines because of negative earning shocks, there will be a transfer from the special capital account to the normal capital account. The dividend restrictions would allow the special capital account to be built back up. After it is back up to the regulatory mandated level, the dividend restrictions could be lifted, and the bank would go back to paying dividends as it did before.

As is mentioned above, shareholders own this account in the good states, and regulators own this account if the bank is not solvent. The special capital account (SCA) could be made countercyclical in the spirit of one of the components of Basel III, and so the capital ratio could be raised in good times and built up. Instead of asking banks to raise external equity, the special capital account could be built up through earnings retentions and dividend restrictions. This avoids the adverse selection costs that are associated with having to raise equity, which is the cost that people usually refer to when they argue against asking banks to raise additional equity. In this case, there also is no discretion for regulators. The trigger for transferring capital from the SCA into the normal capital account and restricting dividends is mechanical. Every time a bank falls below the mandated regulatory level on the special capital account, there is an automatic mechanical trigger, and predetermined dividend restrictions are put in place. No information is revealed, so there are not the kinds of self-fulfilling prophecy problems that occur with contingent convertible bonds (CoCos), for example. It provides the best of both debt and equity discipline because both shareholders and creditors can have a lot of skin in the game. And because the special capital is invested in Treasuries, there are not the kinds of issues that everyone worried about during the crisis (like asset fire sales and downward price spirals). Ideally, there is enough liquidity in this market for U.S. Treasury securities that these concerns are not an issue.

The countercyclicality of the special capital account also deals with another issue that I discuss in Thakor (2013). Whenever times are good, risk-taking incentives inevitably go up, and incentives that regulators can use to put the brakes on risk-taking are at their weakest. People at the Federal Reserve have told me that when things were going well before the 2008 crisis, economists at the Fed found it difficult to convince their bosses that bank risk-taking had to be restrained. In the financial system, it is difficult politically to talk about higher capital requirements or restrictions when things are going well. The banks can resist any additional regulatory restrictions politically on the grounds that they are doing well and that there is no proof that there are problems or risks that justify more stringent regulations. A countercyclical special capital requirement deals with this issue as well—to deal not with what happens after the crisis but with the probabilities that certain situations eventually lead to a crisis.

Finally, I note some concerns that have been presented to me. First, if we ask banks to hold 15 or 20 percent capital, will this hurt bank values? Will it hurt shareholder returns? Will it make it more difficult for banks to raise capital? Some interesting pieces of research have been published or are in working paper form that indicate that these concerns may not be relevant. Malcolm Baker and Jeffrey Wurgler (2013) show that over the past forty years in the United States, the equity of better-capitalized banks had both lower systematic risks and lower unsystematic risks than the equity of banks with lower amounts of capital. They also show that these banks enjoyed higher rates of return for their shareholders. They interpret this finding as indicating that the shareholders of high-capital banks had higher expected returns than the shareholders of low-capital banks, so shareholders viewed banks with higher capital as being riskier and viewed the higher realized returns as compensation for this higher risk. However, an alternative interpretation is that investors may have overestimated the de facto and de jure safety nets that would be available to banks and thus underestimated the risk-protection benefits of capital. Thus, high-capital banks delivered higher returns with lower risk for their shareholders than investors expected ex ante—a positive surprise of sorts. This is consistent with results in Hamad Mehran and Anjan Thakor (2011).

In this paper, we looked at the relationship between bank equity capital and total value in the cross-section and found that the better-capitalized banks have higher values after controlling for a whole list of factors. All of this research seems to point to the fact that increasing capital in banking is not going to have anywhere close to the dire consequences that some people have predicted, so we may be able to make both bank shareholders and taxpayers better off by increasing capital.

Anil K Kashyap: My remarks might be best viewed as a rebuttal to Tom Hoenig (chapter 4). I agree with a lot of what he says, but I am one of Andy Lo's guys who has a completely different take on the crisis. So I am going to give a different interpretation of what I think was going on. I teach a course on the crisis and have thirty hours of lectures on this topic, so what follows is the ten-minute Cliff Notes version of the class.

What did Dodd–Frank conclude was the problem that needed to be fixed? If you read the twenty-one books that Andy Lo surveyed, you could have at least four themes as to what we had to worry about. The premise for macroprudential regulations is preventing the deleveraging that we saw after the crisis and the associated asset fire sales. That is one possibility. Another is runs. There are also bailouts and institutions that are too big to fail. And there are the other fifteen hundred pages of Dodd–Frank that are about things that had nothing to do with the crisis. So it is not clear what exactly what we were setting out to do. The University of Chicago's Booth School of Business is undertaking a new initiative to communicate our research a little more accurately, and the first thing that has been produced is a summary of the ten mutually inconsistent views that our faculty have about the crisis.

So here is my spin on what the crisis was about. The spillovers into the economy and the things that triggered a lot of the rescues and a lot of the extensions of the safety net came from things that were runs, but they were not the kind of runs that we were used to seeing. What Tom Hoenig proposes is a widespread idea that is consistent with the perspective of the Vickers Commission and the way that the United Kingdom is going, which is to have a supersafe public utility called the "banking system" and a casino on the side where anything goes. My biggest complaint with this proposal is that we just watched five runs that would have been in the casino and that nonetheless we had to bail out. It will be more crazy next time if those things are pushed out and we are told that market discipline is all we are going to have—because I doubt that standing by and letting a run continue unabated is the best way to go.

The Five Runs of the Financial Crisis

Many hundreds of billions of funding were lost in the asset-backed commercial paper (ABCP) market during the fall of 2007. Multiple papers now show that people stopped rolling over this form of funding. Even after controlling for all the fundamentals that are the characteristics of the assets being funded, there were still indiscriminate refusals to roll over funding. So that was the first run. It did not require the government to do anything, but it put a lot of stress on the banking system because banks had to honor many backup lines of credit. So the banks found themselves extending credit to replace the funding that disappeared from the ABCP market.

A second run occurred for triparty repurchase agreements (repos). If you ask people at the New York Fed why Bear Stearns was saved, they will tell you that if Bear Stearns went under, nobody would be willing to lend to Lehman, Merrill Lynch, Goldman, and Morgan Stanley on the following Monday. The $1 trillion of funding that was rolled over every day in that market would have disappeared, and it would have been the end of the financial system as we knew it. We just were not ready. On Bear's last day of life, it could not repo its Treasuries. That suggests that the infrastructure was so deeply screwed up that nobody was willing to be a counterparty on Treasury repo.

Another thing that surfaced (which was present in Bear but became much more visible in the Lehman bankruptcy) was the ways that prime brokers get funding that subjects those brokers to runs. This comes about because of the loopholes that exist in the ways that derivatives are treated. By convention, a broker-dealer that has a derivatives counterparty contract with somebody commonly has not posted all the margin that it would have against that contract. It would even be possible not to have posted any margin if the broker-dealer has a good enough credit rating. That was basically AIG's game. It had a triple-A credit rating and obtained a lot of leverage by avoiding having to post any margin. When it was downgraded, it got a $30 billion liquidity call that it could not meet. So by convention, the derivatives contracts allow companies to conserve on liquidity.

How does the run work? When a customer says, "I'd rather face Goldman Sachs than you," and you owe money on the derivatives contract, you have to settle up and post the margin when you transfer the contract to Goldman. Every time your position weakens and somebody wants to step away and face another counterparty, the funding that you were extracting by not fully margining has to be provided on the spot, and no institution in the middle of one of these bouts of doubt is going to say, "I won't novate that contract because I need the liquidity." So they have to do it, and this drains liquidity and creates incentives for others to step back too.

The fourth run was on prime brokers. Darrell Duffie has calculated that in the week after Lehman, Morgan Stanley lost $80 billion of funding. About $50 billion of it was from customers pulling their accounts from Morgan Stanley. How does Morgan Stanley extract liquidity from prime brokerage? You might think that a prime broker is a custodian because it takes the securities and then simply keeps track of the accounting that needs to be done with them. But the broker has a variety of ways to use the securities for funding. If a customer wants a loan of securities, a prime broker can make the loan with securities that it owns, take idle securities that are sitting in the account of another customer and loan those, or pledge the idle securities from the customer as collateral in a repo transaction. If a customer walks away from the broker, the funding must be replaced. So Morgan Stanley lost $50 billion in a week. Goldman suffered a big runoff as well up until the Paulson intervention in October 2008. Prime brokerage is fundamentally vulnerable to runs.

Some might say, "We don't want customer securities to be used in these ways." But if this is not allowed, then a lot of collateral will be trapped, sitting idly throughout the financial system. So it would not necessarily be free to restrict prime brokers in these ways.

Finally, there is the problem of runs on money market mutual funds. In the crisis, a blanket guarantee was passed for them. Money market mutual funds are basically a bank that holds no capital. And they came under stress.

Dodd–Frank and Financial Runs

So those are five runs, and they have nothing to do with too big to fail but everything to do with maturity transformation. These things were at the center of the rescues. What does Dodd–Frank do about this? Essentially, nothing is done on asset-backed commercial paper. That class of securities is dead. There are a few rules saying that you have to have some skin in the game if you securitize. But the ABCP is probably gone. There is nothing on prime brokerage. There is a little bit of language saying that it must be easy to figure out who owns securities in the event that a company goes under. But there are no hard rules on segregation that say that customer funds cannot be used for extracting liquidity. That would be a hard conversation to have because we do not have a benchmark for the social value of liquidity or of the liquidity provision that goes with collateral value. Although I do not know how to calibrate how much liquidity transformation to allow, there was no discussion of it.

There is nothing in Dodd–Frank about money market funds. The SEC took one set of actions to try to improve the rules in 2010, and an SEC chair stepped down because she could not convince the rest of the SEC to go along with a reform that would have put either capital or floating net asset value (NAV) in there.

I think that floating NAV is impractical for money funds because most of the assets that they hold do not trade in anything like a liquid market. How is the mark-to-market value established for something like General Motors' thirty-seven-day commercial paper? Money funds are marked to market every day and report values like 1.000000000000000001 or 0 0.9999999998. So these things are never going to float because there is no secondary market for underlying assets they hold. It is not like an equity market. The accounting rules allow mark-to-market values to be set at historical costs for anything that is under sixty days to maturity. Right now, we do not even try to get real quotes.

This is short-term maturity transformation, and to do something about it, the accounting rules would have to be changed, and a market in really illiquid securities would need to be created. If the SEC goes ahead with the floating NAV proposal, I fear that we will find ourselves with a problem again if we get into crisis.

Dodd–Frank says nothing about triparty repos. The New York Fed formed a working group that had little success by the end of the working group's mandate. Since then, the New York Fed has kept pushing, and some progress may be in the works. Some optimists think that by the end of 2014, triparty repos will be less vulnerable to runs.

Finally, Dodd–Frank does say a lot about derivatives. The only thing it says about runs, though, is the possibility of imposing a one-day stay on qualifying financial contracts if an institution is being resolved. In the new Dodd–Frank resolution regime, if Lehman failed again, the government would have one day to move all of their derivatives book to a bridge bank. How does this influence the incentive to run? If investors saw that there was a chance that the one-day stay was probable, they likely would step out of the derivatives trade a month earlier than they would have before because nobody wants to become entangled in the stay. So I think that the runs problem regarding derivatives probably has been made worse through Dodd–Frank.

My takeaway on all this is that Dodd–Frank is based on a narrative, some of which is right but a lot of which is wrong. The remedies do not address what I see as the problems, and the FSOC is being counted on to step in and try to do stuff. The first example of this was the attempt to discipline the money market funds, and it was a complete failure. I think the situation we are in is somewhat safer with respect to a large number of risks, but a lot of maturity transformation is still going on, and we essentially have the same bad choices if something goes wrong.

Questions and Answers

Question: If the new clearinghouse requirements for derivatives are completely effective, it is claimed that they would sharply reduce the risk of runs. Do you agree?

Kashyap: In principle, I think it is a very good idea. One of the things that I am worried about is the proliferation of clearinghouses and how in the short run we might end up with so many of them that we are left with very inefficient netting of contracts. We may make that problem better for the medium term, but I think in the short run we are going to have a lot more collateral sitting in all these clearinghouses—one in Singapore, one in Hong Kong, one in Japan, another one in New York, another one in maybe Frankfurt or Paris, another one in London. If there are six or seven clearinghouses, they are not going to do most of what we want them to do. The other thing is that the institutions have strong incentives to keep transacting over the counter because it is very profitable for them. They are going to fight this, so it will take much longer than you would have imagined.

Question: Don't you think that we are going to end up with essentially one clearinghouse for each product?

Kashyap: No. And I do not even think you would want to do that because you would certainly want at least currencies and interest rates to be cleared in the same place because there is so much duplication there. Then you would want to have a lot of the biggest contracts all trading in a single place. I just do not think that the political economy works to get you there.

Question: What should we do about the shadow banking sector? Do you think it poses more of a problem for than the regulated banking sector?

Kashyap: With banks, we have the Basel Committee on Banking Supervision. So when you have a crisis, you have a committee, and the committee meets and makes some changes. So far, they have planned changes regarding capital, liquidity regulation, and even stress tests. The biggest problem for the shadow banking system is that the form of the shadow banking system is different in every single jurisdiction. I think of the shadow banking system as regulatory arbitrage. Because the rules start out differently everywhere, the way that you arbitrage it looks different in, for example, the United Kingdom, Canada, and the United States. So if you wanted to have a Basel committee on shadow banking, you would send insurance regulators from one place, money fund regulators from here, and nonbank bank regulators from another. And then if you can get them together, you have the problem that they do not speak the same language. So solving this problem is going to be difficult.

I think that some things that might be done include paying more attention to repos and trying to do something on margins and haircuts because much of this stuff is funded through repos. So this would mean no more triple A exemptions from margins. And we could require a minimum level haircut. I think that would be a good thing. If we got clearinghouses for some of these things, that would be desirable. But I think that the shadow banking system is, in the U.S. case, the biggest problem that we face, and it is not like there is a playbook you can use to easily fix it.

Question: How should a regulator balance the costs from regulations (like the Volcker Rule) and the derivatives rule against benefits that can be difficult to measure (like reductions in systemic risks)?

Walsh: This is a particular challenge for securities regulators who must actually do cost-benefit analysis and can then be challenged on it in court by the industry. As a bank regulator, I was always glad that we did not have to do that. We asserted, as I think Dodd–Frank does, that the cost of systemic bank failures is so horrific that whatever the price to put these regulations in place is worth it, so put the regulations in place. The cost-benefit analysis that the banking agencies do for these regulations is not a meaningful measure of their cost, in any sense of the term. It is more often a matter of pursuing the lowest-cost method of achieving the objective. But when all is said and done, on the banking side of things, it is an assertion that the benefits outweigh the cost. McKinsey has been doing some work with a government client in this area, trying to find better ways to do that kind of analysis. It is an area where more work is needed.

Question: It seems that the shadow banking system was used by the large, complex institutions—the large banks and investment banks—to avoid capital requirements. So I don't think you can separate the banking sector from the shadow banking sector. I have not been a fan of Dodd–Frank, but can't you argue that parts of Dodd–Frank may rein in the behavior of large complex firms?

Kashyap: They are putting in incentives to do more of it. If you make it fifty times more costly than it used to be to be a bank and the banks used to do crazy amounts of regulatory arbitrage before, what are you going to get afterward? More.

Walsh: The Dodd–Frank requirements do have the effect of pulling activities that were done through all sorts of off-balance-sheet gimmicks inside the accounting and regulatory net, which I think does promote safety and soundness.

Question: At least they are regulating these institutions more than before. It is not like a hedge fund. The question is whether something completely outside the regulatory framework is going to emerge, but at least they have been in the regulatory framework.

Kashyap: The surprising thing about the crisis is that when hedge funds got into trouble, it was not a big deal: they either failed or were bought out. It's the guys doing maturity transformations whose weaknesses threatened the system and necessitated bailouts.

Question: How would you propose to regulate shadow banking?

Kashyap: Repos are usually overnight funding that supports something with a longer maturity. So I would start by making heat maps of where maturity transformation is occurring and then try to think about what can be done in case something goes wrong. The Office of Financial Research is starting to do this. I don't think I have run into anybody who has a great answer for this, but if you want to go to an extreme, you could say that you want a capital requirement for every funding transaction. You could go to something that approximates asset-level capital charges so that no matter how it ends up getting funded, there is some equity tranche that is loss absorbing that moves with the asset. That would be a revolution. For this to go anywhere, you would almost need to have a maturity transformation regulator that would be out there looking for this.

Question: Anjan, I am curious as to how your proposal for special capital compares to contingent equity. Is your approach better than contingent equity? Is it complementary? How do the two relate to each other?

Thakor: First, there is not one contingent capital proposal. There are many. The special capital account is different from contingent equity. It is, in fact, noncontingent equity. The equity is always there. It is not a convertible, so it is equity in the sense that it is always there. The difference between that and normal equity is in the control rights and the transfer of contingent insolvency. With normal equity, if the bank is in trouble and the value of everything falls below its liabilities, all the assets just accrue to the creditors. Here, because it is the special capital account, it is invested in a designated asset like Treasuries that you can keep track of. The idea is that you do not want to make that available to the creditors because you do not want to dilute their incentives to impose market discipline on the bank.

S&P and Moody's and major rating agencies have noted that they give a two to three notch ratings advantage to banks because of their implicit bailout guarantee that is embedded in too big to fail and other forms of protection. That is something that makes leverage very attractive for banks. Why would I take equity if I can get price advantage from unsecured debt? So that is the issue that this is trying to address. We want this equity to be invisible to the creditors, but at the same time, we want it to be meaningful enough to provide all of the risk-attenuation incentives for the shareholders of the banks. We are trying to get the best of both worlds. The other way in which it is different is that there is no conversion trigger. There is no regulatory discretion on when to convert something to equity. It is always equity. With contingent capital, the market value is not independent of where you set the threshold for the trigger. Instead, you get multiple equilibria because anticipation of the trigger affects the market value.

References

Acharya, Viral, Hamid Mehran, and Anjan Thakor. 2012. Caught between Scylla and Charybdis? Regulating Bank Leverage When There Is Rent-Seeking and Risk-Shifting. CEPR Discussion Paper No. DP8822.

Acharya, Viral, and Anjan Thakor. 2010. The Dark Side of Liquidity Creation: Leverage-Induced Systemic Risk and the Lender of Last Resort. Working Paper, New York University.

Baker, Malcolm, and Jeffrey Wurgler. 2013. Do Strict Capital Requirements Raise the Cost of Capital? Banking Regulation and the Low-Risk Anomaly. Working Paper, Harvard University.

Coffee, John C. 2012. The Political Economy of Dodd–Frank: Why Financial Reform Tends to Be Frustrated and Systemic Risk Perpetuated. Columbia Law and Economics Working Paper No. 414.

Farhi, Emmanuel, and Jean Tirole. 2009. Leverage and the Central Banker's Put. *American Economic Review* 99 (2):589–593.

Gorton, Gary. 2009. Slapped in the Face by the Invisible Hand: Banking and the Panic of 2007. Working Paper, Yale School of Management.

Lo, Andrew. 2012. Reading about the Financial Crisis: A Twenty-One-Book Review. *Journal of Economic Literature* 50 (1):151–178.

Mehran, Hamid, and Anjan Thakor. 2011. Bank Capital and Value in the Cross-Section. *Review of Financial Studies* 24 (4):1019–1067.

Stiglitz, Joseph. 2010. *Freefall: America, Free Markets, and the Sinking of the World Economy.* New York: Norton.

Thakor, Anjan. 2013. Skill, Luck, and Financial Crises. Working Paper, Washington University.

6 Panel Discussion on Stability, Resolution, and Dodd–Frank

James R. Barth, John Dearie, David Skeel, and Arthur Wilmarth

Arthur Wilmarth: Our panelists have published excellent work analyzing Titles I and II of the Dodd–Frank Wall Street Reform and Consumer Protection Act of 2010, which are closely connected. Title I includes sections 165 and 166, which mandate enhanced prudential standards for systemically important financial institutions (SIFIs). We are not going to address at any length the procedure for designating systemically important nonbank institutions under section 113, but that certainly is an important topic in its own right. We are primarily going to talk about bank SIFIs with over $50 billion in assets. If the Financial Stability Oversight Council (FSOC) has also identified a group of systemically important nonbank financial institutions or nonbank SIFIs, how should these institutions be regulated to prevent a recurrence of a crisis similar to the financial crisis of 2007 to 2009? In looking at Title I, we focus on the issue of enhanced capital requirements.

The Basel III accord proposes a regime where the largest, globally significant SIFIs would have total tier 1capital including surcharges and buffers reaching up to 9.5 percent of their risk-weighted assets. More recently, in this country, discussions have gone well beyond Basel III. The Brown-Vitter bill would require a 15 percent equity capital ratio on a leverage basis for the largest SIFIs—those with over $500 billion in assets. In addition, at least three members of the Federal Reserve Board—Jeremy Stein, Dan Tarullo, and Janet Yellen—have indicated in recent speeches that they see a need to go beyond the Basel capital requirements without specifying exactly how much further they would go. One question is whether enhanced capital is really where we should focus our efforts under Title I. If so, how might that affect other requirements, such as liquidity requirements, limitations on concentrated exposures, and so on?

Title II establishes the Orderly Liquidation Authority (OLA). The Federal Deposit Insurance Corporation (FDIC) has attempted to set out a roadmap for the OLA, most recently through discussions of the single-point-of-entry concept. The OLA process raises issues about bail-ins for bond holders or subordinated debt holders. Who gets bailed in and under what circumstances? But talking about capital structures for bail-in purposes cycles back to Title I, so I think there is a close connection between the two areas—enhanced prudential standards under Title I and OLA under Title II.

John Dearie: Three years into the implementation of Dodd–Frank, a lot has been accomplished, and a lot remains to be accomplished, as the various reviews and analyses of Dodd–Frank have noted. Assessments by Davis Polk and others indicate that we are about 40 percent of the way through implementation. Nevertheless, we are three years in and about to celebrate (if that is the right word) the third anniversary of the signing. So this is a terrific time to consider where we are, what has been accomplished, and where we go from here.

In reading many of the of the articles, commentaries, and papers that tend to appear before the anniversary of a major piece of legislation, it seems to me that there currently are four principal criticisms of Dodd–Frank. First, Dodd–Frank is absurdly long and complex. Second, which is related to point one, the Act is is too difficult to implement, which is why we are only 40 percent through the implementation three years after enactment. I think the Volcker Rule is probably the most notable example of point two. I was just reading an article today about some comments made by SEC commissioners who described the Volcker Rule still as a "jump-ball" among regulators. Third, the Act was largely silent on several causes of the crisis, particularly the Federal National Mortgage Association (Fannie Mae) and the Federal Home Loan Mortgage Corporation (Freddie Mac). Fourth, which is a Republican criticism, Dodd–Frank failed to address some of the major causes of the financial crisis (particularly too big to fail) and may actually have institutionalized those problems.

All these criticisms have merit, deserve discussion and debate, and have some and perhaps a lot of truth to them. But taken together, these legitimate criticisms have contributed to (here in Washington certainly, in the media, and around the country) a broader and deeper narrative that is unfortunate because it is not true. That broader narrative is that nothing has really happened since the crisis: nothing has really changed, we are really no better off, there have been no meaningful improvements, and our banking and broader financial system remain just as vulnerable to instability as they were in 2008. And that is certainly not true. A great deal of progress has been made since 2008. Important changes have been made, and the banking system is far stronger and more resilient today than it was in 2008.

What We Have Accomplished since the Crisis

Today capital and liquidity are at nearly twice the levels they were in 2009. According to the results of the Federal Reserve's latest stress test, tier 1 common equity capital (money provided by banks' shareholders and the highest loss-absorbing form of capital) has increased more than 90 percent, from $420 billion in 2009 to more than $800 billion. That additional capital has raised the average ratio of tier 1 common to risk-weighted assets for the eighteen largest banking companies from about 5.5 percent to more than 11 percent, and liquidity is at nearly twice the level that it was in 2009. Leverage has been reduced, in some cases by half. Asset quality is far stronger, with problem loan balances and charge-offs having been reduced quarter after quarter to levels not seen since before the crisis. Risk management, internal controls, and corporate governance procedures have all been significantly enhanced.

In addition, compensation structures at most banks have been reformed to more closely align the personal incentives of bank executives with the long-term safety and soundness of the banks. Large portions of compensation are being awarded in stock that does not vest for five years. The idea is the bank had better be around in five years, or executives do not get paid. And clawback provisions are now incorporated in compensation packages. Some of these provisions were activated in the aftermath of the JP Morgan Chase's 2012 London Whale episode.

These changes have occurred at a time when, according to the FDIC, capital in the banking system is at or near record levels. Together these changes strongly suggest that we have a banking system and broader financial system that are much stronger and more resilient than before the crisis.

Responsibility for these improvements is shared among the banking industry (which has taken the initiative and made many important improvements), the regulators (who have done the hard work of rule writing), and the Dodd–Frank Act itself. The panel is going to take a close look at Title II, its credibility and workability, but any meaningful discussion of Title II has to begin with a discussion of the importance and significance of Title I—because the whole point of Title I is never to get to Title II.

Title I and Enhanced Supervision

To prevent or minimize the occurrence of financial instability among large financial institutions, section 165 of Title I establishes a special regime of "enhanced prudential supervision" for bank holding companies with total assets equal to or greater than $50 billion and for nonbank financial institutions designated by the Financial Stability Oversight Council (FSOC) as "systemically important." Enhanced prudential supervision of systemically important financial institutions (SIFIs) entails standards and requirements that, in the language of the statute, "are more stringent than the standards and requirements applicable to nonbank financial companies and bank holding companies that do not present similar risks to the financial stability of the United States." Aspects of safety and soundness for which Title I mandates "more stringent" standards for SIFIs include capital, leverage, liquidity, asset concentrations, and single counterparty exposures. Although designating certain institutions as "systemically important," whether by statute or by the FSOC, raises concern regarding moral hazard and implied government support within the context of too big to fail, enhanced supervision of large institutions will minimize the occurrence of financial instability among these institutions.

Title I also requires large institutions to produce so-called living wills. Under the Dodd–Frank Act, bankruptcy is the preferred resolution framework in the event of a failure of a systemically important institution. To make this prospect achievable, Title I requires that all large institutions prepare living wills that serve as a detailed blueprint of the organization and its plan for a rapid and orderly liquidation under the Bankruptcy Code in the event of its failure.

The living-will exercise, although reportedly arduous and expensive for some institutions, has tremendous value. First, meaningful living wills require that large and complex institutions regularly review their corporate structures, including a careful and precise inventory of their many business lines and legal entities. Knowing what businesses one is in and in what ways, is essential to effective organizational and risk management. Second, the living-will requirement enables both the firm and its regulators to understand and address those parts of the consolidated institution that could create complications or even systemic consequences in the course of liquidation.

Certain aspects of enhanced prudential supervision deserve careful scrutiny and continuing discussion, particularly the role, significance, and supervisory purpose of capital. In recent months, capital has emerged as a centrally important issue and even a silver bullet solution to virtually every supervisory challenge. Whether the challenge is large institutions, funding structures, or particular asset categories, more capital is increasingly proposed as the solution. I am a former bank supervisor and understand the importance of capital. But I also remember my supervisory training, which was that a given level of capital has little supervisory meaning if it is divorced from or considered apart from other equally relevant metrics of safety and soundness—such as the structure and quality of the bank's earnings, the nature and structure of its balance sheet, the reliability of its liquidity, the quality of its management, the rigor and effectiveness of risk management, internal controls, corporate governance, and so forth. So I worry about this heightened focus on capital. Capital is not without cost or consequence. In fact, there are certain circumstances in which ever-higher capital can become perverse incentivizing e greater risk-taking within the institution, which is not the objective of the higher-capital policy.

To conclude, great progress has been made since 2008., and Any discussion of the Dodd–Frank Act must acknowledge that fact because it has important implications for identifying the issues that remain with regard to implemention of the Act and where we go from here.

Wilmarth: James Barth is going to provide his views about what we learned or should have learned from the financial crisis regarding the virtues and perhaps the shortcomings of capital regulation and what those lessons might tell us about the implementation of Title I.

James R. Barth: I would like to make a few quick observations at the outset. First, Charles Calomiris (chapter 8) notes that national banks were not involved in real estate—were prohibited from it, in fact—for a number of years after their inception in the 1860s. In their early years, if a national bank failed, that was considered prima fascia evidence that the owners and managers of the bank had engaged in fraud. Another interesting fact is that in the 1970s the savings and loan industry was subject to risk-based capital requirements. There was a minimum statutory capital requirement, but Congress eliminated it and told the regulatory authority to set one somewhere between 0 and 5 percent. The requirement was set at 3 percent, which says something about the role that regulatory authorities play in not imposing stringent regulations on the institutions they regulate.

At a 2011 conference, Jamie Dimon of JPMorgan Chase asked Ben Bernanke, chair of the Federal Reserve System, the following question: "Has anyone bothered to study the cumulative effect of these regulatory market fixes?" Numerous economists are engaged in research within the Federal Reserve System, but Bernanke's answer was that the central bank does not have the quantitative tools to study the net effect of all the regulatory market changes during the last three years: "It's too complicated." This type of admission clearly did not deter the Congress from rushing to undertake a major reform of the financial sector.

Not everybody is convinced that the Dodd–Frank Act has solved the too-big-to-fail problem. Richard Fisher, president of the Federal Reserve Bank of Dallas, for example, favors breaking up big banks. He has 520 banks in his district, and 95 percent of those banks have assets of less than a billion dollars, which may be part of the reason that he is in favor of breaking up the big banks. Sheila Bair, former chair of the FDIC, has also talked about breaking up the big banks. Simon Johnson, of the Massachusetts Institute of Technology, has called for setting a cap on the size of big banks, with a ceiling of total assets not to exceed 2 percent of U.S. gross domestic product. This is an arbitrary cap and fails to account for the globalization of banking. Perhaps bank asset size relative to the aggregate GDPs of the countries in which a bank operates should be included if such a cap is imposed.

The Origins of the Crisis

In my view, the recent U.S. financial crisis began in the housing sector. The crisis began to emerge more fully in the summer of 2007, spread throughout the financial system, led to the recession that began in December 2007, and ended in the summer of 2009. The recession exacerbated the crisis but was not the initiating factor. Over the last 120 years, in 40 percent of those years housing prices declined, and in 60 percent of the years, real home prices increased. If a firm relied on the assumption that home prices would only go up, then that would be a flawed business model. The rate at which home prices were rising before the recession was not sustainable. Home prices peaked in the spring of 2006 and then plummeted. The home ownership rate also reached an all-time high while home prices were rising. The rate increase benefited by relaxed lending standards that provided a greater opportunity for every risk class to obtain a mortgage to buy a home. The real estate sector accounted for more than 5 percent of GDP at its peak.

The real estate market is where we should focus when looking for the origin of the financial crisis. Banks were holding approximately $4 trillion in real estate assets on their balance sheets, so everyone had to know that if home prices declined, it would cause problems for a lot of banks and for the securities that were backed by home mortgages.

Anil K Kashyap (chapter 5) notes that there were five runs on firms in the shadow banking sector. I believe that these five runs occurred in no small part due to the real estate–oriented collateral behind the liabilities. So some of those runs can be attributed to both a maturity mismatch and a high number of assets that were tied to the real estate sector.

Leverage of Financial Institutions

Lawrence J. White (chapter 3) looks at leverage and the common equity-to-asset ratio for CitiGroup. In the third quarter of 2008, before many of the big banks were bailed out, I looked at CitiGroup's tangible capital-to-asset ratio and found that it reached a low (based on reported data) of roughly 0.5 percent. This implies a leverage ratio of 200 to 1. In this regard, I agree with Thomas M. Hoenig (chapter 4) that one should look at tangible capital ratios, not equity or risk-based capital ratios. Nobody paid attention to risk-based measures. No reasonable investor during the financial crisis paid attention to anything other than tangible equity capital ratios or market-value ratios, and at the time, each of these provided similar information about the solvency situation of a bank.

CitiGroup reported that its total assets were $2.1 trillion. According to Simon Johnson, however, the assets of CitiGroup were a lot larger than this, and JPMorgan Chase does not have $2 trillion in assets (Johnson and Kwak 2010). He is right in some sense about the figures reported by these and some other big U.S. banks. JPMorgan Chase has roughly $4 trillion in assets, and it is the biggest bank in the world but only when International Financial Reporting Standards (IFRS) are used. Under U.S. generally accepted accounting principles (GAAP), which banks here rely on, the bigger asset figures are not reported. The difference in the two accounting treatments is that U.S. GAAP allows for the netting of derivatives, and IFRS does not. As regards Basel III, I think the expectation is that the leverage ratio will be calculated based upon U.S. GAAP—that is, the netting of derivatives will be allowed. The use of IFRS would require gross netting, which would lead to bigger asset numbers so that much more capital would have to be held at the banks to meet the new and higher capital requirements.

In some of his work, Simon Johnson talks about JPMorgan Chase, Bank of America, CitiGroup, Goldman Sachs, and Morgan Stanley as global financial institutions. According to the Financial Stability Board, these five and three other big U.S. banks comprise eight of twenty-eight global SIFIs. All eight U.S. big banks, moreover, exceed Johnson's cap of 2 percent of GDP. PNC Financial has assets of about $300 billion, or roughly 2 percent of GDP, and appears to be a bank that would not have to be broken up. However, Washington Mutual with $300 billion in assets was also a bank at the cutoff point, and it collapsed in 2008. This suggests that relying on an arbitrary measure to determine which banks should be broken up is a flawed goal. Size is not the problem. The problem is excessive risk regardless of size.

The Role of Bank Holding Companies

The holding companies of the eight large banks are also large, and the way that their assets are funded is important. CitiGroup, for example, had $600 billion in assets in its holding company as of the third quarter of 2008 and $900 billion some time earlier, so the size of the holding company was reduced over time. Bank of America had assets of $500 billion in the holding company, and JPMorgan Chase had $350 billion. Before the Dodd–Frank Act, the FDIC could seize the subsidiary banks but not the holding company. If insolvent, a holding company was resolved through bankruptcy proceedings. However, as a source of strength, the FDIC could gain access to the assets of the holding company so that the liabilities, with the exception of short-term debt, could be required to absorb losses. I have always wondered why the holding company structure was needed. Historically, it was used to acquire banks in more than one state, but a problem arose because the holding company (not the individual subsidiary banks) became too big to fail. If the holding company experienced problems in rolling over its liabilities, that could create problems for both the holding company and its subsidiary banks, but regulators might bail out the former due to its being too big to fail.

With holding companies of savings and loans, there was a problem with whether the assets of the parent company were required to be used to support the subsidiary depository institutions. IndyMac, Inc., for example, was a holding company with IndyMac Bank as its subsidiary. Roughly 99 percent of the assets of the holding company were in the FDIC-insured subsidiary banking institution. There was a legal suit over whether IndyMac, Inc. should have been a source of strength for IndyMac, the bank itself that failed and was seized by FDIC, and the bank directors were alleged to have thrown good money after bad when the holding company injected money into IndyMac Bank. Under the law at the time, there apparently was no requirement that the holding company be a source of strength for the subsidiary bank, as was the case for holding companies of commercial banks. So an interesting issue is why holding companies that controlled FDIC-insured institutions were needed. Was it simply a way to escape the seizure of the holding company by the FDIC prior to the Dodd–Frank Act? Was it a delaying tactic to allow shareholders of the holding company to take more money out of the subsidiary bank by continuing to pay dividends and salaries to officers and directors at the holding company level before the FDIC could act? So if 90 percent or more of all of the assets of a holding are the assets of the subsidiary FDIC-insured institutions, why are holding companies needed?

Supervising the Regulators

In *Guardians of Finance: Making Regulators Work for Us*, my coauthors (Ross Levine and Gerard Caprio) and I note that the regulatory authorities failed in their responsibilities to regulate and supervise banking institutions properly (Barth, Caprio, and Levine 2012). The Federal Reserve, for example, allowed banks to reduce capital through the use of credit default swaps, which contributed to the significant leverage of CitiGroup and the other institutions. AIG was involved as a counterparty in many of those credit default swaps. Yet the Fed and other regulators did not seem to worry about the financial condition of AIG. Although I believe that the regulatory agencies had evidence that was provided by the institutions themselves indicating problems, nothing was done to deal with those problems.

Another example discussed in *Guardians of Finance* relates to the Prompt Corrective Action Provisions of the Federal Deposit Insurance Corporation Improvement Act (FDICIA) of 1991, which requires the FDIC to take prompt action when it sees that capital at a bank is deteriorating. The FDIC is excellent at identifying problems. The evidence indicates that it has identified the causes of 79 percent of bank failures years before they actually failed. Even going back to the 1980s, the same picture emerges with the problems plaguing savings and loan institutions. In the more recent case involving the FDIC, its own material loss reviews note that 95 percent of the time, the agency did not act promptly and correctly to address a known problem. This raises some questions about how to get the regulatory authorities to enforce existing laws and thereby do what they are obliged to do to protect taxpayers.

A major point that relates to regulatory failure is that every major financial law in the United States since 1790, ending most recently with the Dodd–Frank Act of 2010, was enacted after a financial crisis, not before to prevent a crisis. After every crisis, more laws and more regulations are passed, and more regulatory authorities are created as well. A few laws were enacted in response to changing market forces and an acknowledgment that laws ought to be changed because banks were adapting to a more modern environment and changing their business models. A point that Charlie Calomiris (chapter 8) makes is that business models of banks change over time, and the models are different among different banks, which has to be acknowledged when determining how to regulate institutions and whether to break up institutions.

Furthermore, the U.S. regulatory structure is complex. Since the 2007 to 2008 crisis, one new agency (the Consumer Financial Protection Bureau) has been established, and one agency (the Office of Thrift Supervision) (OTS) has been eliminated, which was a good decision since it did a poor job regulating the institutions assigned to it. Some might wonder why the OTS engaged in forbearance with respect to big institutions like Countrywide, IndyMac, and Washington Mutual. Because these three institutions paid the OTS 40 percent of the fees needed to run the agency, the OTS would not want to lose them. Countrywide had a commercial bank that converted to a savings and loan institution, so it would be regulated by the OTS. Mortgages could then be put onto the books of the savings and loan association, which might receive more favorable regulatory treatment by OTS than by its former regulator. Time ran out, however, and the institution was seized by the FDIC.

The complex U.S. regulatory structure exists because of the Congress. If a regulatory body is eliminated, a congressional committee might also be eliminated, and the committee chair and ranking member may then receive fewer financial contributions when they run for office. So this situation is probably a barrier when trying to consolidate our regulatory system. It is hard to start over and establish a more simplified and effective regulatory system.

In *Guardians of Finance*, Jerry Caprio, Ross Levine, and I state that we need to impose more discipline on the regulatory authorities and hold them more accountable for their actions. To accomplish this task, we propose a sentinel—a new agency without any regulatory powers. You may recall that an OTS regulator allowed IndyMac to backdate a capital infusion so that it was able to maintain its well-capitalized status. This is an example of the problems that are created when regulatory authorities deliberately avoid enforcing existing laws and regulations. We believe that a sentinel would serve as a check and balance on the behavior of the regulatory authorities. It would serve as a sort of unbiased referee. The idea of a sentinel is based on a book written by a University of Chicago professor and a *Sports Illustrated* writer who pointed out that referees, over time and in all types of different sports, tend to be biased in favor of the home team (Moskowitz and Wertheim 2012). To eliminate or reduce that bias, the introduction of things like instant replay was introduced so that a referee's decisions can be questioned and perhaps a bad decision reversed.

We see an analogy between regulators and referees. Regulators do not have an incentive to be evil, but at times they do bad things. Perhaps, like sports referees, they are simply biased, which can lead to bad decisions. In the case of banking, the home team is the regulated institutions, and the away team is the public. This means that regulators may be biased in such a way that their decisions favor the regulated institutions. I believe that establishing a sentinel would be beneficial, even if it is a controversial proposal.

The Financial Stability Oversight Council

Some may argue that a sentinel is not needed now that Title I of the Dodd–Frank law has established a new Financial Stability Oversight Council (FSOC). The FSOC's mission is to identify, monitor, and address any systemic risk posed by large, complex financial firms and by the financial products and activities found at many financial firms throughout the country. It consists of nine federal financial regulators, one independent member with insurance expertise, and five nonvoting members (including three state regulators). The secretary of the Treasury Department serves as chair.

The FSOC is also responsible for identifying systemically important nonbank financial firms for regulation by the Fed. The law is silent on how to measure systemic risk and therefore how the FSOC is to fulfill this duty. The FSOC also is authorized to make recommendations to the Fed on standards for systemic risk firms, including capital and liquidity requirements, with the exact standards left to the discretion of the Fed. The problem, as has been the case in the past with reform legislation, is that the Fed remains unaccountable for whatever happens based on the standards that it sets, and the establishment of the FSOC does not correct the situation.

To support the FSOC, a new Office of Financial Research (OFR) is established within the Treasury Department. Its responsibilities include promoting best practices for financial risk management, monitoring and reporting changes in systemic risk, and evaluating and reporting on stress tests for banks. It is doubtful that the OFR will now accomplish what all the other regulators collectively failed to accomplish in the past. After all, the OFR is located within the Treasury Department, not within an independent agency, and this makes it more vulnerable to political pressures.

At first glance, the FSOC might seem like a good idea to the extent that the individual regulators previously failed to devote enough attention to systemic risk because each was focused too narrowly on its own segment of the financial system. Yet the FSOC membership consists of nearly all the same regulatory agencies that were in charge prior to the crisis and that not only failed to prevent the crisis but actually contributed to it.

The Dodd–Frank Act does authorize the FSOC to extend regulation to include firms in the "shadow" financial sector, such as hedge funds and private equity funds. However, the circumstances that would trigger such an extension by the FSOC and the ways that it would proceed in a timely manner to address looming problems are unclear. It is important to remember that regulators have historically focused rather narrowly on their own specific areas of oversight and that their focus has been on institutions rather than financial instruments, such as credit default swaps and repurchase agreements, despite the potential for the latter to create problems in financial markets. So it is hard to believe that the FSOC will sufficiently focus on changes in the composition of the financial system and the accompanying changes in systemic risk.

Nonfinancial Firms and Banks

Finally, perhaps we should allow nonfinancial firms to own banks. Larry White (chapter 3) mentions GE Capital, but GE owns a bank. Walmart wanted to acquire a bank a few years ago. Harley-Davidson owns a bank. If an individual goes to a bank wearing a black leather outfit with big boots and says to a loan officer, "I want a loan to buy a motorcycle," the loan officer might not make the loan. Harley-Davidson, on the other hand, may be better able to provide loans to motorcycle buyers because it knows the customers of motorcycles better and is in a better position to know the value of the collateral should a motorcycle have to be repossessed because of nonpayment. CMS Energy, Target Corporation, Toyota, and Flying J also own banks for similar reasons. Since they began in the early 1900s, not a single industrial loan corporation (ILC) has ever failed. A Toyota executive once told me that if the ILC failed, it would hurt the reputation of the far more important parent company, and so the parent holds the ILC to stricter standards than the regulators. It might be time to support the ownership of banks by more nonfinancial firms. China allows nonfinancial firms to own banks. Only four other countries out of 126 prohibit nonfinancial firms from owning banks.

Wilmarth: David Skeel will address the Orderly Liquidation Authority under Title II of Dodd–Frank and possible bankruptcy law alternatives to the OLA.

David Skeel: At this point, the problems and complexities that have been talked about seem to suggest that the most promising reforms are politically impossible and that it is not clear that the adjustments that are feasible are likely to work. I hope that at least a few of the things I present do not fall into either of these categories.

First, I will start with the resolution rules for systemically important financial institutions in Title II of the Dodd–Frank Act. I begin by pointing out that the analogy that was used to justify Title II was somewhat dubious and then give an overview of the Title II framework.

Second, I talk about the single-point-of-entry strategy that the FDIC has developed for implementing the new resolution rules. After describing the single-point-of-entry technique, I outline what I view as its principal virtues and vices.

Finally, I describe how the benefits of single-point-of-entry resolution could be achieved in bankruptcy, with a small number of adjustments to the bankruptcy laws that I refer to as chapter 14.2. Chapter 14 is a set of proposed bankruptcy reforms devised by a working group at the Hoover Institution. Chapter 14.2 is a new iteration of the earlier proposals that would mirror the benefits of single point of entry.

Title II: The Orderly Liquidation Authority

As Congress was debating the legislation that eventually became the Dodd–Frank Act, the Treasury and FDIC argued that the FDIC had done a fabulous job of resolving banks for seventy-five years, so we simply needed to give it the same kind of resolution powers to resolve systemically important financial institutions that it already has with ordinary banks. That argument has a nice sound to it, and it was repeated over and over. But it was misleading. For most of the past seventy-five years, bank resolutions were relatively uncommon. When banks did start to fail, the FDIC did an adequate but not great job. The FDIC got better after Congress introduced prompt corrective action requirements in the wake of the savings and loan and banking crisis of the late 1980s. But most of these banks are small and medium-size, and the FDIC's strategy for resolving them has little to do with the resolution of a large financial institution. The FDIC's modus operandi is that they talk with potential buyers of the bank, choose a buyer secretly, come in on Friday afternoon to close the bank, and transfer the deposits and the assets to the buyer, and on Monday morning, everything opens back up and it's business as usual.

The FDIC's complete discretion to determine who gets what and how the bank is resolved would be offensive except that the government is the real party of interest in these bank resolutions because 96 percent of the bank's liabilities are deposits. Because the government has guaranteed the deposits and there are very few other creditors, the FDIC (and the deposit insurance fund) is the principal beneficiary of a successful resolution and the victim of a poor one. From that perspective, the FDIC's discretion and the absence of ordinary rule of law protections are somewhat defensible for small and medium-size banks. But it has nothing to do with big financial institutions. Systemically important institutions differ from small and medium-size banks in several important ways.

One difference is that government-insured liabilities are a much smaller part of the balance sheet for these large financial institutions.

These institutions have real, nontaxpayer-guaranteed creditors. Giving the FDIC unbridled discretion by forgoing ordinary rule-of-law protections is thus more worrisome in this context. In addition, the traditional FDIC strategy would create a "Damned if I do, damned if I don't" scenario if it were applied to systemically important financial institutions. Someone who is trying to find a buyer for a giant institution over a weekend might not be able to find a one. Financial institutions that are capable of acquiring another large financial institution are not thick on the ground. That's the "Damned if you don't" danger. If a buyer is found, the purchase may make a very big and systemically important financial institution even bigger and more systemically important. That is essentially what regulators did with JPMorgan Chase in 2008.

The resolution rules work begin when the so-called three keys turn. The three keys are the main bank regulators—the Fed, the Treasury, and the FDIC. Each has to agree that it needs to take over this financial institution and that there is a risk of adverse systemic effects if the regulators do not act. If the regulators decide to take over the institution, they file a petition with the federal district court (at the federal trial level court) in Washington, D.C. There is a secret hearing, and the court has twenty-four hours to decide whether to allow the takeover. The only grounds for not allowing the takeover at this secret hearing are that it is not actually a financial company—that the bank regulators mistook General Motors for a bank or that the institution is not in default or in danger of default. Any institution that the three bank regulators want to take over is in danger of default as a result of that very move, even if it was in perfect health the moment before the intervention So there is no way to counter the takeover. After the takeover occurs, the FDIC is put in place as a receiver to "liquidate" the systemically important institution. The FDIC is required to kick out any managers who are "substantially responsible" for the failure. Shareholders are supposed to take losses, and creditors are supposed to take losses. And there are a number of provisions borrowed from bankruptcy for the purposes of OLA, although the reality is that the FDIC can do whatever it wants to do.

The Single-Point-of-Entry Strategy

With the big banks and the law firms that represent them, the FDIC has devised a single-point-of-entry approach for implementing Title II. The idea is that when the FDIC takes over an institution under Title II, it will intervene only at the holding company level, and most or all of the financial institution's subsidiaries will remain intact. The FDIC will transfer the holding company's assets, secured debt, and short-term debt to a new bridge institution and leave behind the shareholders and long-term unsecured debt, which is primarily going to be bond debt. It will take a few months to sort out the details, but the initial move will be quick and will leave behind the shareholders and bondholders. The shareholders will likely end up getting nothing. The long-term debt that is left behind will be written down by a still unknown amount. Short-term debt will be protected.

Single point of entry is a creative use of the resolution rules, and it seems better than the approach that the Title II rules appear to have in mind. One virtue of the single-point-of-entry approach is that it is a quick, surgical solution as long as there are no major disasters at the subsidiary level. If there are huge disasters in the subsidiaries, it is going to be a lot harder to pull off. Another virtue is that single point of entry takes advantage of the quirky capital structure of large U.S. banks. U.S. holding companies have relatively few assets other than stock of their subsidiaries, and they have substantial bond debt. This is unusual from a worldwide perspective. The parent corporation of a European financial institution often has substantial operations and relatively little long-term debt. The capital structure of U.S. holding companies is a historical accident that was caused by the limits on interstate banking and other idiosyncrasies of U.S. banking regulation. This may be one of those rare cases where the unintended consequences of past regulation are helpful rather than problematic. Europe is trying to implement similar resolution rules, but the capital structure of its banks is a lot less conducive to this end.

A third virtue of the single-point-of-entry approach is that the FDIC is at least signaling what it plans to do, even if the market might not completely believe it. Although it has complete discretion, it is saying that it is going to write down the long-term debt and protect the short-term debt.

One concern with this approach is that it is going to require more regulation. If a bank's long-term debt might be written down, it is going to be a little bit more expensive, and the bank is not going to want to use as much of that kind of debt. To ensure that systemically important financial institutions have enough long-term debt for single point of entry to work, regulators will be forced to police the institutions' use of long-term debt to make sure they keep an adequate amount. If other too-big-to-fail institutions are the principal holders of the debt, this could create an additional problem—the risk that regulators will be reluctant to write down the bonds in resolution due to concerns about the effect on the holders.

A second, more important concern is that single point of entry promises carte blanche protection to all short-term debt, especially derivatives, repurchase agreements (repos), and the like. It is as if we are giving these financial institutions even more incentive to use short-term debt than they had in 2008. This is probably my single biggest concern with the single-point-of-entry strategy.

Third, as has been mentioned, the single-point-of-entry approach does not address problems at subsidiaries. The FDIC is devising ways to try to stabilize a liquidity-starved or troubled subsidiary, but single point of entry works best if the FDIC can do the quick write-down at the parent-company level without having to worry about subsidiaries all over the world.

A fourth concern is legal. Single point of entry violates one of the key principles of the Dodd–Frank Act, which was that Title II would be used only for liquidation. Senator Barbara Boxer added a "Thou shalt liquidate" provision to Title II late in the legislative process to make sure that the message was received. In my view, the liquidation requirement was a bad idea. In a single-point-of-entry resolution, reorganization is necessary. This is almost precisely the approach that was used in the earliest U.S. reorganizations, most of which involved railroads. This is the way that Chrysler and General Motors were reorganized (with a little government help and manipulation). The FDIC claims that single point of entry satisfies the liquidation requirement because the assets are "sold," but it clearly is a reorganization.

A final concern is whether anybody will ever pull this trigger. In another crisis, will regulators bail out systemically important financial institutions all over again? I suspect that if more than one institution is in trouble, they will, and Dodd–Frank will not change that. A Title II resolution also would not do anything to reduce concentration in the financial services industry. If the resolution worked, we would end up with a big financial institution after the resolution that looks a lot like the big institution from before the resolution. This is one reason, in my view, that the largest banks love this idea. It does not rock the boat as much as they were afraid the boat was going to be rocked.

Chapter 14.2

I have a few final words on the bankruptcy alternative, chapter 14, that was proposed several years ago (Jackson 2012; Scott and Taylor 2012).

In its original incarnation, chapter 14 applied to financial institutions with $100 billion in assets and made a number of adjustments to the bankruptcy laws to facilitate the bankruptcy of a large financial institution. The original draft predated the emergence of the FDIC's single-point-of-entry strategy for resolution. More recently, the group has been discussing the use of bankruptcy to achieve the same benefits as a single-point-of-entry resolution, building in part on the discussion in a recent report issued by the Bipartisan Policy Center (Bovenzi, Guynn, and Jackson 2013). Much as with single point of entry under Title II, the holding company would file for chapter 14, and its assets, secured debt, and short-term debt would be transferred to a newly created entity. Also as with single point of entry, the stock and long-term debt could remain with the bankrupt entity. Bankruptcy's sale provision, section 363 (which was used in the Chrysler and General Motors bankruptcies), would provide the statutory basis for the sale.

There are a couple of obstacles to making the bankruptcy alternative work. One is that currently there is no stay on derivatives in bankruptcy. The rule that creditors cannot cancel contracts, grab collateral, or sell collateral that they have applies to other creditors but not to holders of qualified financial contracts (such as derivatives, repos, and similar contracts). Dodd–Frank has a one-day stay for derivatives that at least ought to be applied in bankruptcy.

A second issue is cross-defaults. Title II forbids creditors of one entity (say, a subsidiary) from invoking a provision that makes the resolution of an affiliated entity (say, the holding company) a default under contracts of that entity. In the absence of such a rule, the holding company's bankruptcy could trigger terminations by contractual counterparties at the subsidiaries. I think Congress needs to add a similar rule to the bankruptcy laws.

Third, Congress needs to ensure that the new entity would have access to the same licenses and operating permits that the financial institution had before filing for bankruptcy.

Finally, the $64,000 question in the bankruptcy of a systemically important financial institution is liquidity. Could you achieve the restructuring without the enormous amount of liquidity that the FDIC has access to in Dodd–Frank? It is not clear that you could. There is an argument that when you do the sale, the new institution would be well capitalized and could borrow money from private markets quickly. I am not sure that it would be fast enough. It is possible, at least with bank holding companies, that the new entity would have access to the discount window. So the big issue right now is whether a liquidity source should be added. And if so, should it be from the Treasury or the Fed discount window? If I had to choose one, I would choose the Fed discount window. This is a tricky issue, however, because a source of liquidity could be misused to bail out rather than to resolve.

Although I have been a critic of the Title II resolution rules, I think that single point of entry is an interesting strategy. I do not think that it ends too big to fail, but it is better than what Dodd–Frank actually says about resolutions. I would be much happier if a few changes were made to bankruptcy to reinforce the idea that bankruptcy is the option of first resort when a systemically important financial institution is in trouble. And the Dodd–Frank Act repeatedly emphasizes the same point—that we should use bankruptcy rather than Title II whenever possible.

Wilmarth: David has illuminated three significant problems with the Title II version of the single point of entry and the chapter 14.2 version of bankruptcy. First, are we going to encourage institutions (particularly those in trouble) to move toward short-term financing because only the short-term creditors (the qualified financial contracts under 360 days) will have any likelihood of 100 percent recovery? This will lead to a Lehman or Bear Stearns on steroids when the next problem comes. Second, and linked to that, who is going to buy the bail-in bonds? And third, where are you going to get debtor-in-possession financing? According to Title II, the source of debtor-in-possession financing is the U.S. Treasury. The Treasury will provide a five-year loan that can be extended for at least another three years. Because the U.S. Treasury is a source of debtor-in- possession financing, Title II is an enormous opportunity for bailouts. But with the bankruptcy alternative, how can debtor-in-possession financing be obtained in a so-called private bailout process?

Discussion

Barth: The Fed is already talking about imposing a minimum requirement for long-term debt, and we have learned that Wells Fargo is afraid that the minimum would be too high. Even if the Fed imposes a minimum amount of long-term debt to be issued by a bank, the question then becomes who would actually buy it. I assume that the Fed will not buy it.

Some proposals have called for capital requirements of 15, 20, and even 30 percent. The Modigliani–Miller theorem is used by some to suggest that equity can be substituted for debt without any negative effects because as debt cost goes down, equity cost goes up, and they would offset each other. Franco Modigliani and Merton Miller were on two sides of that issue. Miller took the view that equity can be swapped for debt with no adverse effects, but Modigliani argued that the increase in equity cost is not offset by the decrease in debt cost. So the two disagreed over this issue, and they both won Nobel Prizes in part for that theorem.

Dearie: At another conference last week, David gave a similar presentation on his critique of OLA and his advocacy of bankruptcy, and someone made the point that the changes to bankruptcy that you are talking about to make it more workable and appropriate for large financial institutions end up making bankruptcy look more like OLA. Moreover, what seems to be a major or perhaps even the major critique of OLA is the discretion that the FDIC has. You noted earlier that the FDIC has become increasingly specific in saying what they are going to do, and if it becomes more specific about how it intends to pursue a single point of entry, then some doubts will be allayed. So there is a kind of convergence between OLA and bankruptcy. If they move toward each other, we might arrive at a workable and credible system.

Skeel: I agree that a convergence is happening, and that is a good thing on all sorts of different levels. If there are substantive differences between the two systems, some will try to game those differences. One example is that there is a stay of derivatives and other qualified financial contracts in OLA but not in bankruptcy. Another difference is that in bankruptcy, the principal decisions are made by the managers and creditors rather than by the regulators. Even those differences are being collapsed a little bit, but the trigger is likely to come from the managers of the company in bankruptcy and from regulators of the company in OLA.

Dearie: The two alternatives that David presented for how debt financing could be arranged in a bankruptcy were either directly from Treasury or, the thing that sends the shiver down my spine, by way of a discount window. That to me is a very bad idea. The discount window is not a backdoor bailout and should not be thought of that way. But if the discount window is used to provide debt financing, that gets awfully close to the flame, which would bother me a lot. So again, I find myself caught in-between. I understand the objections to OLA, but I see the operational difficulties associated with bankruptcy.

Barth: I think the contagion point is fundamental because in virtually every major financial crisis, there is not just one major financial institution teetering or stumbling along the cliff edge. Instead, several institutions are likely to be viewed as interconnected in important ways. Continental Illinois was bailed out because Paul Volcker and others believed that if it was not bailed out, Manufacturers Hanover was going to fail, and later they believed that if Manufacturers Hanover was not bailed out, then Chase was going to fail. They were all considered to be too big to fail in those days.

David's point remains salient, and I think this is the case for a bankruptcy too. Will the regulators pull the trigger on the first too-big-to-fail bank? Because if the first OLA does not go perfectly, any sort of disruption or disappointment of creditors could spread very quickly and affect further resolutions. So a great question is whether the regulators, even with all the tools that they have obtained, would pull the trigger, or whether they would be more tempted to do what they did in 2008, which was to do an open bank recapitalization.

I do agree with something that Barney Frank said. He said that market discipline lasted twenty-four hours: the government let Lehman fail, and then twenty-four hours later it bailed out AIG.

Question: Jim Barth, you mention the need for a sentinel to provide oversight of regulators. It seems to me that the natural oversight of financial regulators is academic research. I think that better access for academics to data from regulators is something we can all support here.

Barth: Yes, if one cannot measure something, then one cannot improve it, which implies the need for available data. Our proposal for a sentinel is controversial. It will not solve all problems, but it is meant to be an independent federal agency that consists of experts, that has the ear of the Congress and the president, and that will be listened to by most people. The sentinel could go before the Congress twice a year (not unlike the Fed does) and raise any issues when there are disagreements between what it believes should be done and what the regulatory authorities are doing. The problem with being an academic is that no matter how good one is and how much one publishes that addresses current policy issues, few people will pay as much attention as they will to a official federal agency.

A little bit of history may help in this regard. In the late 1980s, I wrote a piece with the deputy chief economist at the Federal Home Loan Bank

Board saying that the Federal Savings and Loan Insurance Corporation (FSLIC) was insolvent by a certain dollar amount. The chair of the agency at the time and the ranking majority and minority members of the Senate Banking Committee disagreed with our assessment. After the *Washington Post* published an article about the report that was picked up by other media, the chair testified that the FSLIC was indeed insolvent, and he differed from our assessment by a relatively insignificant amount. The bottom line is that some things that are known about important problems within agencies may never see the light of day. Academics may also have a problem convincing the news media about the seriousness of certain matters.

John Paulson owns a hedge fund and made a few billion dollars betting that home prices would decline. It has been said that he told the regulatory authorities about his concerns about a decline in home prices but that little attention was paid to him. If home prices continued going up at 10 percent a year, year in and year out, eventually even Bill Gates would not be able to afford to buy a home. It was known or should have been known that home prices had to stabilize or decline, which they did. Because banks were holding a total of $4 trillion in real estate loans, when home prices went down, there would be problems for banks and others that were holding securities backed by mortgages. Did nobody within the regulatory agencies know about the potential problems that were developing?

Who has the information and expertise to identify problems that are developing? A lot of it is within the Federal Reserve System. It tends to have a monopoly on timely and relevant information and the personnel with the right expertise. Bloomberg and others had to sue the Fed to find out who was getting money under the Troubled Asset Recovery Program (TARP) and other associated programs. A U.S. federal district court judge finally said that irreparable harm would not be done to the American economy if that information was released. The Fed did not voluntarily release this information. It took a U.S. federal district court judge to make the information available to the public.

Question: Jim, would it be an unfair characterization to describe your sentinel as an expanded inspector general (IG) concept?

Barth: In a way, but an inspector general does not possess all the expertise that we would like to see in a separate and more focused financial regulatory agency or sentinel.

References

Barth, James, Gerard Caprio, and Ross Levine. 2012. *Guardians of Finance: Making Regulators Work for Us.* Cambridge, MA: MIT Press.

Bovenzi, John F., Randall D. Guynn, and Thomas H. Jackson. 2013. *Too Big to Fail: The Path to a Solution.* Washington, DC: Bipartisan Policy Center.

Jackson, Tom. 2012. Bankruptcy Code Chapter 14: A Proposal. Working Paper, Hoover Institution.

Johnson, Simon, and James Kwak. 2010. *13 Bankers: The Wall Street Takeover and the Next Financial Meltdown.* New York: Pantheon.

Moskowitz, Tobias J., and L. Jon Wertheim. 2012. *Scorecasting: The Hidden Influences Behind How Sports Are Played and Games Are Won.* New York: Three Rivers Press.

Scott, Kenneth, and John Taylor, eds. 2012. *Bankruptcy Not Bailout: A Special Chapter 14.* Stanford, CA: Hoover Institution Press.

7   The Origins and Intent of the Volcker Rule

Priyank Gandhi

The Volcker Rule is the popular name for section 619 of the Dodd–Frank Wall Street Reform and Consumer Protection Act.[1] The rule is named after the American economist and former chair of the Federal Reserve Board, Paul Volcker.

Origins of the Volcker Rule

After the financial crisis of 2007, President Barrack Obama created the President's Economic Recovery Advisory Board and appointed Paul Volcker as its chair. Shortly thereafter, in a *New York Times* op-ed article, Volcker argued that actions by regulators to rescue large financial institutions during the crisis had enhanced their incentives to risk-taking and leverage.[2] In his view, moral hazard associated with government bailouts could be eliminated only through structural changes, such as limiting proprietary trading and prohibiting the sponsorship of hedge funds and private equity funds by banks. Volcker further argued that these activities were speculative in nature, better handled by nonbank financial institutions, and had to be prohibited to ensure a robust financial system.

The Volcker Rule is intended to reduce the ability of commercial banks in the United States to take excessive risks by restricting the types of speculative investments that they can undertake. The activities to be banned have been deemed too risky by legislators and are purported to be harmful to the bank's depositors and institutional clients. Although nonbank financial companies supervised by the Federal Reserve are allowed to participate in such activities, they are subject to additional capital requirements. Banking entities are also allowed to participate in certain exempt trading activities if they are related to instruments issued by the U.S. Treasury or government-owned agencies. Other exemptions include underwriting and market-making activities to meet demands of customers, clients, and counterparties, as well as risk mitigation and hedging or trading on customers' behalf. Finally, a banking entity is also allowed to organize and offer a private equity or hedge fund, as long as the banking entity does not guarantee or insure the performance of the fund.

The rationale behind the Volcker Rule is that in recent years, commercial banks have increasingly participated in speculative activities that involve placing bank capital at risk in search of profits rather than responding to customer needs. These include activities such as trading, securitization, investment banking, brokerage, sponsorship of hedge funds, private equity funds, and venture funds. Researches have documented that such activities indeed account for an ever-increasing fraction of a commercial bank's income (Brunnermeier, Dong, and Palia (2012).[3]

Proponents of the rule believe that these activities add further layers of risk to what is already inherently a risky business. They argue that speculative activities present conflicts of interest between bank division managers and customers that (based on past experience) are virtually insolvable with so-called Chinese walls between business segments. In their view, such conflicting activities are better handled by other legally distinct participants in financial markets.

Regulators also are concerned that their extensive efforts during the financial crisis to rescue large financial institutions by extending deposit insurance and lender-of-last-resort facilities to investment banks, mortgage providers, and insurance firms has reinforced the moral hazard problem. Large, complex financial institutions can now always count on public support during times of aggregate economic shocks. Regulators also believe that their actions provide large commercial banks with incentives to increase risk-taking, eventually leading to an even more fragile financial system that will be susceptible to ever-more serious crises in the future.

Similar rules to force banks to divest their risky speculative businesses have been proposed in the United Kingdom and several other countries. In the United Kingdom, the Independent Commission on Banking led by Sir John Vickers requires bank holding companies to erect a ring fence between their commercial banking and investment banking arms. In the European Union (EU), the High-Level Expert Group chaired by Erkki Liikanen, the governor of the Bank of Finland, has proposed that proprietary trading and other significant trading activities should be assigned to a separate legal entity if the activities to be separated amount to a significant share of a bank's business.

Difficulties in Implementing the Volcker Rule

Dodd–Frank and the related Volcker Rule are complex. Regulators are still struggling to interpret the legislation more than three years after the act was enacted. The length of the Volcker Rule hints at its complexity: the original rule as submitted to the Congress as part of the Dodd–Frank Act was just ten pages long. In October 2011, when the Volcker Rule finally emerged for public comment, the text was 298 pages long, and four federal agencies—the Federal Reserve Board, the Securities and Exchange Commission, the Federal Deposit Insurance Corporation, and the Comptroller of Currency—were charged with its implementation.[4] This has resulted in infighting among the regulators and delayed the law's full implementation indefinitely.[5]

One issue that highlights how complex it is to implement the Volcker Rule is the distinction between sovereign debt issued by the U.S. Treasury and non-U.S. government bonds. The Volcker Rule exempts U.S. Treasury securities but classifies trading in sovereign debt issued by other countries, even those by EU nations and Japan, as speculative investments. Regulators in other countries are justifiably concerned that such restrictions will cause U.S. banks to exit the markets for sovereign bonds for those countries, reducing liquidity and hampering the ability of these nations to borrow money by issuing foreign debt. The effect is likely to be particularly severe on smaller nations with thinly traded bonds that rely heavily on large banks to serve as primary dealers to buy their debt at auctions. Regulators in Europe and Japan have indicated that they cannot accept any regulations whose consequences are exported to their countries or they will be tempted to respond in kind, restricting the ability of large foreign banks to hold and trade U.S. Treasury securities. The issue has been muddied further by the fact that in an attempt to level the playing field, U.S. regulators require that the Volcker Rule will apply to U.S. divisions of foreign banks and will also cover activities of any bank with a connection to the United States, even a single branch in one state.

Another issue with the implementation of the Volcker Rule is that it effectively requires regulators to micromanage how market making—the process by which a market participant accepts the risk of holding a certain inventory of securities in order to facilitate trading in that security by its customers—is conducted by banks in the United States. Postimplementation, U.S. and foreign banks will have to prove that all buying and selling of securities amounts to market making for clients, not proprietary trading.

This has led to an outcry from U.S. banks. Banks complain that it is easy for them to divest independent trading units that are devoted entirely to proprietary trading. However, it is often difficult, if not impossible, to distinguish between proprietary trading and other activities (such as market making and portfolio hedging), and there is a fine line between classifying such activities as trading for their own accounts and buying and selling on behalf of clients. As a result, instead of bearing related regulatory costs, banks may simply decide that it is more efficient for them to exit certain markets altogether. By some industry analyst estimates, the cost of issuing corporate debt may increase annually by $360 billion if banks exit these markets.

In light of the banks' reaction, it is vital that regulators reexamine the proposal and conduct and unbiased, data-driven, careful analysis of the economic issues at the core of the Volcker Rule. This will allow the regulators to assess the costs and benefits of restricting certain activities, convince market participants to accept the final version of the rule when issued, and implement the rule without delays and disruption to the financial markets. In the remainder of this chapter, I highlight a few of these key economic issues.

At the outset, regulators must convince market participants that activities that are now banned under the Volcker Rule played a central role in the financial crisis. Researchers more or less agree that the financial crisis can be traced not to trading portfolios of banks but to losses suffered by banks in the housing markets. Gary B. Gorton and Andrew Metrick (2009) show that in the run-up to the crisis, banks used sale and repurchase agreements (repos) frequently to finance short-term investments. Such repo transactions were often collateralized with securitized bonds. As losses mounted, first on the securitized subprime-housing assets and then on securitized prime-housing assets, banks faced increased funding costs and received ever-lower values for posted collateral. This, combined with insufficient capital held by banks to cover unanticipated losses effectively lead to the insolvency of U.S. banks (Acharya and Richardson 2009).

Banning Proprietary Trading: Pros and Cons

Several alternative arguments have been put forward to support the ban on trading activities at commercial banks. The laundry list of these justifications includes potential unresolvable conflicts of interest, increased risk taking, increased systemic risk, increased complexity, reduced transparency, increased cost of risk management, and complications in the event of a bankruptcy. The academic literature suggests that evidence supporting any of these arguments is mixed at best. Although a full review of this literature is beyond the scope of this chapter, a few key results are worth mentioning. Researchers have documented that despite potential conflicts of interest, allowing banks to engage in nontraditional activities is overall socially beneficial as banks always seek to establish a reputation for quality (Kroszner and Rajan 1994; Ang and Richardson 1994;, Puri 1994, 1996). Instead of increasing risk, diversified financial institutions are shown to be less exposed to income shocks and therefore more stable (Templeton and Severiens 1992; Altunbas, Manganelli, and Marquez-Ibanez 2011). Although banks with higher noninterest income contribute more to systemic risk (Brunnermeier, Dong, and Palia 2012), complementary activities at different units also often serve as natural hedges for each other and may in fact reduce risk (Cumming and Hirtle 2001). Rather than increase risk-management costs, participation in trading allows banks to manage risks better, reduce costs, and increase credit supply (Brewer, Minton, and Moser 2000). Financial institutions are definitely more complex and informationally opaque as compared to the average nonfinancial firm (Flannery, Kwan, and Nimalendran 2004; Iannotta 2006), and this can make resolution in bankruptcy cumbersome. Yet the fact that special procedures are required for winding down large diversified financial institutions cannot per se be an argument for restricting participation of these banks in certain markets.

Regulators should ask why banks choose not to specialize in a narrow range of activities but instead choose to diversify their business models to include trading and market making. In academic finance, a well-established literature analyzes the costs and benefits of diversification (Lang and Stulz 1994; Berger and Ofek 1995; Servaes 1996). For a bank, a diversified business model may offer several advantages and disadvantages, but the existing literature on restricting banks from nontraditional activities is silent on whether diversification has any significant costs or benefits for the diversified bank and its customers. This suggests that we should not pursue the Volcker Rule without further research.

Additional analysis can reveal hitherto hidden benefits of combining traditional banking activities with proprietary trading. For example, in a working paper that I coauthored with Patrick C. Kiefer, we show that for the aggregate banking sector in the United States, interest income and income from trading activities are negatively correlated (Gandhi and Kiefer 2013). Between 1987 and 2012, the correlation between interest income and income from trading activities was -0.79. This correlation is statistically significant. Furthermore, since we use interest and trading income for the aggregate banking sector in the United States, it is unlikely that this correlation is spurious or results from mismeasurement or misreporting of incomes, a phenomenon that is more likely to occur at the individual bank level.

We also examine the correlation between interest income and trading income for the cross-section of bank holding companies. Of the 719 bank holding companies in our sample, the correlation between interest income and trading income was negative for 558 bank holding companies or 78 percent of our sample. This indicates that bank holding companies (and the aggregate banking sector in the United States) effectively employ income from trading activities as a natural hedge to income from lending activities, on average.

We refer to this trading behavior as a natural hedge for the following reason. Income from loans is procyclical, and it is difficult to form a long loan portfolio that performs well in down cycles. However, when banks have access to trading, positions can be taken to counteract the procyclical exposure of the loan portfolios. Trading positions are more versatile (virtually any exposure can be synthesized) and can be used to hedge the stickier positions in a bank's loan portfolio, thus smoothing income across cycles. Most important, even if the divisional managers' trading activities are not explicitly motivated by hedging, rational internal capital markets can operate in a way that allows trading activities to be undertaken as if hedging were the explicit motivation.

In fact, our most surprising result emerges when we compare the lending behavior of banks that employ trading as a natural hedge to lending of banks where trading and lending incomes are positively correlated. We find that banks that employ trading as a natural hedge are able to maintain more stable lending policies as compared to other banks. To the extent that banks have active internal capital markets, access to trading appears to smooth credit supply across cycles, on average.

We are still investigating the source of this higher stability in lending policies. It may be that banks with more diversified income streams have lower income volatility and are able to maintain more stable investment policies through the active operation of their internal capital markets. If diversified banks have lower income volatility, they may also benefit from lower funding costs. Such banks may pass on savings from funding activities to customers and hence may be able to provide credit at lower costs. This effect may be most pronounced during economic downturns when the average cost of credit is high or when other banks (with more positively correlated income streams) may be increasing the cost of credit or reducing the size of their lending books. Our preliminary analysis suggests that this may indeed be the channel that allows for stable lending policies. Banks with more diversified income streams have a cost of capital that is lower by more than 250 basis points as compared to nondiversified banks. Most of this spread is accounted for not by lower idiosyncratic risk but via lower exposure to systematic (market) risk.

The motivation of the Volcker Rule is to protect depositors and clients from the risk borne by proprietary (prop) trading divisions at banks, to mitigate the moral hazard tendency created by the implicit bailout guarantee, and to curb systemic risk. On the other hand, banning prop trading may feed back into the real economy through credit supply and adversely affect some of the agents that the rule was intended to protect. It is possible that amplifying credit-supply cyclicality by banning trading can make systemic risk more pronounced. Furthermore, firms that rely on bank loans could experience greater financing costs in the presence of barriers to a bank's ability to smooth income. The implications of shutting down these banks' internal capital markets should be studied carefully so that unintended externalities of the law can be minimized.

Several points—preliminary results from our working paper, the tentative liquidity costs associated with banks' potential exit from certain market-making activities, the concerns highlighted in chapter 8, and the unanswered question of how best to mitigate the moral hazard associated with federal guarantees—highlight the importance of fully assessing the costs and benefits of the Volcker Rule. In a recent statement to the U.S. Congress, Sheila Bair, the former head of the Federal Deposit Insurance Company (FDIC), stated that the recent regulation proposed to implement the Volcker Rule is extraordinarily complex and may try too hard. A very precise regulatory regime might be the most effective way to achieve the stated goals of the legislation, and the design of such a regime should proceed carefully and consider our evolving understanding of how the banking sector interacts with the economy.

Notes

1. Section 619, Prohibitions on Proprietary Trading and Certain Relationships with Hedge Funds and Private Equity Funds, H.R. 4173 (2010), pp. 245–256, http://www.sec .gov/about/laws/wallstreetreform-cpa.pdf.

2. See the *New York Times*, http://www.nytimes.com/2010/01.31/opinion/31volcker .html?pagewanted=all.

3. For the ten largest commercial banks in the United States, noncore activities such as trading, sponsorship of funds, and advisory fees account for 18 percent of total income in 1989 and 59 percent of total income in 2007.

4. A helpful forty-seven-page summary of the Volcker Rule as it exists now has been prepared by Sullivan and Cromwell, a law firm. See http://www.sullcrom.com/ Volcker-Rule-10–12–2011.

5. See http://www.foxbusiness.com/economy/2013/06/05/dodd-frank-reforms-may -take-years-to-implement.

References

Acharya, Viral V., and Matthew Richardson. 2009. Causes of the Financial Crisis. *Critical Review* 21 (2–3):195–210.

Altunbas, Yener, Simone Manganelli, and David Marquez-Ibanez. 2011. Bank Risk during the Financial Crisis: Do Business Models Matter? ECB Working Paper No. 1394. European Central Bank, Frankfurt am Main.

Ang, J. S., and T. Richardson. 1994. The Underwriting Experience of Commercial Bank Affiliates prior to the Glass-Steagall Act: A Re-examination of Evidence for Passage of the Act. *Journal of Banking & Finance* 18 (2):351–395.

Berger, Phillip, and Eli Ofek. 1995. Diversification's Effect on Firm Value. *Journal of Financial Economics* 37:39–65.

Brewer, E., B. A. Minton, and J. T. Moser. 2000. Interest-Rate Derivatives and Bank Lending. *Journal of Banking & Finance* 24 (3):353–379.

Brunnermeier, Markus K., Gang Dong, and Darius Palia. 2012. Banks' Non-interest Income and Systemic Risk. Working Paper.

Cumming, C., and B. Hirtle. 2001. The Challenges of Risk Management in Diversified Financial Companies. *Economic Policy Review* 7 (1).

Flannery, M. J., S. H. Kwan, and M. Nimalendran. 2004. Market Evidence on the Opaqueness of Banking Firms Assets. *Journal of Financial Economics* 71:419–460.

Gandhi, Priyank, and Patrick C. Kiefer. 2013. Costly Liquidity Provision and Bank Trading. Working Paper.

Gorton, Gary B., and Andrew Metrick. 2009. Securitized Banking and Run on Repo. NBER Working Paper.

Iannotta, G. 2006. Testing for Opaqueness in the European Banking Industry: Evidence from Bond Credit Ratings. *Journal of Financial Services Research* 30:287–309.

Kroszner, R. S., and R. G. Rajan. 1994. Is the Glass-Steagall Act Justified? A Study of the U.S. Experience with Universal Banking before 1933. *American Economic Review* 84 (4):810–832.

Lang, Larry, and Rene Stulz. 1994. Tobin's q, Corporate Diversification, and Firm Performance. *Journal of Political Economy* 102:1248–1291.

Puri, M. 1994. The Long-Term Default Performance of Bank Underwritten Security Issues. *Journal of Banking & Finance* 18 (2):397–418.

Puri, M. 1996. Commercial Banks in Investment Banking Conflict of Interest or Certification Role? *Journal of Financial Economics* 40 (3):373–401.

Servaes, Henri. 1996. The Value of Diversification during the Conglomerate Merger Wave. *Journal of Finance* 51:1201–1225.

Templeton, W. K., and J. T. Severiens. 1992. The Effect of Nonbank Diversification on Bank Holding Companies. *Quarterly Journal of Business and Economics* 31 (4):3–16.

8 Panel Discussion on the Volcker Rule

Charles W. Calomiris and Matthew Richardson

Matthew Richardson:[1] Given the Dodd–Frank Wall Street Reform and Consumer Protection Act of 2010, the question is whether we are better off with or without the Volcker Rule. For all of the contributing authors in this book, there is probably much less unanimity about Volcker than anything else. In this chapter, it is NYU/Columbia, pro-Volcker/anti-Volcker: really exciting stuff.

First, I will take a quick step back and give what I think may be the right approach to regulation and note why Dodd–Frank does not do it and why it may be second best. Second, I am going to give the logic of the Volcker Rule. Third, I will acknowledge that principal trading was a big factor during the crisis. People have pointed to the quality of loans and shadow banking, but it all ended up being channeled through securities trading on the part of banks. Fourth, I will talk about why capital regulation is not sufficient within Dodd–Frank and why a structural reform might be needed, Volcker being one example. Fifth, I will look at criticisms of the Volcker rule that get the most play. Finally, I will talk a little bit about implementation.

The Theory of Regulation

The economic theory of regulation is clear. Governments should regulate where there is a market failure. It is a positive outcome from the Dodd–Frank legislation that the act's primary focus is on the market failure of the recent financial crisis—namely, systemic risk. The negative externality associated with such risk implies that private markets cannot efficiently solve the problem, which thus requires government intervention.

More concretely, current and past financial crises show that systemic risk emerges when aggregate capitalization of the financial sector is low. The intuition is straightforward. When a financial firm's capital is low, it is difficult for that firm to perform financial services, and when capital is low in the aggregate, it is not possible for other financial firms to step into the breach. This breakdown in financial intermediation is the reason that there are severe consequences for the broader economy. When a financial firm therefore runs aground during a crisis period, it contributes to this aggregate shortfall, leading to consequences beyond the firm itself. The firm has no incentive to manage the systemic risk.

With respect to systemic risk, therefore, if a financial firm takes certain kinds of risk, those risks may impose costs on other firms in the financial system and more broadly on the overall economy. Because firms do not internalize the costs of these risks, too much systemic risk is produced (Acharya, Pedersen, Philippon, and Richardson 2010). One solution to the problem of systemic risk is to place a surcharge on financial institutions so that they internalize these risks, and the model in Acharya, Pedersen et al. (2010) shows how a systemic risk tax can be proportional to the level of systemic risk. In terms of financial regulation, a regulatory system needs to focus on the problem of the risk that is being produced at these firms. When these surcharges are imposed, behavior changes, so although these firms may still produce some systemic risk, they would now pay for it. As a result, these firms would organically choose to be less systemically risky—that is, they would choose to be less levered and choose a different risk profile with less systemically risky assets.

But this is not the way the Dodd–Frank legislation ended up addressing systemic risk. Aside from a new and significant regulatory apparatus, it puts hard constraints on financial institutions' leverage and places some restrictions on the type of assets that institutions can hold or trade. To the extent that this is the outcome that you get from a first best system, Dodd–Frank approximates this outcome by dictating what those leverage levels and asset holdings might be. So in that big-picture sense, Dodd–Frank fits into the overall regulatory framework, albeit not as a first best solution.

The Logic of the Volcker Rule

What is the logic behind the Volcker Rule and its restrictions on proprietary trading? Many activities are systemically risky. For example, lending to corporations and lending to households are risky activities. Washington Mutual lent to households and went under. It was a big institution and probably created systemic risk on the system. Fee-related businesses like M&A's advisory work is systemically risky. This work disappears in a crisis, and the business no longer generates fees. Any firm that borrowed against the market value of those businesses is hurt in a crisis. And principal trading is systemically risky. Many things are systemically risky, not just trading on a financial firm's own account.

There is a big literature about why a bank is a bank (Fama 1985; Diamond 1991; Petersen and Rajan 1994). Certain activities are core to banks and cannot be duplicated outside the banking sector. Lending to corporations and households is one. Banks have certain comparative advantages in the way that they fund themselves and the way that they monitor. These activities cannot be done outside the banking system, so they cannot be touched even if they are systemically risky. But with principal trading, it is not clear that it is core and cannot be done elsewhere. There are various funds (such as mutual funds, pension funds, sovereign wealth funds, and hedge funds) that buy and sell the same types of securities. Those institutions are much less levered and do not have access to the government safety net.

One reason for taking principal trading out of the banking sector is that these activities add risk to the banking sector. The banking sector is already more systemically risky than other parts of the financial system like mutual funds and other less levered trading operations. This is one reason to exclude principal trading from banking. Another reasonable point that Volcker makes is the question of whether a part of the financial system that has access to the safety net (through deposit insurance or through too-big-to-fail implicit guarantees) should be allowed to transact in a noncore part of the market. Allowing institutions with access to the safety net to engage in noncore activities is going to increase leverage in the system, and this is going to increase systemic risk as well.

The Risk of Principal Trading

The relevant questions are whether principal trading is a source of systemic risk and whether it was relevant to the crisis. I argue that it was highly relevant. During the initial 2008 failure of the financial system in the United States and abroad, banks had near-fatal invest-ments in asset-backed securities. These firms exploited loopholes in capital regulation to take highly levered, directional bets on credit-related securities, especially those tied to the residential mortgage market (Acharya, Cooley, Richardson, and Walter 2010a). One way to avoid capital requirements was to securitize the loans, sell them off, and bring them back on their balance sheets, all with less capital. They did this activity in a variety of ways.

Going into 2007, UBS had $50 billion of asset-backed securities on its books, CitiGroup $55 billion, and Merrill Lynch $70 billion. Most of these holdings were financed overnight through repurchase agreements (repos) or through other short-term liabilities. There was a similar problem in the French banking system and the trouble that the French banking system ran into during the past few years. They were holding a large amount of peripheral debt in the euro system, especially Portugal and Spain. Were the French banks holding that much peripheral, sovereign debt so that they could make a market in sovereign debt for its clients, or were they taking a big bet? They were holding this debt because it offered a spread and no regulatory capital was required. These institutions have certain advantages (such as government guarantees), and they are going to take actions that other institutions cannot afford to. Principal trading has been a source of a lot of the problems that have occurred in the last five or six years (Richardson 2011).

Why Capital Regulation Is Not Enough

In theory, capital regulation can solve this problem. Capital regulations can make institutions delever and change their asset holdings, so maybe regulators can focus on capital. But I think there are two reasons that we probably cannot do that, at least in the way that Dodd–Frank is written. The first reason is that with Dodd–Frank and even with the Basel capital regulation, the regulation produces very linear capital rules. These rules do not address the cases in which financial institutions conduct trades that provide small gains with high probability and large losses with a low probability. These include carry trades and regulatory arbitrage trades. Financial guarantee insurance has a similar risk profile.

Existing capital regulation is pretty inefficient because what we should really care about is those low probability states, which tend to coincide with the systemic risk states. Firms need to hold a lot of capital in those states. But if these firms are required to hold all this capital, then they will hold too much capital in 95 percent of the states when the firms do not need much capital. Under these linear capital rules, capital is going to be too little or too much—too little because it does not cover the losses in the bad states and too much because it covers too much in the good states.

The second reason that the focus cannot be on only capital regulation is that it is difficult to measure leverage at the institutional level because Wall Street is always ahead of the regulators. There was, for example, off-balance-sheet financing in the asset-backed commercial paper market. A study conducted by the New York Federal Reserve Bank showed a lot of gaming around quarterly reports. It is difficult to pinpoint leverage at the institutional level. Even if capital requirements are defined, banks are going to find ways to get around them. The firms that effectively failed during the financial crisis were all well capitalized on a regulatory level. If these firms used current rules, they still would be well capitalized. So capital might be important but may not be enough.

There are also questions of the right level of capital and the cost of capital. Are banks highly levered to take advantage of the safety net and the tax advantage of debt? Or are there real costs of holding too much capital on your books? This issue needs to be addressed before firms can start relying primarily on capital regulation.

Criticisms of the Volcker Rule

One criticism of the Volcker Rule is that it will increase risk because it is going to decrease diversification. Regulators will no longer allow banks to invest in certain securities, which will increase the volatility of their portfolio. I think that this is a bad argument because it confuses idiosyncratic with systematic risk. In a crisis, we care about systematic risk. This is when it emerges. When proprietary trading is added to a portfolio, the total risk (that is, idiosyncratic and systematic risk) of your portfolio on a per asset basis might be decreased, but the amount of systematic risk is not decreased. It is not being diversified away. There is a big literature on this, both precrisis and postcrisis. Many papers look at the individual and aggregate risk of financial institutions with or without proprietary trading, and the evidence is pretty strong that proprietary trading does not reduce systematic risk.[2]

On synergies, I think that there is a much stronger argument against Volcker.[3] If financial firms are more active in primary markets and underwrite, it is easier for them to be active in secondary markets. If firms underwrite corporate bonds, they will know which investors purchased them and which investors may have wanted them. These firms also will have a big database of investors. Underwriting corporate bonds makes it easier for firms to make markets in these bonds because their search costs are much lower. A firm may know, for example, that Fidelity owns a lot of these bonds and likes them, so that firm can sell to Fidelity when another investor wants to sell its bonds. There are synergies between primary and secondary markets, which is why I think that the Volcker Rule's concern about market making is well founded.

Market making and hedging are important, but they are not key financial activities. These activities could be restricted through the Volcker Rule to affect liquidity and pricing in the market. These costs may more than offset the benefits of Volcker, and we have to be worry about that tradeoff.

The Volcker Rule and Market Liquidity

I have three points about liquidity that go in a little different direction. First, a recent study by Oliver Wyman Group (2011) about how the Volcker Rule is going to end the corporate bond market as we know it relied on a paper by Jens Dick-Nielson, Peter Feldhutter, and David Lando (2012). This paper showed that during the financial crisis, if a dealer firm that was the underwriter of a particular bond ran into trouble, the firm began to disintermediate, and the bond became less liquid. Those results have been interpreted by others (such as the Oliver Wyman study) as pointing to what could happen when you remove market making or restrict market making. The argument is that there will be a big liquidity shock and much worse pricing.

It could be argued, however, that the Dick-Nelson, Feldhutter, and Lando paper actually supports the Volcker Rule. The paper focuses on a particular time period—the financial crisis. Liquidity is most important during a crisis and much more freely available during normal periods. This raises the question of whether we really want to concentrate all the market-making activities at systemically risky financial firms. These firms are not going to step in front of the train, and in fact, they cannot during a crisis period because of their systemic nature. The Volcker Rule is already being taken into account, and recent volatility in the bond market as interest rates have pushed up has hurt liquidity because dealers have not been stepping in front. It has been claimed that the Volcker Rule has already hurt liquidity, but dealers in over-the-counter (OTC) markets tend not to stand in front and buy if everyone is on one side trying to sell. Dealers may try to facilitate trades between buyers and sellers, but they have never been willing to take that risk head on. Quotes are only indicative in the OTC and corporate bond markets.

There is a second point here. We are trying to write a rule that measures trading intent. Most agree that there is trading intent when firms make decisions to take a directional bet or not. The problem is whether a regulator can measure it or write a rule based on it. So the rule should not be written based on measuring trading intent.

The third point is that the Volcker rule will make it a little more difficult to make markets. In the short-run, liquidity will be affected. But it is not clear what is going to happen in the long run. Financial markets adjust and move. If the current system is a bad system, we might need to have a different system. If large, complex firms dominate market making, they might be more efficient or have access to a safety net.

The Volcker Rule is getting very complex, but I do not think we should give up on creating a simple version of the rule. Complex rules are easy to game and keep regulators from focusing on the big picture. Complex rules might give the regulators cover. If firms dot the *i*'s and cross the *t*'s, they are in compliance and so are good to go. I think that regulatory supervision is enhanced with simple rules. Simple rules are not easy to write, but it also is not rocket science. Consider how AIG wrote $530 billion of credit default swaps (CDSs). It was gross exposure. Firms like Goldman Sachs took out the insurance and then passed it on elsewhere in the financial system. Goldman had very little net inventory, although it was a big player in that market. Merrill Lynch was a big buyer of insurance from Goldman. When Merrill Lynch figured out that it could go directly to AIG and bypass Goldman, it did. And when AIG got away from the market, Merrill Lynch decided to hold onto that risk. So the inventory positions provide a pretty good idea of who is taking risks and who is not taking risks.

Implementing the Volcker Rule

In terms of implementing the Volcker Rule, the two things that we care about are systemic risk and market liquidity. Systemic risk is systemic risk whether it is from market making, principal trading, or activities that cannot clearly be identified as market making or trading. This does not change. If a firm is holding $100 billion of triple A, nonprime mortgage-backed securities on its books, that risk is the same no matter what it is called. The relevant question is how to manage that risk. From a societal point of view, if a firm were holding that to provide liquidity to the marketplace, improve pricing, and provide better information flow, then those benefits may outweigh the costs of holding that risk.

I think that a simple rule that creates safe harbors is needed (Richardson 2011). The regulator needs to place limits on the gross inventory or net inventory on the book of financial institutions. Perhaps the limits would be relative to the assets that the institution is holding. As long as the firm is below those ranges, it can do whatever it wants. If the firm goes over those limits, it would have to convince a regulator that it is actually making markets. For example, suppose that one day a financial institution underwrote $1 billion of Exxon corporate bonds, something happened on that day, and it could not sell the bonds. The firm is left holding a $100 million on its books, and it is over its inventory limit. It might have to speak to a regulator and describe what happened: "We issued $1 billion of these bonds, and we couldn't sell them. It's going to take us a while to unload them." That's fine. But if a firm is holding $40 billion of Portuguese government debt (sovereign debt) on its books with no capital, it is going to have to justify why it is doing that. So I think that a safe harbor with supervisory permission outside of that safe harbor would be consistent with the spirit of the Volcker Rule but might get around some of these complex issues.

Charles W. Calomiris: There is a deep question at the heart of the controversy over the Volcker Rule and also the extension of the Volcker Rule to prohibit all securities-related activities, which is being proposed by the vice chair of the Federal Deposit Insurance Corporation (FDIC), Thomas M. Hoenig. The question is whether we want to risk destroying U.S. global universal banking. Those may seem like strong words, but I argue that this may be at stake in the debate over the Volcker Rule and other structural reforms that are being considered.

Is Proprietary Trading a Core Activity of Banks?

Many commentators tell us that proprietary trading is not a core activity of banks. I wonder how they know that. I do not think that it is true. What constitutes a core activity in banking changes over time, and I can think of several ways to argue that proprietary trading, not just market making, might now be a core activity of global universal banks.[4] Before explaining why, let me agree with the now universally held views that underwriting of clients' securities offerings and market making are core activities. That perception of underwriting was not the established view in the United States until the 1990s. As late as the 1980s, on the basis of faulty reasoning and the absence of serious research, many people argued that there was no good reason to combine underwriting and lending within the same bank and much potential harm in doing so. A few years later, based on a substantial body of evidence, it became the established view that there were clear benefits and no identifiable costs from combining lending and underwriting.

Are we so sure today that we know which banking activities should be considered core and which should not? I am going to take you through some arguments about why proprietary trading might be a core activity of banks. Do not misinterpret those arguments as expressions of knowledge. I am not really sure whether proprietary trading is a core activity of global universal banks, and I do not think that I am alone in my ignorance: the evidence simply is not in on this question.

It could be argued that we cannot afford to wait for the evidence because proprietary trading is so potentially destructive that we have to shoot first and ask questions later to avoid systemic risk. Is there a good reason to believe that proprietary trading is an activity that contributes to systemic risk? I think the answer to that question is clearly no. Matt Richardson correctly said that holding securitized mortgages contributed to systemic risk leading up to the crisis. But as far as I can tell, securitization is not prohibited under the Volcker Rule, and neither is mortgage lending. Banks will still be able to originate and hold real estate–backed loans and securities. And I doubt that anyone would argue that mortgage lending and securitization, which also necessarily entail being able to hold securitized debts as investments, is a noncore activity of banks. In any case, holding these mortgage-related investments, which were at the heart of the recent crisis, is not the issue in the Volcker Rule's prohibition on proprietary trading, as far as I can tell. We learned during the crisis that if banks suddenly want to undertake a large amount of risk in an effort to exploit a safety net subsidy, they can do so through lending to risky borrowers. Prohibiting proprietary trading, therefore, will not prevent too-big-to-fail banks and other banks from taking on excessive risks or from being bailed out when they do.

The recent crisis is not the only example of the connection between risky lending and systemic risk. In the United States, too big to fail got a big boost in the 1980s with the bailout of an energy lender named Continental Illinois at a time when many banks and thrifts with exposure to energy loans were failing. Continental operated only a handful of branches in Chicago. By current standards, it would not be considered a large bank and certainly not a global universal bank. Paul Volcker, ironically, was the person who pushed for the bailout of Continental Illinois, incorrectly arguing that its failure might jeopardize many other banks (in fact, deposits of other banks in Continental generally were small enough to be fully covered by deposit insurance, as critics of the bailout noted at the time). The precedent of bailing out Continental was particularly damaging because it was small and unimportant. If we could not muster the courage in our regulatory community to allow a bank like Continental to go bust, then it was clear that we were going to bail out just about everybody.

The Costs of the Volcker Rule

The Volcker Rule is not going to prevent risk-taking by banks or solve the too-big-to-fail problem. Its benefits, if any, will be very small. I wish I could say the same for its social costs. One obvious and potentially large social cost, which Matt Richardson discussed, is the chilling effect that the Volcker Rule could have on market making. More broadly, the Volcker Rule could disadvantage U.S. global banks and reduce the use of U.S. capital markets as a place to issue and trade securities. I believe that Matt understates those potential costs. Furthermore, narrowly prohibiting proprietary trading (even if it could be done without interfering with market making) would entail further hard-to-estimate costs to the extent that proprietary trading is an important activity to preserve within global universal banks. I review the reasons to think that it might be.

The Volcker Rule was passed quickly as part of the hurried Dodd–Frank Wall Street Reform and Consumer Protection Act of 2010, with little consideration of its potential costs, based on the advocacy of Paul Volcker and little presentation to Congress of anything that could be called evidence. To those familiar with the 1930s banking legislation, Paul Volcker's role here was a remake of the 1933 performance by Carter Glass. Glass had a strong ideological antipathy to mixing commercial and investment banking and had been trying to limit the activities of commercial banks for more than two decades (based on a theory of credit called the "real bills doctrine" that currently has no adherents). Glass got his opportunity in 1933, when he used a logrolling strategy to incorporate his prohibition into the far-reaching banking regulation of 1933. Glass's success did not reflect any connection between the securities underwriting activities of banks and the banking crises of the Great Depression. On the contrary, all of the academic literature on commercial bank involvement in underwriting (written in the 1980s and 1990s) shows that commercial banks' involvement in underwriting in the 1920s and early 1930s was beneficial. It reduced the risk of bank failure and provided valuable services for clients. Nonetheless, Glass was able to get his way, partly by using the "findings" of the 1932 Pecora Hearings—and the public animus toward large banks in reaction to those hearings—to justify taking action against the big commercial banks (Calomiris 2010). Similarly, Paul Volcker finally got his chance to turn back the clock a bit after the 2007 to 2009 crisis in an atmosphere that was extremely hostile to large banks. If it had been up to Volcker, we never would have allowed Glass-Steagall underwriting prohibitions to be relaxed in the 1980s and 1990s. If Paul Volcker had his way in the 1980s, we would not be agreeing today about how obvious it is that underwriting should be viewed as a core activity of commercial banks because we never would have had the benefit of seeing how useful it is to permit commercial banks to be underwriters. Regulators would still be confidently and wrongly assuming that underwriting was not part of the core function of large banks.

My review of the potential costs of the Volcker Rule starts with its potential effects on markets. I very much agree with Matt that proprietary trading is not going to be distinguishable as an activity from market making. The two activities are not observably different on a transactional basis but reflect different intent, which is not possible to observe. The risk, therefore, is that the Volcker Rule will end up prohibiting banks from engaging in market making. A recent theory paper by Arnoud Boot and Lev Ratnovski (2013) shows why making markets entails huge economies of scale, which gives global universal banks a comparative advantage as market makers. There are no other financial firms that are large enough to substitute for global universal banks as market makers.

What were global capital markets like before these global behemoths existed? I remember studying Ronald I. McKinnon's work on the problems of global capital markets in the 1970s—before the era of global universal banking, which was ushered in by London's Big Bang in 1986 and the deregulation of U.S. underwriting and branching limits in the 1980s and 1990s. *Money in International Exchange: The Convertible Currency System* (McKinnon 1979) bemoaned the consequences for market inefficiency of the lack of liquidity in foreign-exchange markets. That book and many other studies of the shortcomings of the capital markets of the 1970s remind us that markets did not always function as well as they do now. I do not want to return to that world of illiquid and inefficient markets.

But there is little risk of doing so. If U.S. banks cannot make markets, European and Asian banks will fill the gap, although they may fill that gap by trading in different markets—that is, in capital markets located outside the United States. That is not a far-fetched possibility. Some people who have a stake in the potential effects of the Volcker Rule on the efficiency of capital markets are warning us about these risks. These are not global universal banks; they are experienced economic policy-makers at the Bank of Mexico and other central banks. For example, Agustin Carstens has expressed great concern about the effects of the Volcker Rule on market liquidity because of its effects on U.S. banks and on all banks with operations in the United States. In its effort not to disadvantage U.S. banks too much, the Volcker Rule covers all banks with operations in the United States. Because the Volcker Rule's net is so far-reaching, the Bank of Mexico is concerned about the consequences for the liquidity of markets for Mexican sovereign debt and the peso, which depend on global universal banks as market makers. They have concluded that because of its wide reach, the Volcker Rule would affect the Mexican banking system almost to the same extent as it would the United States.

If it turns out that the only way that a global universal bank can operate in Mexico and other countries is to stop operating in the United States—and that may mean reducing its physical presence in the United States and moving its trading to other capital markets—we should be worried. The global market's ultimate adjustment to the Volcker Rule may be to shift resources to non-U.S. banks, to shun New York as a financial center, and to move away from the dollar as a reserve currency.

Given the importance of defusing the threat that the Volcker Rule poses for U.S. banking and capital markets, I agree with Matt Richardson that if we have to limit proprietary trading because of an ill-conceived rule, then we should make sure that we do so without hobbling market making. I like Matt's idea of creating a safe harbor based on some simple rules that limit the size of securities inventories, which inherently would favor market making (for example, a limit on inventory-to-capital ratios). Other misguided proponents of reform (such as Thomas Hoenig) would like to include market making in the list of proscribed activities. I think Tom's proposals have devastating implications for U.S. capital markets and global corporations.

Does It Make Sense to Limit Proprietary Trading?

Does it make sense to limit proprietary trading by banks, using an effective safe-harbor approach like the one proposed by Matt? The social costs of such limits on proprietary trading must be understood in the context of their relationships with clients. One way to think about the synergies of global universal banking is that these banks should do what their global nonfinancial clients need them to do. Contrary to Tom Hoenig's view, prohibiting bank involvement in the creation of hedges for clients would be undesirable because designing and executing those hedges is a central part of the bank-client relationship between global banks and global nonfinancial clients. If a firm is managing someone's underwriting, lending, and cash-flow disbursements globally, then it also is the one best positioned to help that client measure its risks and design the right means to lay off risks that it does not want to retain. Global universal banks are likely to be the most efficient providers of strategic outsourcing of risk analysis and management for global nonfinancial companies. Global banks do this by maintaining "client teams" that track the strategies of their clients and constructing ad hoc "deal teams" as needed to manage the transactions that arise out of those multidimensional relationships. Deal teams design and execute hedges as part of those client relationships.

But what do these client-related synergies in hedging have to do with proprietary trading? To see the connection, consider this question: Who is going to be sitting on the deal team that identifies the need for a hedge and that constructs the right hedge for the client? Today, that team typically includes people who have substantial experience as traders and who may have designed some of the instruments that are being considered for hedging. Eliminating proprietary trading from a bank amounts to what I call the "Volcker lobotomy": it removes from the banking organization the human capital of people who understand these financial instruments best. When JP Morgan sits down with Hewlett-Packard or Shell Oil to figure out how to do a complicated global hedge, it wants to rely on the advice of someone very smart, and that tends to be someone who designs and trades financial instruments for profit. Those people know how best to structure and execute an important transaction for a client.

Proprietary trading, therefore, may be part of the core activities of the bank because its existence within the bank ensures that the bank possesses the human capital needed to provide knowledgeable advice to clients about complicated transactions at crucial moments. Outsiders cannot do that for the client just as well because the client needs someone to provide a holistic analysis of its corporate finance strategy, which takes into account its corporate capital structure, its hedging strategies, and its cash-flow management. It hopes to obtain such an analysis and the execution of transactions that accompanies it from its relationship with a global universal bank.

How big are the benefits from these synergies between proprietary trading and other activities? Some might regard them as small, but no one has been able to measure them. Doing so requires access to detailed data that are currently available only within banking organizations. A few years ago, I began a research project to do this (which I undertook with no financial support from the subject bank). When Dodd–Frank was passed, the bank that had allowed me to begin the study (presumably because it believed that I would find large synergies) decided that there was no longer enough upside for them to make it worth their while to grant me such unprecedented access to highly sensitive data. So Dodd–Frank's shoot-first-and-ask-questions-later approach put an end to the only attempt underway at that time to measure the size of client-based synergies related to trading, hedging, and other services, which would have helped gauge the extent to which proprietary trading is a core activity of global universal banks.

In conclusion, the Volcker Rule is a threat to the continuing global importance of U.S. banks and capital markets. It will achieve little or no good and will do so at a potentially high social cost. At the very least, we need to make sure that the rule is implemented in a way that does not disrupt market making by global universal banks. Even the successful construction of a regulatory safe harbor that insulates market making from the rule may place U.S. banks at significant comparative disadvantage and result in substantial losses of client relationships to universal banks that operate outside the United States. The Volcker

Rule highlights the dangerous tendency of Washington to react boldly to crises based on superstitious or ill-informed beliefs. The Volcker Rule and the process that produced it is, above all, a reflection of some of the most disappointing aspects of our democracy.

Questions and Answers

Question: The idea of a safe harbor having simple rules is intriguing and seems much more workable than the Volcker Rule in its current form. Which regulator would monitor and enforce this? Would something like this prevent problems like the recent London Whale episode?

Richardson: It would be the regulatory institution that supervises banks, like the Fed or the FDIC. It would not be the Securities and Exchange Commission (SEC) or the Commodity Futures Trading Commission (CFTC). There is no doubt that it relies on effective regulators. If you don't think regulators have the ability to regulate, then that says something about our regulatory system. But I think the idea of a safe harbor is that you do not worry until you hit certain inventory limits, and then you go in and find out what is going on.

In theory, the example of the London Whale is the kind of thing that would probably be caught in this system. They had a position, they put on a hedge, they took off the hedge, and they doubled down in the markets. This would show up as a big position, and the regulator would go in and say, "What are you doing?" So if the regulator was good, I think that the London Whale trades would have been caught with the Volcker Rule that included some safe harbor. Would you catch everything? Probably not, because banks will figure out ways to get around it. But you do the best that you can. The Volcker Rule will make trades like the London Whale trades more uncommon. The worry is what happens if London Whale kinds of trades coincide with a financial crisis.

Separately, with respect to Volcker exemptions, I believe that the exemptions in the Volcker Rule are agency-backed securities and Treasuries, not asset-backed securities. Depending on how the rule is written, these may be subject to the Volcker Rule.

Calomiris: The banks are involved in credit card receivables and mortgages and in other types of lending when securitizing and retaining junior positions as part of the origination process in their securitization conduits. I think that we have to acknowledge that problems arose from holding these mortgage securities. This was not a trading issue, per se. Those securities were not short-term trading instruments. The markets for them were actually quite illiquid markets for the most part. So in my view, there was never an intention in the Volcker Rule to stop banks from securitizing in a mortgage market, which necessarily entails holding some of the securities being offered to the public.

Richardson: Charles, it is not a question of whether banks can securitize these loans: they can. The issue is whether they can bring them back on their balance sheets like they did—that is, with favorable capital treatment.

Calomiris: Well, do we feel better if they hold only the junior instruments? I am not so sure. Also, they need to be able to retain senior debt tranches when they find that those tranches cannot immediately be sold at desirable prices in the market.

Richardson: It depends on how much capital is underneath, right?

Calomiris: Trading—proprietary trading—is a red herring because they were holding positions in originated subprime and derivative securities. It really was not about trading. It was about originating, securitizing, and making long-term investments.

Richardson: That is where the losses were. It is trading on their own accounts whether they are holding it for a short or a long time. The prices are changing daily, and it is not like they can sell it any time for par. They have to sell at the market price. The banks are not forced to hold them for a year or two years or five years.

Calomiris: Yes, but in practice, those were long-term investments.

Richardson: Financed with overnight repos.

Calomiris: I am just saying that if we want to have a conversation about whether banks should be involved in securitizing mortgages, then let's have that conversation. We could also be asking whether they should be involved in real estate finance generally. Banks are heavily involved in these activities because of the regulatory and political actions that shoved them into it, going back to 1913 and especially since the 1990s. We could go through that regulatory history, and it would show that, for political reasons, a large amount of real estate lending by banks will persist because Congress has a political agenda that is served by such lending. But that is a different issue, right? And we should note that real estate exposures are primarily where systemic risk comes from—not just in the recent crisis but in most crises.

Question: We are a long way from implementing the Volcker Rule, but banks are already reacting to it. You see them spinning off proprietary trading units. On the other hand, there is very little reaction to things like the conflict minerals rule or mandatory swap clearing. Is this an admission that proprietary trading is too risky?

Calomiris: I think that it is pretty clear that when a regulator frowns on something, then a bank sees an advantage in avoiding it. Doing so is an indication of not anything fundamental but just the fact that the regulators decided to make it costly for banks to do it. I would also say that I don't think banks have gotten rid of their market making businesses yet. I asked some people at Goldman Sachs to explain to me how profitable market making is and how risky it is. They went through a list of different business lines, all of which they said had Sharpe ratios (ratios of expected profit relative to standard deviation returns) of less than one. But the Sharpe ratio for market making was greater than ten. In other words, Goldman Sachs believes that market making serves an important social function and is highly stabilizing for banks like them because of its favorable ratio of profit to risk. Sharpe ratios are an imperfect measure of risk (there are also peso risk issues about the tails of the distribution), but when the Sharpe ratio is an order of magnitude higher than other lines of business, it likely indicates a robust difference. So I doubt that the banks have stepped away from market making yet because it is very profitable and they know it.

Regulation can change that. In a recent research paper, my coauthor and I (Calomiris and Nissim 2013) found that banks are not getting much respect from the market for their recurring noninterest income, which we think is reflective in part of the risks to market making from the Volcker Rule. Controlling for everything else, prior to the crisis the market rewarded an extra $1 of recurring fee income with a $5 increase in market value. Today it is a $1 for $1 increase. The market has little respect for current earnings. Instead, the market respects dividend announcements. The postcrisis market reaction to dividend increases is three times the size it used to be. Dividend announcements are the regulators' green flag telling a bank and outsiders that they are not constrained from growing. So the general problem is that we are now in a world where the markets' reaction to what banks can do and how investors perceive them is largely driven by regulators. It is driven by the regulators' stress tests and dividend permission decisions. Banks are responding to what markets are telling them, but markets are responding to the actions of regulators.

Richardson: This is going to sound like rabid support for the Volcker Rule because it makes me sound like a big supporter of Dodd–Frank. Again, my remarks should be taken in the context that Dodd–Frank is the law. I agree with Charlie on market making. Studies have shown that it has a very high Sharp ratio. But you cannot get that Sharp ratio holding a big inventory. It is not possible. The only question is whether removing or placing restrictions on trading hurts your ability to understand markets and make markets, which is what Charlie talked about. As for the drop in level 3 assets (assets whose fair value is not observable), I do not know if firms have reduced them because of the impending Volcker Rule. But there is an argument that Goldman Sachs might not be the right institution to own a golf course in Japan. Maybe Lehman Brothers should not own a big property development in California. Other firms that are not as systemically risky can own those properties. I think that whether the Volcker Rule addresses these activities or asset-backed securities that are held longer-term depends on how the rule is written. But I do not think that it is a bad thing that level 3 assets have decreased at these systemically important institutions.

Calomiris: I don't think so either.

Question: If we go back to 1986, when universal banks came about, and ask ourselves why they came about, I think a lot of it has to do with how the commodity bubble in the 1970s blew up in an ugly way. Does this mean that we are going back to an era where the commodity trading houses are going to be sources of potential systemic risk?

Richardson: You mentioned commodity trading as one of your core functions in fact?

Calomiris: I agree with you that, with respect to hedging, corporate strategies for capital structure and risk management have to do with commodity trading, too. Commodities that are especially important now include oil for one, but eurodollars are a commodity, too, and the next major threat to global financial stability is the coming rise in interest rates. Firms around the world will be gearing up to hedge against that.

By the way, when I was referring to 1986, I was talking about the United Kingdom because that was the date of Margaret Thatcher's Big Bang and a securities market deregulation of the London Stock Exchange. But the Big Bang had ramifications that transcended its effects on stock trading. Within five years of Margaret Thatcher's Big Bang, the ratio of private bank credit to gross domestic product tripled in the United Kingdom. It is one of the most amazing changes in bank credit that we have ever seen. It might have happened because there are large synergies between lending and trading within global universal banking. What is striking to me is that we know very little about what drives value creation in this new U.S. and UK global universal banking model.

Question: There has not been much discussion about the metrics that the Volcker Rule uses or would use to judge whether a trade is proprietary trading or market making. The point has been made that these metrics will induce perverse behavior. Any comments on that?

Richardson: I am in agreement that if we cannot define it, then it is going to be difficult to write a rule based on it. That is why I would prefer a simple safe harbor where you just look at the balance sheet and see the holdings. That is not perfect, but it is going to be tougher to game because it is simple. So on the precise metrics, I think you are right.

Calomiris: I am supportive of Matt's idea that something simple like an inventory limit might be a good way to implement this, given that we are required to do so by the law. But in one of your comments, I thought you were saying that maybe the regulators think that the law specifically uses the word *prohibition* and so this kind of approach would be dead on arrival. Could you remark on whether it would be possible to do something like simple inventory limits?

Richardson: Just to get around Charlie's point, I guess you can say anything in safe harbor is market making and anything outside of safe harbor is not.

Question: Charlie, you mentioned that the issues that the Volcker Rule addresses basically had nothing to do with the financial crisis or were not a fundamental cause of the financial crisis. Matt seemed to suggest that there is systemic risk associated with some proprietary trading. Matt, I wonder if you would agree or disagree with Charlie and say that proprietary trading was indeed a fundamental cause of the financial crisis? A second related question is whether there is some misunderstanding between the two of you about the exempt securities from proprietary trading. You mentioned agency securities and Treasury securities. I wonder if you would allow for additional exemptions if you were putting together a rule along the lines of what Charlie seemed to suggest, such as private-label mortgage-backed securities. Would you go beyond the two exemptions?

Richardson: Look at what the large banks and investment banks did during the crisis. Their large losses were in asset-backed securities that did not have capital underneath them. That is why they ran aground. There were some firms, like Washington Mutual and IndyMac, whose problems were almost entirely loans. That said, many firms were heavy, heavy, heavy into nonprime mortgage-backed securities and some other asset-backed securities, so I think that should be part of Volcker. Whether you call it prop trading, principal trading, trading on your own account, or whatever trading, to me it is the same thing.

The mortgages have the same risk no matter who holds them. The questions are "Who is holding them, and are they systemic?" Because of regulation that Charlie mentioned, we are concentrating agency securities in Fannie Mae, Freddie Mac, and these large banks. Those are the big guys that held them in the financial crisis. So I would not exempt those guys, but in the statute they are exempt. I certainly would not add to the exemptions.

Notes

1. Some of the comments that I make here are included in *Regulating Wall Street: The Dodd–Frank Act and the New Architecture of Global Finance* (Acharya, Cooley, Richardson, and Walter 2010b; see also Richardson 2011). One of the book's claims to fame is that it is actually longer than the Dodd–Frank Act. When people write a book, they ask well-known people to endorse the book because that helps sell copies. Paul Volcker's endorsement included the words "not a quick read," which probably did not help copies fly off the shelf. The book includes chapters by professors at New York University's Stern School of Business and ends up being fairly critical of the Dodd–Frank Act.

2. See Viral V. Acharya, Christian Brownlees, Robert F. Engle, Farhang Farazmand, and Matthew Richardson (2010), Olivier De Jonghe (2009), Robert DeYoung and Karin Roland (2001), Xavier Freixas, Gyongyi Loranth, and Alan Morrison (2007), Kevin Stiroh (2004), Kevin Stiroh and Adrienne Rumble (2006), and Wolf Wagner (2010).

3. A large related literature looks at economies of scale for large banks. The evidence is mixed. See, for example, Lieven Baele, Olivier De Jonghe, and Rudi Vander Vennet (2007), A. N. Berger and D. B. Humphrey (1991), Gayle Delong, (2001), Ralf Elsas, Andreas

Hackethal, and Markus Holzhauser (2009), Luc Laeven and Ross Levine (2007), Markus Schmid and Ingo Walter (2009), and Ingo Walter (2010).

4. In this chapter, I use the word *bank* to refer to chartered banks (which have narrowly defined functions that exclude, for example, underwriting) and to bank holding companies (which include nonbank affiliates that are engaged in activities not permitted within the chartered banks).

References

Acharya, Viral V., Christian Brownlees, Robert F. Engle, Farhang Farazmand, and Matthew Richardson. 2010. Measuring Systemic Risk. In *Regulating Wall Street: The Dodd–Frank Act and the New Architecture of Global Finance*, ed. Viral V. Acharya, Thomas Cooley, Matthew Richardson and Ingo Walter, chap. 6. Hoboken, NJ: Wiley.

Acharya, Viral V., Thomas Cooley, Matthew Richardson, and Ingo Walter. 2010a. Manufacturing Tail Risk: A Perspective on the Financial Crisis of 2007–2009. *Foundations and Trends in Finance* 4(4).

Acharya, Viral V., Thomas Cooley, Matthew Richardson, and Ingo Walter, eds. 2010b. *Regulating Wall Street: The Dodd–Frank Act and the New Architecture of Global Finance.* Hoboken, NJ: Wiley.

Acharya, Viral V., Lasse Pedersen, Thomas Philippon, and Matthew Richardson. 2010. Measuring Systemic Risk. Working Paper, New York University Stern School of Business, New York.

Baele, Lieven, Olivier De Jonghe, and Rudi Vander Vennet. 2007. Does the Stock Market Value Bank Diversification? *Journal of Banking & Finance* 31 (7):1999–2023.

Berger, A. N., and D. B. Humphrey. 1991. The Dominance of Inefficiencies over Ale and Product Mix Economies in Banking. *Journal of Monetary Economics* 28:117–148.

Boot, Arnoud, and Lev Ratnovski. 2013. Banking and Trading. Amsterdam Center for Law and Economics Working Paper No. 2012-08.

Calomiris, Charles W. 2010. The Political Lessons of Depression-Era Banking Reform. *Oxford Review of Economic Policy* 26:540–560.

Calomiris, Charles, and Doron Nissim. 2013. Crisis-Related Shifts in the Market Valuation of Banking Activities. Columbia Business School Research Paper No. 13-31.

De Jonghe, Olivier. 2009. Back to the Basics in Banking? A Micro-analysis of Banking System Stability. *Journal of Financial Intermediation* 19 (3):387–417.

Delong, Gayle. 2001. Stockholder Gains from Focusing versus Diversifying Bank Mergers. *Journal of Financial Economics* 59 (2):221–252.

DeYoung, Robert, and Karin Roland. 2001. Product Mix and Earnings Volatility at Commercial Banks: Evidence from a Degree of Total Leverage Model. *Journal of Financial Intermediation* 10 (1):54–84.

Diamond, Doug. 1991. Monitoring and Reputation: The Choice between Bank loans and Directly Placed Debt. *Journal of Political Economy* 99:688–721.

Dick-Nielsen, Jens, Peter Feldhutter, and David Lando. 2012. Corporate Bond Liquidity before and after the Onset of the Subprime Crisis. *Journal of Financial Economics* 103 (3):471–492.

Elsas, Ralf, Andreas Hackethal, and Markus Holzhauser. 2009. The Anatomy of Bank Diversification. *Journal of Banking & Finance* 34 (6):1274–1287.

Fama, Eugene F. 1985. What's Different about Banks? *Journal of Monetary Economics* 15 (1):29–39.

Freixas, Xavier, Gyongyi Loranth, and Alan Morrison. 2007. Regulating Financial Conglomerates. *Journal of Financial Intermediation* 16 (4):479–514.

Laeven, Luc, and Ross Levine. 2007. Is There a Diversification Discount in Financial Conglomerates? *Journal of Financial Economics* 85 (2):331–367.

McKinnon, Ronald I. 1979. *Money in International Exchange: The Convertible Currency System.* New York: Oxford University Press.

Oliver Wyman Group. 2011. The Volcker Rule: Considerations for Implementation of Proprietary Trading Regulations. Securities Industry and Financial Markets Association (SIFMA), New York.

Petersen, Mitchell A., and Raghuram G. Rajan. 1994. The Benefits of Lending Relationships: Evidence from Small Business. *Journal of Finance* 49 (1):3–37.

Richardson, Matthew. 2011. Why the Volcker Rule Is a Useful Tool for Managing Systemic Risk. Working Paper, New York University Stern School of Business, New York.

Schmid, Markus, and Ingo Walter. 2009. Do Financial Conglomerates Create or Destroy Economic Value? *Journal of Financial Intermediation* 18 (2):193–216.

Stiroh, Kevin. 2004. Diversification in Banking: Is Noninterest Income the Answer? *Journal of Money, Credit and Banking* 36 (5):853–882.

Stiroh, Kevin, and Adrienne Rumble. 2006. The Dark Side of Diversification: The Case of U.S. Financial Holding Companies. *Journal of Banking & Finance* 30 (8):2131–2161.

Wagner, Wolf. 2010. Diversification at Financial Institutions and Systemic Crises. *Journal of Financial Intermediation* 19 (3):373–386.

Walter, Ingo. 2010. The New Case for Functional Separation in Wholesale Financial Services. Working Paper FIN-09-17, Department of Finance, New York University Stern School of Business, New York.

9 Panel Discussion on the Consumer Financial Protection Bureau

Jeff Bloch, Shane Corwin, and Todd J. Zywicki

Shane Corwin: Our panel will discuss the Consumer Financial Protection Bureau (CFPB) that was created under Title X of the Dodd–Frank Wall Street Reform and Consumer Protection Act of 2010. If any aspect of Dodd–Frank could be considered more controversial than the others, this one certainly could be it. The CFPB is an independent bureau housed within the Board of Governors of the Federal Reserve that has rulemaking supervisory and enforcement authority over most firms that are involved in business-related consumer financial services.

The CFPB's mandate is to protect consumers from unfair, deceptive, or abusive financial practices. As such, it has very broad rulemaking and supervisory authority. Among other things, it regulates mortgages, credit cards, other consumer loans, payday lending, check-cashing services, electronic transmission of funds, real estate settlement services, deposit-taking activities, and real estate appraisals.

The CFPB was established in 2010 but has hit the ground running. By the end of November 2012, it had more than a thousand employees. In its first two years, the CFPB handled more than 175,000 consumer complaints about credit cards, mortgages, auto loans, student loans, and savings accounts. It has ordered credit card companies to pay $425 million to consumers for misleading sales tactics. It has also written regulations on equal credit opportunity, electronic fund transfers, credit reporting, debt collection, and many other practices.

There are few checks on the CFPB's rulemaking authority. Congress does not allocate funds for the CFPB and does not control it through the power of the purse. The CFPB is an autonomous bureau within the Federal Reserve. It is funded by the Fed, but the Federal Reserve has no say in its operation or personnel.

The chair of the Financial Stability Oversight Council (FSOC) may issue a temporary stay of a CFPB rule if petitioned to do so by a member agency. A permanent stay of the rule requires a two-thirds majority vote by the council. In practice, though, it requires a larger majority. There are ten voting members of the FSOC, one of whom is the director of the CFPB. To overrule a CFPB regulation requires the votes of seven of the ten members or seven of the nine members other than the CFPB director. The council cannot challenge a CFPB rule just because it is a bad rule. It can challenge only rules that threaten financial stability.

The CFPB has a single director who is appointed to a five-year term by the president with the advice and consent of the Senate. This is a departure from the governance structure of other regulators. The Securities and Exchange Commission (SEC), Federal Trade Commission (FTC), and Commodity Futures Trading Commission (CFTC) have boards of five commissioners that vote on regulations. If the Senate does not approve a successor for a CFPB director, the director can remain on the job.

Jeff Bloch: In my brief remarks, I will outline the top issues of concern that the banking industry has with regard to the CFPB and its activities. This is not a static list. In a year from now, this list could be very different. But these are the industry's current issues of concern.

Industry Concerns: The CFPB Governance Structure and Exam Process

We have and continue to advocate for a commission structure for the Consumer Financial Protection Bureau (CFPB) instead of the current structure of a sole director who has virtually unchecked powers. We also believe that funding for the CFPB should be through appropriations from Congress instead of through access to hundreds of millions of dollars from the Federal Reserve without any significant oversight. In addition, we advocate giving the Federal Stability Oversight Council (FSOC) or perhaps another entity greater ability to overturn CFPB rules that are problematic. This is a political issue, especially in the current environment in which a Democratic president has nominated the first director as head of a new and powerful government agency. But it does not have to be. A commission structure, for example, would benefit Democrats in the future when a Republican president has the opportunity to make a CFPB nomination in that such a nomination would be for a position to a board or commission in which various viewpoints will be heard and considered.

The next issue of concern is the exam process. The first cycle of CFPB exams was not going to run as smoothly as the exam processes conducted in the past by other banking regulators because the CFPB is a startup agency and it has been difficult for the CFPB to attract a large number of qualified examiners. But several issues of concern have arisen with the exam process. The first issue is the presence of enforcement attorneys at exams, which was not a common practice in the past by the other banking agencies. At a minimum, this chills the give and take of the exam process between banks and examiners and can turn it into more of an adversarial process as opposed to a collaborative effort. An analogy here would be marriage counseling where one spouse brings a divorce lawyer.

Another issue is information requests. When the CFPB comes in for an exam, the amount of information that it requests of the bank is often staggering and far exceeds the requests made by the other banking agencies. This is costly and time consuming for banks. The CFPB has said that banks are free to push back if they believe that some requests are unreasonable or unwarranted. Banks have had some success in this area in that the CFPB has been accommodating in certain instances. However, the reality is that banks do not want to get into these types of disagreements with the regulator, so they tend not to make these requests as often as they would like. For this reason, we view this as a problem.

Another issue of concern with regard to exams is the final exam report. Some banks had exams over a year ago and have not yet received a report from their examiners. This can affect banks in a number of ways. The primary problem is that it interferes with a bank's ability to innovate and introduce new products and services because there are concerns about how examiners will respond to these innovations. Similar to other exam issues, this delay in issuing exam reports is also a function of the CFPB's being a startup agency (with all the problems associated with being a startup) and also of its taking a deliberative approach to ensure that exams are being conducted consistently among banks. The bureau is working to expedite this process for future exam cycles, and we look forward to improvements in the future.

Coordination with the other banking regulators is also an issue of concern. Banks are now examined by the CFPB and also by their safety and soundness regulator. We do not believe there has yet been sufficient coordination between the regulators, but the bureau has recently issued a framework to improve this process. We look forward to seeing how this plays out in future exam cycles.

Fair Lending

For fair lending, I am going to switch gears a little. The CFPB is focused now on fair-lending issues and has stated that its top areas of focus are mortgages and auto loans. We are concerned with its focus on the disparate-impact theory with regard to fair-lending violations. This is not a new theory, but one that has received increased attention from the CFPB and is problematic because lenders may be responsible for disparities in treatment among different groups of people even if there was no intent to discriminate. This is especially problematic in indirect auto lending, an area that is of interest now for the CFPB. Indirect auto lending is the process through which dealers negotiate car loans, which are funded by banks or other types of lender. Under long-standing policy, banks are expected to take corrective action if dealers set rates for these loans in a discriminatory manner. Banks support fair lending and do not support illegal discrimination. Not only is fair lending always the right thing to do, but banks have every incentive from a business perspective to lend to all qualified borrowers. However, from an industry perspective, a number of problems arise when applying the disparate-impact theory in the context of indirect auto lending. I now outline two significant concerns in this area.

First, unlike in mortgage lending, the bank does not know the race or ethnicity of the borrower. In an indirect auto loan, the dealer is arranging the transaction and is completing and submitting the applicable documents to the lender. In these situations, the borrower does not interact directly with the lender, and the lender is not aware of the borrower's race or ethnicity. In mortgage lending, the borrower is asked to indicate race and ethnicity on the mortgage loan application, which is not the case for auto loans. For indirect auto lending, proxy analysis has to be used, which, in essence, is taking other information to make an educated guess on race and ethnicity. This can be done in a number of ways, such as making educated guesses based on surname or the location of the borrower's residence. Such proxy analysis is not always accurate for a number of reasons. For example, a married woman may have a Latino surname if she uses the name of her husband who is Latino, even though she may be a member of another ethnic group. This problem of using proxy analysis is compounded by the fact that different types of methods may be used in such analyses and the CFPB has not provided sufficient information as to the type of methodology that banks should use.

A second issue in the area of indirect auto lending is that banks are expected to analyze the entire loan portfolio for rate disparities in addition to whether any particular auto dealer is engaged in discrimination. For example, a bank might engage in indirect lending with just two dealers. One dealer gives all of its customers a 5 percent rate, and the other dealer gives all of its customers a 3 percent rate. If the dealer that gives the 5 percent rate is giving more loans to minority groups than the other dealer, then there can be a finding of discrimination based on disparate impact because it appears that, overall, minority groups are paying higher rates. This is problematic in that it is clear that neither dealer is engaging in discrimination because each is giving all customers the same rate. To the extent there are discrepancies between dealers, the reasons can be totally unrelated to fair lending. For example, a dealer in an urban area, which may have a large concentration of minority customers, will likely incur higher operating costs than dealers in more rural areas, due to factors such as higher land and labor expenses. One option is for dealers to recoup these higher costs by charging a higher rate.

It is not just the industry that is concerned with the CFPB's actions in this area. A number of House Democrats, including several members of the Congressional Black Caucus, have sent a letter to the CFPB that expresses concerns with this issue. Their concern is similar to ours in that the auto industry is a bright spot in an otherwise sluggish economy, and we all want to ensure that CFPB actions do not threaten the vitality of this industry.

Mortgage Rules

As required under the Dodd–Frank Act, the CFPB recently issued several mortgage rules, including the qualified mortgage rule (also referred to as the ability-to-repay rules), mortgage servicing, and the mortgage loan originator compensation rules. Numerous issues are raised by these rules, but our main concerns fall into a couple of categories. The first is implementation time. These rules will be effective as of January 2014, but the CFPB continues to issue clarifications and changes. The industry does not yet have all the pieces of the puzzle to allow us to comply with these rules. We welcome the bureau's guidance and clarifications and want this to continue, but there are still a number of outstanding issues, and it will be at least a few months before these are all addressed, if then. That means that there is very little time between then and the January compliance deadlines.

A second issue with mortgages relates to fair-lending concerns. We are concerned that compliance with the qualified mortgage and ability-to-repay rules will subject lenders to claims under the disparate-impact theory. Again, under the disparate-impact theory, lenders may be liable for discrimination even if there was no intent. The concern here is that compliance with these and other mortgage rules will tighten credit overall to the extent that this could lead to disparate outcomes for minority groups and fair-lending challenges for banks. Banks might focus primarily on making qualified mortgage loans because these types of loans provide strong legal protections, but minority groups may have a harder time obtaining qualified mortgage loans if, for example, they have greater difficulties meeting the 43 percent debt-to-income ratio that is required for qualified mortgages.

The next issue of concern is student lending. Increasing college tuitions have forced students to borrow record amounts of money to finance their education. College debt now exceeds credit card debt, and I have heard that college debt now also exceeds auto loan debt in this country. The problem for the industry is that the CFPB is looking at making changes to the private student loan market (which consist of loans made directly by the banks) and not the federal student loan program. The problem here is that private student lending currently only accounts for 7 percent of student loan originations while 93 percent of the loans are made directly by the government under the Federal Direct Loan Program. It is hard to resolve a problem when looking at only 7 percent of the picture. Other factors that have created the current student loan crisis also should be addressed, including tuitions that have risen faster than the rate of inflation and family incomes over the past thirty years, as well as declining state support for higher education.

Other Issues

Since its inception, the CFPB has focused on setting up a repository for collecting complaints and having banks respond to them, which is a specific requirement under the Dodd–Frank Act. This complaint portal (as the CFPB calls it) is up and running for a number of retail bank products. There is value in having an organized complaint system to address customer concerns, and banks generally have their own processes for addressing complaints. However, the CFPB complaint portal, which is posted prominently on its website, publicly posts complaint information before it is verified. The customer asserts the complaint, which becomes public if the bank acknowledges that there is a customer relationship (without addressing or verifying the complaint) or if certain period of time has gone by in which the bank has not provided any response. We feel that it is unfair to publicly post unverified complaints. Also, the complaint portal does not include complaints from financial institutions that have less than $10 billion in assets and are therefore not supervised by the CFPB. Those complaints are handled by the institution's prudential regulator. This exclusion gives the appearance that complaints are directed only to large banks and nonbanks rather than small banks. The largest banks may receive the largest number of complaints, but the reason may be that these banks have the largest number of accounts and not undue problems with their business practices.

Finally, overdraft protection, deposit advance products, and prepaid cards are all products that the CFPB is currently reviewing in the context of consumer protection, and we have no problem with that. These deposit advance products are short-term lending products that some banks are developing as an alternative to payday lending.

As for overdraft protection, we have two overall concerns that also apply to the CFPB's review of deposit advance products and prepaid cards. One is that other banking agencies—the Federal Deposit Insurance Corporation (FDIC), the Office of the Comptroller of the Currency (OCC), and the Federal Reserve System—may act in this area, which can lead to potential confusion and inconsistencies with regard to the regulation of these products. Another concern is that the regulatory actions that may result may limit consumer choice and access to these products and thereby force consumers to use less appealing alternatives. So the banking industry currently has a wide range of issues and concerns with the CFPB.

Todd J. Zywicki: I agree with everything that Jeff said, although he said it in a much more mild-mannered way than I would or will. The Consumer Financial Protection Bureau (CFPB) is a good example of an issue that the framers of the Constitution wrestled with at the beginning of the country—the tradeoff between independence and accountability. The CFPB falls completely into the independence camp, and I think that there are some fairly predictable consequences of creating this sort of superregulator that is completely unconstrained and unchecked. So my goal is to take Jeff's remarks, put them in a broader context, talk about agency structure, and cover some of the same ground that he did with respect to some of the things that CFPB is doing. The CFPB's actions are a logical and predictable consequence of CFPB structure, and so the reforms that Jeff proposes are important.

I agree with the idea of having a single regulatory agency for dealing with consumer financial products. The prior system was balkanized among many different regulators and therefore did not work well. But I think that the single regulator should have been the Federal Trade Commission (FTC). We did not need a new superagency, but I agree with the idea of centralizing it.

CFPB Independence

The defects in the CFPB's agency structure matter for understanding the defective policies that we are already seeing (see Zywicki 2013a). I think of it as the revenge of Richard Nixon. The CFPB is a model of agency independence on steroids, and it is different from every other agency that we have had. The Federal Trade Commission (FTC) has been around for a hundred years and has exactly the features that Jeff was describing: it is a bipartisan commission that is subject to congressional appropriations and active oversight. The CFPB does not have those features. We learned in the 1970s why we should not have superagencies that are unconstrained by active oversight by Congress and various other checks and balances. During the 1960s and 1970s, we saw the demise of the New Deal state in the sense that we adopted a belief that agency bureaucrats are technocrats who do not have any political views and act as automatons. But when regulatory policy in the 1970s damaged the American economy, whether via the Interstate Commerce Commission (ICC), the Contract Appeals Board (CAB), or the SEC, many of these agencies were abolished because they were unresponsive.

We have had thirty or forty years of study of regulatory policy since then to help us better understand the tradeoffs between independence and accountability. Predictable, bureaucratic pathologies manifest themselves when there is an unconstrained agency, like the CFPB. These include tendencies such as a tunnel-vision focus on its mission relative to other social priorities, type 1 versus type 2 error problems, and agency imperialism (a tendency for agencies to expand their power and budgets). Getting rid of checks and balances (such as a multimember commission structure or congressional appropriations power) does not get rid of political decision making. It permits bureaucrats to indulge their own political preferences without constraint. In light of the Internal Revenue Service's unequal scrutiny of conservative organizations that were seeking section 501(c)(4) status, it appears that politics influence decisions by the agency's employees and that bureaucrats do not always act in a nonpolitical manner when insulated from oversight. The CFPB has demonstrated itself to be extraordinarily political. I think that it is one of the more political agencies in Washington. Elizabeth Warren used it as a springboard to run for the Senate, and it is now being run by Richard Cordray, who most people speculate has higher political aspirations as well. Politics has not been eliminated by setting up this agency with no oversight and no multimember commission structure.

Over time, we have learned that there are two ways to structure regulatory agencies. (Zywicki 2013a). One way is as an executive department. Accountability comes from the president's power to fire the person who runs it. The public does not get to scrutinize the agency's policies but can make it accountable through the electoral and political processes. The other way is an independent commission with a bipartisan board. Multimember agencies essentially substitute deliberation in an internal adversarial process for the accountability of the executive branch. For example, although the president cannot remove commission members, the multimember structure provides an opportunity for internal deliberation and external dissent through the right to publicly dissent. I worked at the FTC, so I am familiar with this process.

The CFPB is neither type of agency. The CFPB is an independent agency inside of another independent agency. The director is appointed for a five-year term and removable only for cause. The board receives a large amount of money every year from the Fed without any questions asked. The budget of the CFPB is about double the budget of the entire Federal Trade Commission, which does all the other consumer protection policy in the federal government as well as half of the government's competition policy.

The CFPB and Evidence-Based Policymaking

Has this defective agency structure manifested itself in practice? Are its actions consistent with what scholars of regulation would predict? The CFPB has said that it is different from other agencies and that, if left unchecked, will not exhibit the defects in outputs that typically result from a dysfunctional structure: it does not need to have to have these traditional checks and balances because it is engaged in evidence-based policymaking. Members of the board are looking at the facts as good engineers of consumer credit policy. The basic idea is that there are no politics here. So the question is whether there is any justification for making the CFPB different from, say, the FTC. Have we been doing consumer protection policy completely wrong for a hundred years at the Federal Trade Commission by having the checks and balances?

A look at CFPB's record so far might reveal whether it really is engaged in a disinterested search for the truth. Jeff gave an overview of the qualified mortgage rule, but I want to focus on one aspect of it—the provisions of the rule that deal with so-called complex mortgages (such as negative amortization mortgages). The CFPB cites only one academic study (that I am aware of). It was a study from the Chicago Fed titled "Complex Mortgages" that concluded, "Unlike the low income population targeted by subprime mortgages, complex mortgages are used by households with high income levels and prime credit scores" (Amromin, Huang, Sialm, and Zhong 2013, abstract; see also Zywicki 2013b). Foreclosure rates have been high, but the study says that's because complex mortgage contracts attract sophisticated borrowers who are more strategic in their default decisions. The basic thrust of the study is that the problem with negative amortization mortgages was not a payment problem or a problem of peddling mortgages to poor people because the borrowers who took the mortgages overwhelmingly have high incomes and high credit scores. Those who took out complex mortgages were sophisticated and rational in their decisions. When their house went down in value, they recognized that it was a terrible investment, and they walked away from it. The study found no evidence that the problem with complex mortgages was a payment problem or that the high-income sophisticated borrowers who took out those mortgages could not afford to pay. They simply realized that their home had become a negative-value investment and rationally chose not to pay.

What does the CFPB say to justify what amounts to a ban on negative amortization mortgages? "In their later incarnations," the CFPB says, "interest-only and negatively amortizing loans ... were often sold on the basis of the consumer's ability to afford the initial payments and without regard to the consumer's ability to afford subsequent payments once the rate was recast" (Consumer Financial Protection Bureau 2014, 563). The rulemaking continues, "The lower payment possibility for these loans allows borrowers to qualify for loans that they otherwise may not have been able to afford; but this comes with the same risks just described. The performance of many of these loans was also very poor, and worse than expected, with the onset of the downturn" (Consumer Financial Protection Bureau 2014 [citing the "Complex Mortgages" study], 563–564). In other words, the CFPB took a study that said that these loans were given to high-income, sophisticated home owners who strategically and rationally walked away from a bad investment and turned it into a conclusion that there was payment problem to justify its rules that treat all mortgage loan defaults as a payment problem.

The board also effectively banned teaser rates even though there is no evidence that teaser rates contributed to the crisis. The qualified mortgage rule also reveals a mindset that treats everything as a consumer protection problem and assumes that consumers are hapless dupes who can't take care of themselves and are constantly taken advantage of by banks. For instance, products that did contribute to the foreclosure crisis were the no-downpayment mortgage (which allowed people to have no equity in their home) and the cash-out refinancing (which allowed them to strip the equity from their home). When the house fell in value, it became a bad investment, and they walked away. Although some foreclosures were caused by problems of unaffordability, the primary reason for high foreclosure rates was that houses were under water: they were worth less than their mortgages. That is not a payment problem. That is an incentive problem to which people rationally responded.

Nevertheless, the qualified mortgage rule does not say that if we want to address the foreclosure problem, we should raise downpayment requirements. The CFPB is implementing provisions of the Dodd–Frank Act that preserve so-called antideficiency or nonrecourse laws. These laws basically limit the bank to taking the house back from the borrower when they default. Estimates are that foreclosure rates are about two to three times higher in states that have antideficiency laws versus those that allow banks to sue for a deficiency. These rules do not address the underlying problems that cause the foreclosures. Instead, they create new moral hazard problems by preserving laws that treat people as dupes when they rationally respond to the incentives that they are facing. They are creating moral hazard problems and ensuring that in the future foreclosure rates will be higher than they otherwise would be.

The other thing about the qualified mortgage rule is that it violates what Congress intended when it set up the CFPB. One of the goofier ideas in the original Dodd–Frank proposal was the plain, vanilla mortgage. Basically, lenders would have to offer so-called plain, vanilla products that people that would have to decide to opt out of. Congress laughed that proposal off the Hill when it first came up. So through the QM rule, the CFPB is saying, "We're not going to force you to offer plain, vanilla products. Instead, if you offer plain, vanilla products, then you get a safe harbor, but if you don't, you take your chances." The CFPB is not going to tell banks that they have to do it, but they will get big incentives to offer plain vanilla mortgages. But they get a safe harbor for consumer protection purposes but not from fair-lending rules. The CFPB can sue you for making or not making the same loan to the same person. For instance, if there is a correlation between, say, credit scores and certain demographic attributes, qualifying under the QM rule does not protect you from a disparate-impact suit. They can get you coming or going.

CFPB Regulation of Auto Dealers

The second thing I want to talk about is auto dealers, which Jeff mentioned. CFPB has an exclusion for auto dealers. This is a special-interest provision that came about when the dealers' lobbyists were on the Hill lobbying for special rules during the auto bailouts to prevent closures of auto dealers. Section 1029, Exclusion for Auto Dealers, says that the CFPB may not exercise any rulemaking supervisory enforcement or any other authority over auto dealers. Because the CFPB cannot reach the auto dealers directly, they instead reach those who lend to the auto dealers and turn private parties into the regulatory arm of the CFPB.

There really is not any basis for doing this. The board does not cite any justification for it. The argument seems to be, "People sit across from each other and negotiate these loans, and that could lead to discrimination. It's rife with potential for discrimination." That is not much of an argument, but it is the argument by which CFPB is going to remake the entire system of compensation for giving auto loans in this country. Essentially, the only way to get out of it is to adopt a completely different compensation scheme—a flat-fee compensation versus the way that it is done now.

That may be a good idea, but it does not seem like a good idea to do it in this way. Why would they do it this way? They cannot reach the auto dealers directly, and it is a way to avoid cost-benefit analysis and the other sort of things they would have to do if they wanted to do rulemaking. So enforcement (or in this case, enforcement by bullying and a veiled threat of enforcement) is used to evade the modest checks and balances that are in the system to slow them down.

Agency Design

Finally, agency design matters. Jeff alluded to the CFPB's complaint database. Bloomberg has counted the database's complaints by ZIP code, and most of them come from those poor, downtrodden people on the East Side and upper West Side of Manhattan and in Boca Raton and Palm Beach. Apparently, they are being taken advantage of by credit card issuers. I do not see any regulatory value in allowing people from Manhattan to complain that they do not like their credit cards. It is just giving people a place to gripe.

I think the point is that nothing that the CFPB is doing justifies the extreme level of independence that it has in its agency structure. These structural defects are being manifested in policymaking and decision making, such as the misuse of the study on complex mortgages. That would not happen at the FTC because the FTC has an independent Bureau of Economics and a bipartisan commission where different views can be aired and even a dissent can be filed. Inherent in this is politics. Bureaucrats are not just disinterested bureaucrats. There is always judgment. And I think that the reforms of putting them on budget and making them more accountable are our business.

Questions and Answers

Corwin: Todd has written that part of the motivation for the Consumer Finance Protection Bureau was that consumers were taking on products (loan products, in particular) that were harmful to them either because they were unsophisticated or irrational or perhaps just outright tricked by the financial institutions. And there seems to be evidence that many of these consumers don't understand some of the features of these products. I think making sure that people have the information is a great goal, but that does not seem to be the CFPB's objective. For example, it does not seem like the mortgage rules are designed to make sure that people understand mortgages. It seems like the mortgage rules are designed to limit available mortgages to a subset that are very simple. I look at the recent discussion of overdraft fees in a similar way. There was an article in the *Wall Street Journal* this week that discussed overdraft fees. I was surprised to read of the CFPB's concern that people who use overdraft protection pay on average, I think it was $900 a year more than people who don't use this overdraft protection. It seemed to me they are using a service, and they are paying for the service. As long as they understood the service ahead of time, that's fine. So I was curious if you would comment about how much we need to be concerned with making sure consumers understand financial products versus limiting the products or deciding what products should be offered.

Audience: I did some research on this topic, and people seem to understand the dollar amount of the overdraft or payday loan. What people don't understand are the implications of their decisions over time. They don't add it up, and they don't translate it into rates. You can affect decisions on repayment behavior by onsite disclosure that makes people think forward. I think people do have a good sense of their budget and what these dollar fees are, but I think going down the path of more information about the future is where you help people make decisions on full information. That is my instinct.

Zywicki: I read the overdraft report Tuesday when it came out (see Flores and Zywicki 2013). It is a good example of how sophisticated, serious economic thinking could help because it is a terrible report. The basic thrust of the report is that the only goal of regulators should be to minimize the amount of overdraft fees in society. But let's think about overdraft. Overdraft and payday lending are competing products. Nowhere in the overdraft report do they ask the question, "If people aren't using overdrafts, what are they using?" A lot of them are probably using payday lending instead. Payday lending is often cheaper than overdrafts, but you can't know whether people are better off or worse off without access to overdraft until you know their alternatives. That question is beyond the scope of the report.

And it is the same thing in the payday report in the opposite way. The evidence is that payday lending and overdrafts compete with each other. According to research by Donald Morgan, consumers choose between payday lending and overdraft protection in a way that is basically rational, and they choose overdraft protection and payday lending because they can't get credit cards. People who use payday lending are people who do not have credit cards or would max out their credit cards. That would be more expensive because they have to pay all the penalty fees. So there is a pecking order. If you have credit cards, use credit cards. If you don't have credit cards, use payday lending and overdraft protection. If you can't get payday lending, use pawnshops. And this is common sense. This is rational decision making for consumers who are subject to constraints. Does the CFPB ever ask the question, "If you take away payday lending, what happens to people? Are they better off being forced to use pawnshops?" I don't see it in the CFPB's payday lending research or overdraft research. But I think that is an example of something that is perfectly common sense to economists, but I don't think it is to the CFPB. People who use overdraft protection more are more likely to opt into overdraft protection. Why? The implication is because they have got limited alternatives. They are using overdraft protection because, even though it is not a great product, it is better than a pawnshop or a payday loan for a lot of these people. These are the kinds of questions that I think are important to understand.

Bloch: I agree with everything Todd said, so I won't repeat it, but I want to say a couple of words about disclosures in general. The banking industry is all for disclosures and ensuring that consumers understand the terms of their transactions. The problem is that scores of disclosure regulations have been issued over the past forty years or so, with the result that consumers are faced with layers upon layers of complicated disclosures that they don't understand. The reams and reams of disclosures we receive when we apply for and receive a mortgage to buy a home is a classic example here. As confusing and complex as the rules are, banks must comply with them, even though streamlined, less complicated disclosures would certainly be in the best interest of consumers and the industry. With overdraft programs, people use the product, as Todd said, because it has benefits for certain people, and there are certain people who are in a situation where they need to use them or be faced with less appealing alternatives, such as bouncing checks, which leads to more fees in addition to embarrassment. The bottom line is that the banking industry is a competitive market and banks want to serve their customers, so if overdraft programs are a viable option and benefit for certain consumers, then banks should be able to offer them without excessive regulatory obstacles.

Audience (Spatt): I disagree with limiting product choices. I have thought about mortgage contract terms for several decades. I have written papers on mortgage contract terms going back to the 1980s. It seems to me that different contract terms serve different borrowers. Some of the variations are things like trading off initial payment in the form of points versus rate. Some people prefer adjustable loans because of the nature of their labor-market risks. Some people prefer adjustable-rate loans because of issues of the opportunity to get a teaser. There are sophisticated borrowers who have done better than the banks at some of this because when the banks offer options to people, the more sophisticated borrowers can cherry pick.

What really has me nervous here is that when government says, "We know best," that is often exactly when they do not know best. In other contexts, I see the same kind of issues playing out. Another area where I have a lot of expertise is taxable and tax-deferred investing. When I have talked to people in the benefits space, like human resources people, I find that they have paternalistic views about which choices are good, but typically, their paternalistic views lead their personnel astray. I understand that there are some folks in society who don't understand whether 2 plus 2 equals 4 or equals 6. Frankly, to the extent that some of us do understand what 2 plus 2 equals, it seems to me that our society ought not to get messed up by trying to protect the other people. But it seems to me that to the extent that regulators don't necessarily fully understand the trade-offs in these contracts them-selves, they ought not to circumscribe these issues. They ought not to declare that if a lender offers a product in a certain space, there is a presumption that this product will mostly be taken by confused individuals. A lot of this just seems to me to be crazy.

Zywicki: Something that has really bothered me about the CFPB's thrust is the overwhelming mentality that consumer credit should fit into a public utility sort of model. We see it in the auto dealer regulation. What they want is posted pricing where everybody gets the same price. The auto dealer regulation shows that they distrust negotiation and shopping because they see it as rife for discrimination rather than a possibility to get a good deal. But the overwhelming idea (and this goes back to Elizabeth Warren's idea of setting up the CFPB) is that simplicity is kind of an end in itself, whether it is plain vanilla mortgages or very simple credit cards. They are going to do the same sort of thing to credit cards that they did to QM and the like.

One of the terrible legacies of this whole financial crisis is that we are going to end up stuck with this stupid thirty-year fixed-rate mort-gage with an unlimited right to prepay. It is going to further entrench this product, and that is sort of what they are trying to do. We are pretty much the only country in the world that has a thirty-year, fixed-rate, self-amortizing mortgage with an unlimited right to prepay, and that is one of the reasons that our foreclosure rate is ten times higher than the rest of the world. In the United States, what happened was that when people's houses went up in value, they refinanced, they stripped out their equity, and when their houses fell in value, they gave the house back to the bank. England had the same price patterns as the United States, but people could not strip their equity, so they kept their equity intact. In the United States, you pay about 100 to 120 basis points extra to get a fixed-rate mortgage, so you are paying 120 basis points a year to get an interest-rate insurance twenty-nine years from now. The average American owns their house for five years. And some people think it is a good idea to make people pay 120 basis points to get interest-rate insurance twenty-nine years or thirty years from now. Plain vanilla products are great for plain vanilla consumers, but I have yet to meet the plain vanilla consumer. I meet different people who have different situations. So we can step up and make disclosure work better for people and make competition work better for people, but I see this idea of simplicity for simplicity's sake coming out of this agency. And that, I think, is dangerous.

Bloch: One of the primary goals of the Dodd–Frank Act is to ensure ready access to the financial system by consumers. I see that goal as having two components. One is to make sure that consumers have the knowledge to choose the products or services that they need and want. The second is to ensure that the financial institutions can have the means to provide them. I see nothing in Dodd–Frank about changing people's behavior as an objective. That is not the proper role of government when it comes to providing consumers with financial products and services.

Question: At the beginning, you said that the CFPB centralizes consumer financial regulations in one place, but the more I listened to you, the more it seems that it's not possible to do that. On the one hand, the CFPB's concerns interact a lot with antitrust. I mean, should banks be broken up? The answer to that question has a lot to do with the terms that consumers negotiate. To me, that creates big difficulties in separating antitrust from CFPB. And similarly, in the negative amortization mortgage, if somebody rationally negotiates to be able to walk away from a mortgage, that bank is probably not really going to take all the risk. It will pass it along to the taxpayers, and so you have a systemic-risk problem that is being created by that negotiating process. It seems to me that this should be a concern for the Fed and the other agencies that try to limit systemic risk. So I am wondering where you think the boundaries of the CFPB should lie.

Zywicki: First, one key point is that the loans that the banks made were incredibly stupid, but they were not stupid because people did not understand their loans. They were stupid because people understood all too well what their incentives were for a nothing-down mortgage when their house falls in value and they are in a nonrecourse state. One of the myths of the crisis is thinking that what was actually a safety and soundness problem (allowing banks to make mortgages without 20 percent down) was a consumer protection problem. And that gets to the too-big-to-fail and systemic-risk issues. But it is a safety and soundness issue, not a consumer protection issue.

The second thing that I have real concerns about is the competition issue. The overwhelming structure of Dodd–Frank and CFPB, as well, is to promote consolidation of the banking industry. Everybody knows that regulatory burdens disproportionately tax small institutions relative to large institutions. And the combination of that with the entrenchment of the too-big-to-fail subsidy and everything else in Dodd–Frank, I think, is promoting consolidation in the banking industry. I think this tendency to impose a plain vanilla mortgage through the back door does the same thing. Limiting the ability to modify products is going to favor the low-price seller, which will be the big banks and not the banks who know their customers and the people in Jeff's world who have designed products appropriately for their customers.

The last issue is the single-regulator issue. There is an incongruity in Dodd–Frank in that they want to set up a one regulator for the federal government but they have all these preemption rules at the local level. So at the same time that they are doing that, they are basically now empowering the Eliot Spitzers of the world to enforce CFPB regulations. You are going to have state attorneys general enforcing CFPB regulations in a very complicated process. We now have a system where the federal government can regulate local lenders and state governments can regulate interstate commerce in a way that we have never seen before. I think that is a future headache (see Zywicki 2013a, 923–927).

Corwin: As we wrap up, let me ask if either of you has any final comments or concerns related to the CFPB or directions that you think the CFPB should go in the future.

Zywicki: I think that the CFPB is hopeless without fundamental structural reform. I think it is just endemic in the bureaucratic structure of the agency. One last thing is that people have raised the question of the internal organization of economists at the CFPB. The FTC economists have their own bureau. They report directly to the commission, and I think that is a valuable mechanism for preserving the independence of economists—giving economists an independent voice in commission decision making and reporting directly to the board. I can't figure out exactly how the economists are organized in CFPB, but they seem to be just an appendage to the lawyers. I think this is a terrible way to organize economists, and I would be harsher on the lawyers with respect to their motivations. But I think that reorganizing the internal structure of the agency to make it look more like the FTC would strengthen the hand of the economists and maybe rein in some of these problems.

Bloch: As for the future, we completely agree on the need to change the structure of the CFPB. But let me briefly mention a couple of other issues that we did not have a chance to discuss. One important issue is the CFPB's new authority to prohibit unfair, deceptive, or abusive acts or practices (UDAAPs). Before the Dodd–Frank Act, the FTC and others had UDAP authority—the authority to prohibit unfair or deceptive acts or practices. The Dodd–Frank Act added *abusive*, the second A, which allows the CFPB to identify and address what it considers to be abusive actions among the banks and nonbanks that it supervises. Our question here is, "What constitutes an abusive practice?" The CFPB's response has been that there is enough information in the statute to define this and there is no need to write a rule or provide additional guidance. This essentially means that we will have to wait as the CFPB takes actions against banks and nonbanks for what it determines to be abusive actions and then try to assess from these actions what the term *abusive* means, at least from the CFPB's perspective. Our preference would be for the CFPB to provide its views now rather than later. The real downside with the CFPB's approach in defining the term *abusive* is that it will stifle innovation in developing and delivering financial products and services in that the industry will not want to develop a new product or service if there is a chance the CFPB would have issues with it from a UDAAP perspective.

As for the collection of consumer data, a significant and emerging problem is developing here that I did not address in my earlier remarks. The CFPB continues to collect huge amounts of data on individual consumer financial transactions for research purposes. Collecting data and information from banks imposes significant costs and burdens on them, and these costs and burdens are growing as the CFPB collects more and more of this information for research purposes. In addition, the CFPB is also buying a huge amount of this data from other sources, and our other concern here is with the centralization of so much data about consumer behavior and the history of consumer actions. We are concerned not only with the privacy and security of the information but also with the ways that it will be used by the CFPB.

Another issue we are concerned about is that the CFPB seems to be issuing a fair amount of rather prescriptive guidance that looks very similar to rules. However, under the rulemaking process, the CFPB and other agencies are required to proceed with a notice and comment process before issuing a final rule. With guidance, this process can be avoided. The CFPB is certainly not the first or only agency that has been criticized for issuing prescriptive guidance instead of a rule, but there is a concern here that is unique to the CFPB.

CFPB guidance generally applies only to the institutions that the CFPB supervises (the banks with over $10 billion in assets and certain nonbanks) while the CFPB's rulemaking authority applies to the entire industry. One of the purposes of creating the CFPB is to level the playing field so that the entire industry operates under the same set of rules. Issuing guidance that applies to only certain segments of the industry will not achieve this goal.

Finally, with regard to supervising nonbanks, we welcome this and believe that this is an idea whose time has come. However, we are concerned about whether the CFPB will have sufficient resources here. I have no idea how many nonbanks are out there, and I don't think the CFPB does either, but we all know it dwarfs the number of banks. So although we certainly would like to see supervision of these nonbanks, we don't see how the CFPB is going to have the resources for this. For example, I read the other day that there are now more payday lenders in California than there are McDonald's. That gives you an idea of how big that group is.

References

Amromin, Gene, Jennifer Huang, Clemens Sialm, and Edward Zhong. 2013. Complex Mortgages. AFA 2012 Chicago Meetings Paper, December 19. http://papers.ssrn.com/sol3/papers.cfm?abstract_id=1714605.

Consumer Financial Protection Bureau. 2014. Ability-to-Repay and Qualified Mortgage Standards under the Truth in Lending Act (Regulation Z). http://files.consumerfinance .gov/f/201301_cfpb_final-rule_ability-to-repay.pdf.

Flores, G. Michael, and Todd Zywicki. 2013. Commentary: CFPB Study on Overdraft Protection. *Mercatus Research*. Mercatus Center, George Mason University, November 3. http://mercatus.org/publication/commentary-cfpb-study-overdraft-program.

Zywicki, Todd. 2013a. The Consumer Financial Protection Bureau: Savior or Menace? *George Washington Law Review* 81 (3):856–928.

Zywicki, Todd. 2013b. Policy-Based Evidence Making at the Consumer Financial Protection Bureau. Law & Liberty blog, January 21. http://www.libertylawsite.org/2013/01/ 21/policy-based-evidence-making-at-the-consumer-financial-protection-bureau-new -mortgage-rules-show-why-heightened-oversight-is-necessary.

10 Panel Discussion on Derivatives and Dodd–Frank

Amy K. Edwards, Raymond P. H. Fishe, Robert McDonald, Craig Pirrong, and Paul H. Schultz

Paul H. Schultz: The Dodd–Frank Wall Street Reform and Consumer Protection Act of 2010 regulates derivatives, including swaps. In a swap contract, two counterparties agree to trade a series of cash flows. In a traditional interest-rate swap, one party contracts to pay a fixed rate of interest on a notional amount to the second party, and the second party contracts to pay a floating rate to the first. Whoever has the larger payment when a payment is due pays the net amount to the other party. The payments are made on a regular time schedule (say, quarterly). In a currency swap, the two parties agree to make regular payments to each other in different currencies. For example, a U.S. company that sells its products in Japan could agree to swap yen for dollars on a regular basis. Swaps can be used to hedge interest-rate risk, foreign-exchange risk, and many other types of risk as well.

Credit default swaps were a source of concern during the financial crisis. In a credit default swap, one party (the buyer) makes regular payments to the other party (the seller). If there is a default on the loan or security named in the contract, the seller will make a payment (usually the face value of the security) and take possession of it. Credit default swaps can be used to insure an investment in a risky debt instrument.

Credit default swaps figured prominently in the crisis because American International Group (AIG) had sold credit default swaps on $440 billion in debt, including mortgage-backed securities. When these securities turned south, AIG needed an $85 billion federal bailout.

The Bank for International Settlements (BIS) reports that as of June 2013, the notional value of over-the-counter (OTC) interest-rates swaps was $437 trillion, while the notional value of credit default swaps was $24.5 billion (Bank for International Settlements 2013). These are incomprehensibly large values but also meaningless. The gross market value of swaps is the cost of replacing all outstanding contracts at current market prices. The gross market value of interest-rate swaps was $14 trillion at the end of June 2013, and the gross market value of credit default swaps was "only" $728 billion. Gross credit exposures (that is, gross market values after legally enforceable bilateral netting) was less than $4 trillion for all over-the-counter derivatives in June 2013.

Before Dodd–Frank, swaps were largely unregulated and traded primarily over the counter. Lack of regulation and margin requirements may be one reason that they were so popular. But it also made it almost impossible for regulators to learn the true exposures in the swaps market.

How Dodd–Frank Regulates Swaps

I am going to sketch out the provisions of Dodd–Frank that apply to the swap market. First, section 723 requires swaps to be centrally cleared. In this case, a clearinghouse is the counterparty to both sides of the contract. Traders do not need to worry about whether their counterparties will remain solvent. The clearinghouse takes the place of their counterparty. The clearinghouse will require margin from traders. Swap counterparties that are commercial end users are exempt from clearing. Unusual or exotic swaps are not well suited to centralized clearing and will continue to trade in the OTC market. The Securities and Exchange Commission (SEC) and Commodity Futures Trading Commission (CFTC) will determine which swaps need to be cleared.

Second, section 723 requires all swaps subject to clearing to be traded on a board of trade, exchange, or swap execution facility. A swap execution facility (SEF) is a trading platform that provides pretrade bid and ask prices and an execution mechanism. It must have many-to-many execution functionality. That is, multiple buyers must have access to multiple sellers. SEFs must also have request for quote (RFQ) systems that deliver RFQs to at least two and later three market participants. It is hoped that this additional pretrade transparency will lead to lower trading costs and more liquidity in the swaps market.

Posttrade transparency will be increased with real-time reporting of swap transactions that includes price and volume. Block trades will be subject to less stringent reporting requirements. The idea is that a delay in reporting will give a dealer a chance to trade out of a large swap position with a minimum of market impact. This can increase liquidity for large trades. Block trades are not required to be executed on SEFs or exchanges.

Notice that end users that are not financial firms are not required to clear swaps and therefore do not have to execute their trades on SEFs. They can continue to enter into bilateral swap contracts with a single dealer. They are permitted to trade on SEFs, however, and can choose to clear their trades.

Third, the act defines swap market participants. A swap dealer makes a market in swaps, holds itself out as dealer in swaps, and enters into swaps for its own account in the ordinary course of business. A major swap participant is a nondealer that maintains substantial positions in swaps for hedging or risk-management purposes. Section 731 imposes significant compliance responsibilities, including reporting, capital, and margin requirements for both swap dealers and major swap participants.

Fourth, section 716 of the act, the swaps pushout rule, prohibits swap dealers from receiving guarantees from the Federal Deposit Insurance Corporation (FDIC) or access to the Federal Reserve's discount window. This provision of Dodd–Frank, which is also known as the Lincoln Amendment, was designed to make banks push swap activities out to nonbank affiliates. Some market-making and hedging activities were exempted. An error in the original drafting of the rule did not exempt market making and hedging for foreign banks, and regulators have corrected this error through ad hoc fixes. Banks have complained that it is unclear which activities must be separated from the bank. At this point, the Office of the Comptroller of the Currency (OCC) has delayed implementation of the swaps pushout rule until July 2015. It is possible that it will be repealed. In fact, on October 30, 2013, the U.S. House of Representatives voted to roll back the swaps pushout rule.

Security-based swaps, which are mainly credit default swaps, will be regulated by the SEC. The CFTC has responsibility for other swaps, including swaps on broad-based indices, swaps on government securities, and foreign-exchange swaps.

Merton Miller has said that the two great catalysts for financial innovation are taxes and regulation, so it is not surprising to see Dodd–Frank spur innovation in the swaps market. No regulator or other market observer, however, is smart enough to anticipate all the ways that the market will respond to new regulations. In writing Dodd–Frank rules, regulators were rightly concerned about swap trading migrating overseas. Nobody anticipated futurization.

With Dodd–Frank, the regulatory advantage of swaps was diminished or eliminated. Prior to Dodd–Frank, there were no margin requirements for swaps. For many users, this was a big advantage of swaps and a primary reason for choosing swaps instead of other derivatives for hedging. With Dodd–Frank, clearinghouses were required to collect initial margins on swaps that assumed a five-day liquidation period. Futures, which were considered to be more liquid, require margin only to cover exposure for a one-day liquidation period. In addition, a trader that traded more than $8 billion in notional value was required to register as a swap dealer and incur reporting and compliance obligations that futures traders do not face.

Given that regulatory compliance costs have increased for swaps relative to futures, it is not surprising that trading has migrated from swaps to futures. Cash flows of swaps can be duplicated with a series of futures contracts. In addition, futures on swaps have become increasingly popular. Some of these futures even have features that are used to duplicate the cash flows of swaps. But although the swap futures are economically equivalent to swaps, they have lower margins.

Craig Pirrong: I am one of the people who call Dodd–Frank "Frankendodd" because it is basically a monster that has gotten out of the control of its creators. So I would like to echo something that Chester Spatt has said, which was that a lot of what Dodd–Frank tries to do is to reduce systemic risk by essentially redesigning the financial system, and this is particularly true of derivatives markets.

I would like to divide what Dodd–Frank does with derivatives into two basic parts. One part is how market participants manage counterparty credit risks, and the other part is how they execute transactions. And although I have been pretty critical of both of those, I focus a lot of the criticism on clearing—clearing mandates, collateral mandates, and things of that nature. The basis of my criticism is that even though these measures are designed to reduce systemic risk, they have not really looked at the true systemic effects of some of these prescriptions for managing counterparty credit risks. Consequently, there are going to be a lot of unintended consequences that will undo many of the intended effects of Dodd–Frank. Systemic risk will be replaced or reallocated, so the problems might not arise where they did before but have been displaced.

Hedge funds certainly survived the crisis pretty well. A lot of the regulation that was put into place and a lot of the regulatory focus prior to the crisis in 2008 were motivated by what happened ten years earlier with long-term capital management. The view was that hedge funds were the source of the problem, which meant that people took their eyes off the ball and saw later that the problem had moved on. I think that that is a serious concern going forward.

I think that there are going to be a lot of unintended consequences of Dodd–Frank. We have seen of them already in the way that regulators have been caught flat-footed by many things that have happened. For example, I think futurization, particularly in the energy markets, came as a big surprise to regulators. It was something that they really had not anticipated even though in many respects it was baked into the way that the law was written and the way that the rules were written under the law. I think we can anticipate many of these unintended and unexpected consequences going forward.

Robert McDonald: I want to make a few comments about the rationale for derivatives regulation in Dodd–Frank and why that issue is prominent in the legislation. I will also echo a bit of what Craig said regarding derivatives regulation and systemic risk.

Why Dodd–Frank Regulates Swaps

If people are asked why there is a great deal of focus on derivatives regulation in Dodd–Frank, many will point to AIG. AIG infamously wrote hundreds of billions of dollars' worth of credit default swaps (CDSs) on mortgage-related obligations. Many banks purchased these swaps as insurance against their own mortgage-related positions. As was typical in deals between large financial institutions, these CDS contracts paid gains and losses as they accrued, but there was no initial margin. AIG had not been required by counterparties to set aside an initial lump sum as collateral against the possibility of future failure to pay. At a crucial moment during the crisis, AIG was unable to meet a margin call on the swaps. This had the potential to cause AIG to fail, and there was great concern about contagion. The financial institutions that had purchased the CDS contracts sold by AIG would lose their insurance, so losses on their mortgage-related positions would no longer be offset by gains on the CDS contracts. As a result, these institutions potentially could fail, inflicting losses on their counterparties, and so on. It is easy to understand why AIG was rescued. But the truth is that we don't know the effect an AIG default would have had on AIG's credit default swap counterparties. Goldman Sachs, for example, claimed that it had hedged against AIG's credit risk.

In assessing the lessons from this episode, it is important to keep in mind that a lot was going on at AIG at the same time. First, AIG had a securities lending business. The firm loaned out securities (such as corporate bonds) and invested the proceeds in mortgage-backed securities. This activity doubled down on the mortgage market bet that AIG had made by selling CDS. By September 2008, AIG had lost a substantial amount of money doing this. Second, AIG is a colossal insurance company. AIG's insurance subsidiaries were regulated at the individual state level, and state insurance commissioners reportedly were concerned about an AIG default. They were contemplating the seizure of the insurance subsidiaries in a couple of different states. This would have been a mess. So there was a possibility of a lot of things going wrong all at once with AIG. This was not simply a case of a firm that wrote a credit default swap on which it could not make payments.

Given that this big insurance firm had run into problems on multiple fronts, threatening the financial system, you could ask, "What makes sense to regulate to prevent a recurrence?," and you could conclude that you should regulate derivatives because failure to pay on the CDS contracts was a triggering event. AIG aside, however, the derivatives markets appeared to work reasonably well. The enormous over-the-counter interest-rate swap market, for example, did not suffer failures. You might also conclude that you should regulate securities lending because AIG had lost money in that activity. Finally, you could conclude that you should regulate insurance at a national level based on the state-by-state patchwork quilt of insurance regulators, the importance of insurance as a financial contract, and the size of the insurance sector. It would seem natural to have a national insurance regulator come out of Dodd–Frank. Such a regulator would presumably have paid attention to AIG Financial Products Corporation, which sold the CDS contracts. So why did derivatives face increased regulation? One possibility is that they were easy. There was an existing well-established regulatory apparatus—including both the SEC and CFTC—that could be tweaked. There were preexisting clearinghouses using a time-tested clearing and margining methodology, so the role of those clearinghouses simply could be expanded with a clearing mandate.

Prior to the crisis, there was already, in the background, substantial concern about notional overhang in the over-the-counter derivatives market. Many derivatives market participants had roughly offsetting contracts, but they were not perfectly offsetting because they had different counterparties or perhaps slightly different contractual features. There has been talk about $600 trillion in notional outstanding derivatives. Economically, it is not really $600 trillion in exposure, but that notional amount partly reflects the fact that many of these contracts are very similar but nevertheless cannot quite be netted. There was a lot of concern about the difficulty of unwinding all of these positions if there was ever a need to do so. So I think there was probably the idea that derivatives were low-hanging fruit in the regulatory arena.

Benefits of Regulating Swaps

I think some of the increased regulation is beneficial. I remember learning several years ago about a firm that offers a swap reconciliation service. In case that phrase doesn't ring a bell, the basic idea is that bank A and bank B have entered into an over-the-counter derivatives contract. The question is whether bank A's description of the contract matches bank B's description of the contract. A swap reconciliation service goes into each of the two banks and reconciles their trades with each other, making sure that there is agreement about the contract. Historically, one reason for ending up with different descriptions is that firms kept records of derivative deals in Excel spreadsheets with inconsistent fields; sometimes nobody was certain what had been agreed to. This problem has lessened over time, but $600 trillion notional of these contracts is outstanding. Most of it is probably accounted for properly, but perhaps there are contracts at the edges that are not. In any event, a swap reconciliation service goes in and tries to help firms clean up their books.

Given the large notional quantity of OTC derivatives outstanding, the historical sloppiness of record-keeping in this market, and market practices such as not requiring initial margin in some cases, it seems that it was reasonable to be concerned about the derivatives market. If nothing else, compliance with Dodd–Frank will force lagging firms to improve internal systems and controls because they are going to have to do things like price and transaction reporting, which requires them to know exactly what they have bought and sold. In most cases, there will have to be initial margin, which will reduce counterparty risk in cases like that of AIG.

So there was a rationale for derivatives regulation. The follow-up question is whether derivatives regulation will matter for systemic risk, which was an important rationale for the legislation. With the notable exception of AIG, most derivatives institutions worked fine during the financial crisis. I expect that Dodd–Frank reforms will reduce the build-up of the interconnected positions resulting from notional overhang.

The requirement that positions be centrally cleared when feasible will reduce the number of uncleared positions. Given the margining and position limits that will occur with clearing, it seems unlikely that there would be an exact analog to the AIG problem for a firm that is selling centrally cleared swaps. If a problem does occur, it probably will be easier to address (or at least to assess in advance) the fallout from a failure. At the same time, we now have mandated clearing. As a result, as a number of people have pointed out, there are now new too-big-to-fail entities—namely, clearinghouses. The clearinghouses will have access to the discount window, so it is hard to imagine that a mandated, systemically important institution such as a clearinghouse is going to be allowed to fail. It is one thing to let an individual bank fail, and it is another thing to say, "We're requiring you to use a clearinghouse, but by the way, the clearinghouse has failed. You're on your own." So I am skeptical about claims that significant clearinghouses will be allowed to fail. Another consideration (to echo something that Anil Kashyap has said) is that OTC contracts are very profitable for dealers. There is a question about how easily they will give up that franchise and submit everything to exchange trading and central clearing. I think that at the margin, there will be big incentives to avoid standardized contracts and to identify instruments as something other than a derivative.

Finally, when all is said and done, we don't know how many clearinghouses there will be. We don't know what the configuration of risk across these clearinghouses will be. We don't know what the exposure of derivatives to these different clearinghouses is going to be. Offsetting forces are at work: there are natural economies of scale in clearinghouses, and there are risk-management advantages from clearing closely related products, but at the same time, there will be competition to create multiple clearinghouses. We don't really have theory or data to guide us in understanding what the new equilibrium configuration will be and the nature of the risks that it will impose on the system. In the past, the market has configured itself as an outcome of economic competition. We do not know how a clearing mandate will play out. I think there are a lot of issues and a lot of uncertainty about the result of all the new regulations.

Amy K. Edwards: Before I begin I should disclose that what I say on this panel represents my own views and does not necessarily reflect the views of the Securities and Exchange Commission or my colleagues on the staff of the commission.[1] As Craig has already mentioned, the

CFTC regulates more products than the SEC, but the products regulated by the SEC are more security-like. For example, the SEC's jurisdiction includes single-name credit default swaps for both corporate and sovereign reference entities.

The Division of Risk, Strategy, and Financial Innovation (RSFI) has analyzed the Depository Trust and Clearing Corporation's (DTCC) Trade Information Warehouse data to understand the potential economic effects of Title VII of the Dodd–Frank Act. We have produced many statistics that help us understand various features of the credit default swap markets so that we can better support the rulemaking process. For example, we have learned that the median trade size in credit default swaps is around $5 million. The distribution of trade sizes is relatively small. The 25th percentile is approximately $2 million, and the 75th percentile is approximately $8.5 million. Trades in sovereign single-name credit default swaps are a bit larger but not significantly so. A typical single-name corporate credit default swap trades more than a typical bond in the corporate bond market but a lot less than equities. The market is still pretty large today, although it is significantly smaller than it was in 2008. Overall, the data from the Trade Information Warehouse are more comprehensive for the credit default swap market compared to what we know about the total return swap market, which we understand is smaller than the credit default swap market.

Unlike traditional security markets, the credit default swap market does not have clear borders. The credit default swap market does not have a trading floor, and a single transaction can have counterparties from different countries, which may or may not be in a reference entity located in the same country as either counterparty. In single-name credit default swaps that reference a U.S. entity, the majority of transactions have at least one U.S. counterparty. A number of counterparties to trades are affiliated with U.S. entities but actually are located overseas. In addition, some foreign counterparties are guaranteed by U.S. entities. We even observe transactions in U.S. reference names between foreign entities, some of which are located in the United States, and some of which are not. With all the ways that U.S. counterparties can be involved in a credit default swap transaction, drawing a line on what is a U.S. transaction can be complex.

As a final thought, central clearing in credit default swaps can differ from central clearing in other types of instruments. When a stock clears, for example, a trade on day T is guaranteed on day T plus one and clears on day *T* plus three. After clearing, the central counterparty typically has no exposure to the stock. After the buyer has its stock and the seller receives its money, the clearing agency no longer bears credit risk on that transaction. In a credit default swap, the central counterparty is exposed to the contract until expiration. That is very different from equities and not much different from options, but a typical option has a much shorter term than a typical credit default swap.

Raymond P. H. Fishe: The problem with going fourth in a panel of four is that you lose three of your introductory points to other speakers. So at the risk of repeating others' comments, I will offer four points. Because I do consult with the Commodity Futures Trading Commission, what I say represents my own opinions and not those of the CFTC, the commissioners, or the staff.

Title VII of Dodd–Frank does a number of things in the derivatives market. First, it broadly defines *swap*. The legal definition and the regulatory definitions now expand the notion of that word as previously used by the industry and markets. The CFTC had to enumerate exceptions and safe harbor rules to limit the coverage created by the new definition. So the new definition changes the market size. It is not just the notional $600 trillion market, but if the definition is applied without the exceptions, it would include most insurance contracts and nearly all other contracts that exchange payments between parties dependent on another instrument or measurable event. So Title VII is a major change in what we call swap markets.

My second thought relates to the Title VII goal of increasing transparency. It is not clear whether Dodd–Frank chose this market to increase transparency because there was evidence of a real problem or because (as in Jim Overdahl's bar fight example) somebody wanted to take a swing at it. Regardless of the motivation, swaps were largely an OTC market and had little transparency. The structure that has been proposed and is being implemented is an attempt to change that, and I think that one thing we know from academic studies is that transparency can lead to more competition, which will result in gains to many participants. This does not mean that these changes are costless, but with regard to transparency, we are fairly sure about the net positive results.

The third thought that I would like to offer is that clearing mandates are a way to deal with counterparty and systemic risk—whether the money is going to be there, what the quality of the counterparty is, and what the likelihood is that defaults will spread beyond the affected contracts. I do not believe that any solution has been offered to deal with such risks other than some form of mandatory clearing. There are costs associated with mandatory clearing, and when those costs are high relative to the risks abated, regulators have enumerated exceptions to the mandate. Not all contracts are subject to mandatory clearing, and not all entities are subject to the requirement. In the end, it is almost like a controlled experiment because the cases where you have to clear can be compared to those where you do not have to clear. Over time, we will discover whether counterparty and systemic risks are different between these cases.

Some swaps were cleared before Dodd–Frank, so clearing is not something new to this market. Clearing organizations cooperate with the regulators and provide information about the products that have been cleared. Such information is an important input when regulators define the different swap categories and classes of swaps for the purpose of mandatory clearing.

Finally, Craig talked about the unintended consequences and gave futurization as an example. That is an important observation. When the rules become fully effective and implemented, it will be interesting to see how futurization changes these markets and the distribution of risks. It will also be interesting to see which platform emerges as the dominant platform and which contract type survives over time. I do not have an opinion on the likely result because it will be sorted out by the marketplace.

Questions and Answers

Question: A goal of Dodd–Frank is to lower systemic risk. Nevertheless, some have claimed that a single clearinghouse will be riskier than the bilateral clearing that has been used for swaps. Can you comment on why central clearing might increase systemic risk?

McDonald: I don't think there is a clear answer to that, but I will take a crack at it. One thing about clearinghouses is that they have very crisp rules: there is marking to market one or more times daily, and payments are made on a fixed schedule. In the event of some kind of crisis, a clearinghouse might have problems either because there is some kind of freeze in the banking system or because they are unable to make a mandated payment for some other reason. As an example, consider what happened to CDS prices during the crisis. Imagine that you are clearing CDS and there is some large-volume CDS contract where there is a huge move in price and the margin is outstripped. The clearing-house could be in trouble, and we don't know how that would play out. In the over-the-counter market, on the other hand, there is poten-tially more flexibility to deal with failures to pay. There can be negotia-tions and extensions of credit while things are worked out. Clearinghouses tend to be very cut and dry. So there are procedural issues that may make them more fragile under certain scenarios. But there is the offsetting benefit of netting out a lot of these contracts. I don't think that it is clear overall, and it probably depends on the sce-nario whether a firm is better off with everything being cleared cen-trally or with a mix, as we have now.

Pirrong: I definitely second Bob's point. Clearinghouses operate under a very metronomic time schedule. In a tightly coupled system, the necessity of paying variation margin on this tight time schedule can be destabilizing. I remember rumors that went around during the crash of 1987 that the CME Group's clearinghouse was late making a payment, which almost started a run on the clearinghouse. So this can be destabilizing.

Although netting is frequently considered to provide one of the benefits of central counterparties by reducing systemic risk, in reality netting just redistributes risk. It is a way of reestablishing priorities and giving derivatives counterparty priorities over other creditors of a firm. By elevating derivatives in priority by clearing through the netting mechanism, somebody is going to be paid more, but somebody else is going to be paid less. Some of those other entities that are going to be paid less might be systemically important. They might be vulnerable to runs as well. Money market funds and the repurchase agreement (repo) market, for example, are vulnerable to runs.

So netting is one example of where people are not thinking systemi-cally about the effects of certain things involved in central counterpar-ties (CCPs). Collateral is another one. The purpose of collateral is to reduce the amount of leverage in derivatives transactions. But market participants have other ways of taking on leverage, and they will sub-stitute these other forms of leverage for the leverage eliminated from derivative transactions through collateralization. Leverage is fungible. We don't really know how fragile the new capital structures are going to be compared to the preclearing-mandate capital structures. When you think about things systemically, you think about how clearing redistributes risk as opposed to how it reduces risk. You think about how people are going to adjust in equilibrium to these mandated changes. It is not evident that we are going to reduce systemic risk. We might reduce it under some scenarios and increase it under others. I get concerned that people will think that we have solved this problem, so now we can walk way and will not have to worry about it anymore.

Edwards: The SEC has adopted a few rules under Title VII that are relevant to this discussion—one on clearing agency standards and one on the procedures for mandatory clearing. In response to Craig, I would note that the clearing agency standards and mandatory clearing determinations address concerns about whether centrally clearing credit default swaps would increase systemic risk. For one, the clearing standards regulation requires clearing agencies that clear credit default swaps to have more financial resources to cover member defaults than is required of other clearing agencies. Clearing agencies that clear credit default swaps have to be able to cover a default by their two largest members, as opposed to just the largest member, as is required for clearing agencies that do not clear credit default swaps.

In addition, Title VII does not say that anything must be mandatorily cleared, and the SEC has some discretion over what must be mandatorily cleared and the terms and conditions that apply to any clearing determination. Congress laid out several factors that the SEC must consider when determining which swaps must be mandatorily cleared. One is the effect on systemic risk. A consideration of a swap for mandatory clearing must consider the effect of a mandatory clearing determination for that swap on systemic risk.

Fishe: In answering a question about how centralized clearing will affect systemic risk, you have to ask, "Relative to what?" to understand what an increase or a decrease in risk means. If the OTC market is the alternative to centralized clearing, counterparty risk is between the two parties and any subsequent novations. In the OTC world, if you have a very adverse consequence in the economy and then defaults, some of those agreements would go into the judicial system and be dealt with that way. And that was a possibility during the recent financial crisis. But as a matter of history, it did not follow that path because of firm and industry appeals for government involvement. As such, we are not dealing with the question of whether an OTC market is the relevant alternative to understand if risk will increase or decrease.

The question is better examined in the context of what we have now, which is mandatory clearing for some products and entities. Thus, the relevant alternative for whether risk has increased or decreased is more likely to compare centralized clearing for a subset of products/entities to centralized clearing for a different subset of products/entities. In addition to answering the risk question in a meaningful setting, this type of comparison helps to sort out the best coverage of the clearing mandate.

One of the concerns for the regulatory agencies with regard to clearing was the way in which the margins were determined. What is the proper method of risk assessment for swap contracts? The best method may differ between swaps and futures because of the different specifications and liquidity in these instruments. Ultimately, the methods used require judgment and extensive data analysis. As the swaps market does not offer much historical data, regulators may naturally be more cautious in the methods employed for swaps.

Note that the method of determining margins for futures markets is made at the point of market. The designated contract market (DCM) makes that determination for the CFTC regulated markets. In the new swap markets, that is not generally the case. The regulatory agency is making the decision about margin requirements. This may make sense initially, but going forward, I think that is a cause for concern because the contract markets may be better positioned to receive relevant information and make and implement timely decisions to lower default risks.

Question: Clearinghouses will now have access to the Fed's discount window. Will this access be used to prop up failing clearinghouses? Is this a tacit admission that they are too big to fail?

McDonald: My sense of the reason for discount window access for clearinghouses was the scenario I mentioned earlier, which is that you have illiquidity for some reason, the clearinghouse has to make payments, and it cannot get access to funds in a timely fashion. The discount window might provide an alternative route for doing that. The question is whether the discount window could also be used to prop up a failing clearinghouse. I don't think that is what the Fed would tell you is envisioned, and I will leave it at that.

Question: A complication in regulating swaps or other derivatives is that they are traded around the world and by U.S. and foreign banks. How should we regulate derivatives trading of U.S. banks abroad?

Fishe: Generally speaking, this question deals with the following issue. A firm has a foreign affiliate—a bank or a financial institution—and it guarantees in some formal way its capital and its contracts. The problem arises because the foreign affiliate engages in swaps trades. The parent company is the U.S. firm that is contractually on the hook for the capital that is at risk. The U.S. regulators are concerned about whether that connection transfers the risk back into the United States and it then becomes part of our systemic risk calculation.

This issue also involves something called *substituted compliance*. This arises when the non-U.S. firm or the foreign affiliate is in a foreign regulatory environment that U.S. regulators acknowledge is sufficiently similar to U.S. regulation that compliance in the foreign setting is sufficient. In other words, even if you have a connection and claim back to U.S.-based capital sources, U.S. regulation may be unnecessary if foreign-based regulation offers similar protection.

There are different methods for establishing whether the foreign regulator creates the same kind of environment for regulation as the U.S. regulator. One method is to compare the rules one by one, ask if the foreign regulator meets each one of those rules, and check them off. Alternatively, there may be groups of rules. If there are five rules on this issue that regulators consider important, then assess the breadth of these rules, and ask whether this overall breadth is roughly met by the foreign regulator's rules. This approach does not require that the foreign regulator have a matching list of rules to achieve substituted compliance. Whichever method is employed, if substituted compliance can be worked out in practice, then the reach of U.S. laws and the definition of a U.S. person is less problematic for the affected markets.

Pirrong: My head spins when I look at all the details, and I just try to think about the economic consequences of trying to regulate an international market. One thing that comes to mind is that any across-border, extraterritorial rule is likely to affect whether the market is or is not fragmented. If the rules are considered to be too intrusive, some foreign counterparties are likely to be unwilling to deal with U.S. persons, and that is going to lead to fragmentation. That will affect the degree of competition, and it also will affect the sort of the topology of connections between firms and the markets. It is difficult to predict the systemic effect of these rules.

McDonald: My head spins also. But I find it interesting to think about this soon after Apple was pilloried before Congress for its international tax dodges. I am curious to know if there are obvious parallels between the problem of tax avoidance in an international context and the problem of derivatives regulation avoidance by operating internationally. In both cases, there is a similar fundamental setup where entities are economically integrated but are not completely integrated with respect to jurisdictional control. So to understand if there are parallels, the question is, "What are the various routes by which you can evade regulations or taxes in one country by undertaking actions in another?" I realize that tax and financial regulations are different, but I would like to understand the extent to which there are parallels.

Question: With futurization, we have seen OTC swaps converted into exchange-traded futures. Why is this happening? Is it likely to continue? Why wasn't this foreseen?

Pirrong: It started in energy, and it was the low-hanging fruit in the sense that most swaps were essentially look-alike swap products that were easy to convert into futures. I am skeptical about whether there will be a similar kind of transition in other parts of the market. The jury is still out. There are the deliverable swap futures, which are one candidate that leads to a similar movement in interest-rate derivatives. But it is still early, and there are some regulatory ambiguities about whether those would be treated as swaps or futures. But a lot of this will depend on how swaps and futures are treated, particularly in terms of margin. So a lot of it depends on choices that regulators make.

As to whether it was a surprise, I think that there are several senators who were certainly surprised because they wrote a letter bashing the CFTC, asking why it was not registering energy traders like Shell and BP as swap dealers. Given the ease of the transition for those firms, it should have been expected. A large fraction of the swaps that they traded were essentially New York Mercantile Exchange (NYMEX) lookalike or CME Group lookalike kinds of products that were easy to convert into futures. It was basically a name change. They were called swaps, they were cleared before, they were traded a certain way, they are going to be cleared now, they are going to be traded the same way, the contract terms stay the same, so we just call them futures now instead of swaps.

McDonald: I don't understand why there is an issue here. Swaps and futurized swaps are just two ways of attaining the same economic outcome. Presumably the clearinghouse is going to margin both of these contracts based on their economic characteristics. So I don't understand why anyone cares what you call it or what nominal form the contract takes, especially since both are exchange traded and cleared.

Pirrong: I think all those things are right. I think that the differences that show up may be platform differences and distinctions between the swap execution facility (SEF) and the designated contract market platforms. The portfolio margining is an innovation in clearinghouses that makes the contract market makers seemingly better off, and that may change the whole landscape for the swap execution departments in the SEFS. The regulation of these things may have to evolve going forward to even the playing field, but that is what it would amount to. But I agree with the points that these are economically the same thing, so it's six of one and half a dozen of the other.

Fishe: I think this is a great example of what happens when you try to have regulators dictate markets. If you set margin requirements higher on one product than another and they are economically equivalent, then people are going to switch to the lower margin product.

Question: If they are economically equivalent, why do we see higher margins on swaps than futures?

Pirrong: I guess one issue is liquidity. They could potentially be different terms in liquidity. But the liquidity characteristics of the products probably would be driven largely by their economic characteristics. If two contracts essentially have the same set of cash flows (for example, they are both cleared), you would think that they would be similar in liquidity as well. It seems that there was sort of a swap-a-phobia built in when Dodd–Frank was conceived, and we essentially have to punish things that are called swaps even though they are economically equivalent to other kinds of products.

Question: A lot of swaps that trade OTC are customized. Will futurized swaps provide enough flexibility for end users?

McDonald: Eris Exchange trades futurized interest-rate e-swaps. They have a flex product that you can basically customize to resemble an over-the-counter interest-rate swap with arbitrary starting dates. (I should offer the disclaimer that I am an outside director of Eris.)

Question: Regulation of swaps is split between the CFTC and the SEC, with the SEC in charge of security-based swaps and the CFTC in charge of all others. The SEC and CFTC proposals for swap execution facilities seem to be different. For example, the CFTC originally required five requests for quotes but has now scaled it back to two. The SEC has not completed its rule, but it appears that there is no minimum number of requests for quotes. How different are the SEC and CFTC rules likely to be?

Edwards: The Dodd–Frank Act says that if a security-based swap is mandatorily cleared, then it is required to trade on an exchange or a swap execution facility unless no exchange or swap execution facility makes the security-based swap available to trade. This requirement raises several questions. What is a swap execution facility? What does it look like? What does it mean for a swap execution facility to make a swap available to trade? If a swap execution facility or exchange decides to allow trading of any mandatorily cleared swap, does this mean that no one can trade any such swaps over the counter?

To address these questions, the SEC's proposal contains flexibility in how a swap execution facility can be structured, which allows an efficient market mechanism for a swap to evolve. For example, for a request for quotation (RFQ) type system, the proposal specifies that the requirement is to have the ability to request a quote from all participants or fewer than all participants, for example, a minimum of one participant. That effectively means there is no minimum. In addition, the proposal considers various other ways that market venues can be structured. For example, a call auction would satisfy the proposed definition. Finally, the academic literature on exchange trading and over-the-counter trading suggests real benefits to over-the-counter trading for blocks. In consideration of the literature, the proposed definition considers the flexibility needed for blocks. This is one area where the regulations that the CFTC adopted are different from the SEC proposal because the CFTC rule excludes blocks from having to be transacted on a swap execution facility.

Question: What are your major concerns about the swap execution facilities?

Pirrong: You mentioned that contracts must trade on a SEF or exchange if they have been made available to trade there. That is peculiar in some ways. If A and B are consenting adults, why shouldn't they be allowed to decide the best way for them to execute their transaction? Why should C, who might have an economic stake in making them trade on a particular platform, have a voice in making that decision? I think that there is going to be a lot of confusion in getting that sorted out.

And also the RFQ thing is a head scratcher as to why a restriction like that should be imposed. It suggests that dealer customers are essentially like victims of some sort of Stockholm syndrome, are tied to their dealers despite the abuse that they have suffered over the years, and have to be made to shop around more. These market participants understand what the tradeoffs are in terms of incurring execution costs and in terms of getting more bids versus information leakage. They should be the ones that are making that decision.

Question: How did the CFTC come up with five requests for quotes? Why did they have a minimum? And why five?

Fishe: I think that the answer goes back to a previous characteristic of swap markets. The previous market was largely a voice broker type of market. You could call around for quotes, but you incurred search costs, so you might have been less inclined to seek competitive offers. Although the current rules still allow a voice market, there is a clause about transmitting the trade information in the most technologically practical manner, so that might be a restriction at some point on voice brokerage but not now. I think that regulators wanted more competition than was found in the voice brokerage market, so the multiple-quotes requirement was a solution to the perceived need for more competition. The RFQ requirement is the method of generating that competition. Note that in the platforms that include order books, there will also be competition if somebody wants to provide that liquidity in a standing manner. Because the disruptive trading rule says you cannot repeatedly violate bids and offers, orders on these order books will have some type of implied precedence under the law.

Audience (Spatt): As an outsider, the rule of five requests for quotation is one of the rules that I found most curious. My recollection of this was that when Chairman Gensler was pressed on this at one of the hearings at the Senate Banking Committee two years ago, he said, "We got this from the futures markets, and in the futures markets, there is, in effect, an infinite number." I thought that suggested how the CFTC was thinking about some of these issues. They were trying to make the swaps market kind of like futures.

Question: We will now see real-time price dissemination for small swap trades. How will block trades be handled?

Edwards: In Title VII, Congress gave the SEC and CFTC the ability to define what a block trade is in their respective markets and to specify the appropriate time delay for reporting block trades to the public. The idea behind the delay is that if a dealer facilitates a block trade and therefore takes on a big position, then the rest of the market will not see it right away. Real-time price and size dissemination could increase the costs to dealers of hedging or trading out of that position. The increased costs to dealers could result in higher costs and lower liquidity to others.

The regulations in the corporate bond market consider this issue, apply caps on the disseminated trade size, but do not delay the dissemination. Yet the evidence from the corporate bond market indicates that prompt price dissemination results in lower transaction costs for large transactions. We don't necessarily know if the evidence from the corporate bond market is going to apply directly because of differences between corporate bond and CDS markets. The bottom line is that the effect of price dissemination could be different for CDS than it was for corporate bonds.

Fishe: This is a difficult question to answer because it has several parts. There is mostly real-time reporting and transparency, except when blocks are involved, which is not infrequent in swaps markets. Then it is not just a block rule that delays reporting, but there is a cap rule, too, where you are not really reporting the actual size of the trade. Because of the reporting delay, the transparency issue focuses on the information in the real-time trade flow; that is, we are not going to put the trade in the trade flow at the time it occurs but are going to take it out from real-time reporting and place it back in the trade flow thirty minutes later. The question is, "How much distortion does the reporting delay create?" One approach to answering that question is to examine what inferences the market is not able to make for this thirty-minute period of time. In other words, how significantly biased are those inferences as a result of not having this transaction in the trade flow? Statistical analysis can then give you answers to how the knowledge in the market is affected by reporting delays. And that leads to an understanding of where you might want to place your block sizes to reduce these distortions. In effect, you have limited transparency but for economically efficient reasons.

Now the cap rule has a similar effect, but it addresses Congress's intent to ensure anonymity in these markets. At a high notional level, you might be able to infer the party behind the swap trade based on other reporting requirements, such as the footnotes in quarterly reports. The cap rule then is motivated by the goal of keeping participants' trades anonymous.

Question: How are blocks defined?

Fishe: The rule starts out at 50 percent of the notional trade distribution. That means that the block size will be set so that 50 percent of the notional amount of the trades will not be blocks. It will transition to a 67 percent notional rule to expose more trades to the market in real time, but there is a one-year examination period built into the rule so that CFTC may assess the data to gain confidence in this cutoff. If some swaps trade in very liquid markets, then there may be data that support more rapid, broader reporting by increasing the block size. Alternatively, if there is a lot of clustering in these markets, then that will affect where the block cutoff is set going forward. If liquidity concentrates on specific notional values, then dealers may build hedges to the blocks from these liquidity points, which could then increase the coverage of what is reported in real time.

Question: One CFTC commissioner recently complained that the trade reporting was producing too much data in too many fields. Are they overwhelmed? And how is the data quality?

Fishe: The CFTC, which is the smaller agency, has already finalized two-thirds of its rules, more than any other regulator, so it has not been overwhelmed. The swap data have over five hundred fields for information reporting, which may certainly be challenging, but *overwhelming* is not the right word. You have to have sensible questions to ask of the data and then use sensible analyses, and the information typically will provide good answers for your questions.

Edwards: The swap data repository proposal would impose requirements aimed at promoting the accuracy and integrity of the data, and the benefits mentioned in the proposing release signal an expectation that the data from SDRs will improve on data available to the SEC at the time of the release. Like any other dataset, our current data on credit default swaps require a lot of cleaning. In addition, we currently don't have a lot of data on total return swaps. In addition, the proposal for swap data repositories was not prescriptive. It would permit access to the same information SEC staff has access to now, though it will allow for changes in the future.

Question: In 2011, the D.C. Circuit Court shot down the SEC's proxy access rule because of the lack of careful cost-benefit analysis. What are the SEC and the CFTC doing to improve their cost-benefit analysis of these rules?

Edwards: On March 16, 2012, the Division of Risk, Strategy, and Financial Innovation, along with the SEC's Office of the General Counsel, issued "Current Guidance on Economic Analysis in SEC Rulemakings," which created written guidelines on what rule writers and economists need to consider and to include in a rule release. The "Current Guidance" has been very helpful. It is not a checklist. It is very flexible and recognizes that not everything mentioned in the document is appropriate for every rule. Indeed, it gives staff ideas to consider as they are going through the process of doing an economic analysis for rulemaking. The guidance is also useful for guiding the staff in the right direction, especially in internal discussions regarding the relevant content of a particular economic analysis.

Pirrong: I want to bring up some things in the context of cost-benefit analysis. First, cost-benefit analysis is likely to be one of the grounds on which rules will be challenged. Second, there is still a tremendous amount of uncertainty as to how the courts are going to treat the CFTC's cost-benefit analysis. For example, the position limit rule was challenged on cost-benefit grounds, but the judge did not rule on that basis. Finally, I would say I don't know if it would be possible to do a cost-benefit analysis right. I don't know whether you could do it at all. For example, look at the position limit rule. First of all, what would the effect of the rule be? Its motivation was to prevent excessive fluctuations in prices. Can we estimate what the effect will be? What cost is associated with excessive fluctuations in prices? And look at the other side. People say, "If you constrain positions, that might reduce the amount of speculative risk-bearing capacity, that might reduce liquidity, and so on." How do you quantify those sorts of things? I think many of the big impacts of these kinds of rules present tremendous challenges to any sort of analysis.

Audience: In regard to the SEC's economic analysis, I'll follow on Amy's comment to say that there has been a lot of public attention recently on the effectiveness of the SEC's recent guidance in this area, and so I would encourage people to look at that if they have further interest. Law professors and other outside groups have looked over the SEC's recent economic analyses in rulemakings and noted that they feel there has been an improvement since the SEC's "Current Guidance on Economic Analyses in SEC Rulemaking" was issued. And after Title VII's cross-border economic analysis was released, one article noted not only the breadth of the economic analysis but also the transparency of the economic effects.

Question: I appreciate the comments from Bob and Craig on the fact that Dodd–Frank may not have been their particular choice for how to address problems in the derivatives market. Given that the statute is already in place but there are still items left to the regulator's discretion, what do they think are the one or two most important pieces to get right?

Pirrong: One thing that comes to mind is anything having to do with margins relating to clear derivatives. In terms of the systemic issue, I think that is important and needs a lot of careful thought.

McDonald: I guess the things that trouble me most are the sorts of rules that dictate to the market what it ought to be doing. For example, with this question about SEFs versus exchanges, why set a different margin for a swap execution facility? I would hope to see more flexible responses to what the market's telling you about how these things are going.

Question: Let me put an idea out there and see if you can react to it. It seems to me that the swap execution facilities and the idea of putting things on organized exchanges will try to bring the CDS market up to somewhere close to where the stock market was before the 1987 stock market crashed—in other words, multiple decades or a generation behind where it should be. And it doesn't create a centralized market for exchanging things, and it doesn't allow customers to place limit orders that are respected. And if that were mandated, part of the market—the black market—would probably gradually go away, and you would get electronic interfaces and an entirely different market. So thinking about the fact that we are going to be maybe where the markets were before the 1987 crash, it is interesting to use the 1987 crash as an example of what might happen with regard to systemic risk if something really gets screwed up. In the 1987 crash, the NASDAQ dealers didn't answer their phones, and nobody really knew where the market was. That meant that the specialists and even the securities firms did not know whether they were solvent, and the SEC never knew. It was not clear if the SEC could determine whether they were solvent a couple of days after the stock market crash. So having transparent trading is instrumental in being able to measure solvency, and being able to measure solvency is important for systemic risk.

Edwards: The data that we get from the Trade Information Warehouse include positions in addition to transactions. This allows SEC staff to track market participants' exposures in CDS efficiently by counterparty and by reference entity.

Question: Product innovation by the CME Group and the Intercontinental Exchange (ICE) seems to be a step or two ahead of Dodd–Frank and regulatory reform. ICE is launching its CDS index futures soon. It is going to be clearing swaptions, CME's going to be clearing swaptions at some point this year, and LCH in 2014. What role should regulators play in product innovation at self-regulating organizations (SROs) like ICE and CME, especially in light of the futurization they seemed to have missed?

Edwards: I can comment on what the SEC does with respect to new products today. Exchanges have rules regarding their listing standards, and certain potential innovative products are consistent with those listing standards and some are not. If an exchange wants to offer a new product that is not consistent with its listing standards, then the exchange would file a proposal with the SEC to amend its listing standards. The proposal would go out for public comment. The SEC considers that public comment and the consistency of the amendments with the Exchange Act and SEC regulations in deciding whether to approve the amended listing standards. There is an equivalent requirement of public notice and comment for OTC security-based swap products that are not traded on an exchange or SEF but are proposed to be cleared by a registered security-based swap clearing agency.

Fishe: The CFTC is a principles-based agency with twenty-two or twenty-three core principles. That is what will guide a discussion of innovation by ICE and the CME.

Note

1. The Securities and Exchange Commission, as a matter of policy, disclaims responsibility for any private publication or statement by any of its employees. The views expressed herein are those of the speaker and do not necessarily reflect the views of the commission or of the speaker's colleagues on the staff of the commission.

References

Bank for International Settlements. 2013. Statistical Release: OTC Derivatives Statistics at end-June 2013. Monetary and Economic Department, November. Available at http://www.bis.org/publ/otc_hy1311.pdf.

11 Mortgage Reform under the Dodd–Frank Act

Mark A. Calabria

Many, if not most, accounts of the financial crisis of 2008 include a prominent role for the U.S. residential mortgage market. Although other U.S. property markets, such as commercial and retail, exhibited similar boom-and-bust patterns, the elevated level of defaults and associated costs borne by the taxpayer have brought a particular emphasis on American single-family mortgage finance policies. It should be of little surprise that the Dodd–Frank Wall Street Reform and Consumer Protection Act of 2010 contains multiple provisions related to mortgage finance. This chapter offers a review of those provisions, followed by an evaluation of their likely effect and effectiveness.

Significant Mortgage Provisions

Dodd–Frank's sixteen titles contain a number of provisions that affect the mortgage market. The financial services law firm Davis Polk estimates that Dodd–Frank will require forty-nine separate rule makings in the area of mortgage reform alone. Of particular importance are those found in Titles IX, X, and XIV. These three titles most directly affect the mortgage market and are the focus of this chapter.

Many other provisions indirectly affect the mortgage market. For example, the financial stability provisions of Title I could dramatically affect competition in the mortgage market. Before divesting its depository subsidiary, MetLife had established a business plan to become a top five national mortgage originator. To avoid a systemic designation under Dodd–Frank's Title I, MetLife abandoned those plans. MetLife's abandonment of the mortgage market has left mortgage origination less competitive than it would be otherwise. However, these provisions are outside the scope of this review. In general, this chapter focuses on the more direct effects.

Skin in the Game

One of the more interesting approaches to risk management is section 941's "Regulation of Credit Risk Retention," which prohibits the issuance of any asset-backed security under the Securities Exchange Act of 1934 (the 1934 act) unless the issuer retains "not less than 5 percent of the credit risk for any asset that is not a qualified residential mortgage" or meets the definition of a qualified residential mortgage (QRM) that is to be determined by regulations jointed issued by the federal financial regulators, along with the Department of Housing and Urban Development (HUD) and the Securities and Exchange Commission (SEC). Although section 941's risk-retention requirement applies to any asset-backed security (ABS) issued under the 1934 act, Dodd–Frank gives broad discretion to the SEC to make determinations for ABSs that do not contain residential mortgages.

Unlike other classes of ABSs, section 941, which adds a new section 15G to the 1934 act, establishes a number of statutory criteria to guide the regulatory QRM definition. These statutory requirements include documentation of the borrower's financial resources, debt-to-income standards, mitigation of payment shock for adjustable-rate products, consideration of other credit enhancements, and the restriction of loan terms that have been demonstrated to exhibit a higher risk of borrower default.

Dodd–Frank exempts Federal Housing Administration (FHA), Veterans Administration, Rural Housing Service, and Farm Credit loans from the risk-retention requirements. Regulators have discretion to extend that exemption to loans that are securitized by the Federal National Mortgage Association (Fannie Mae) or the Federal Home Loan Mortgage Corporation (Freddie Mac). Although initial versions of the QRM have exempted Fannie Mae and Freddie Mac loans, as long as those entities are in conservatorship, the Federal Housing Finance Agency has chosen to restrict Fannie Mae and Freddie Mac to the purchase of QRM-compliant mortgages. A concern is that such exemptions would further entrench the federal government's current dominant role in the mortgage market, leaving taxpayers vulnerable to additional losses and distorting the pricing and allocation of risk within the broader mortgage market.

By construction, mortgages held in portfolio would be exempt from the QRM requirements. An open question is to what extent the QRM requirements would drive even loans held in portfolio, as the option to later sell those loans into the secondary market could influence initial origination decisions. Even during the height of the housing boom in 2006, a significant portion (approximately a fifth) of both subprime and conforming loans was not securitized. Among jumbo mortgages, the percentage securitized first broke 50 percent in 2007 and declined in 2008 and 2009 to the single digits.

An initial QRM proposed rule was issued by regulators on April 29, 2011. In this initial rule, regulators fleshed out a number of characteristics "that have been demonstrated to exhibit a higher risk of borrower default." The most controversial of these has been a minimum 20 percent required downpayment. There is little, if any debate, over the contribution of lower downpayments to default behavior, but comments submitted to the regulators from financial firms and advocacy groups claim that such a requirement would dramatically reduce mortgage access to low-income and minority households. Commentators have also observed that Dodd–Frank's section 941 is silent on the issue of downpayment. In response, regulators issued a new proposed rule on August 28, 2013, that solicits comments on either a no-downpayment requirement or a higher 30 percent requirement, dropping the original 20 percent requirement. It is widely expected that commentators will support the elimination of any downpayment requirement and that regulators will accordingly offer a final rule with no limitations on loan to value.

Also of interest are the QRM's requirements for debt-to-income ratios. The initial rule sets a maximum front-end ratio of 28 percent and a back-end ratio of 36 percent, which are consistent with the ratios generally observed in the conventional mortgage market although stricter than those observed in FHA.

The final QRM rule will possess the potential to dramatically shape the characteristics of which loans may or may not be sold into the public secondary markets. Because the QRM is also an amendment to the 1934 act, mortgage-backed security (MBS) issues that are later determined to be non-QRM would subject the issuer to liability under SEC rule 10b-5. Given the subjectivity in some of the documentation requirements under QRM and potential rule 10b-5 liability, lenders can expect increased documentation and verification costs.

Dodd–Frank and Predatory Lending

One narrative of the financial crisis attributes the increase in mortgage defaults to predatory lending. Dodd–Frank's attempt to address predatory lending is contained in Title XIV, Mortgage Reform and

Anti-Predatory Lending Act. Despite the title, no definition of *predatory lending* is contained in Title XIV, which is a collection of prohibitions and restrictions. The major substantive provisions of Title XIV are structured as amendments to the Truth in Lending Act of 1968. Title XIV somewhat mirrors the anti–predatory lending statutes passed in North Carolina beginning in 1999.

A theme of mortgage reform before Dodd–Frank was the focus on mortgage brokers versus lenders. Because of their rise from the ashes of the savings and loan crisis of the 1980s, mortgage brokers grew to be a significant share of mortgage originations. For a variety of reasons, including their lack of established reputation and focus on performance-based compensation, brokers were often assigned responsibility for poor underwriting decisions made in the years leading to the crisis. Congress reacted to such concerns in 2008 by including the Secure and Fair Enforcement for Mortgage Licensing Act (SAFE Act) as Title V of the Housing and Economic Recovery Act of 2008.

Dodd–Frank's section 1401 expands the definition of *mortgage originator* and adds new requirements for persons falling under such definition. A *mortgage originator* under section 1401 is a person "who, for direct or indirect compensation or gain, or in the expectation of direct or indirect compensation or gain—(i) takes a residential mortgage loan application; (ii) assists a consumer in obtaining or applying to obtain a residential mortgage loan; or (iii) offers or negotiates terms of a residential mortgage loan." Although the act contains exceptions to this definition, all mortgage brokers and many bank employees (other than administrative and clerical) will be considered mortgage originators and hence subject to both enforcement and litigation risk.

After a person is considered to be a mortgage originator, a variety of duties and restrictions apply, including the requirement to be qualified and licensed under the SAFE Act. Dodd–Frank also prohibits the compensation of originators from varying based on the terms of the loans, other than based on the principal amount. Originators may receive compensation from a party other than the borrower only in instances where the borrower pays nothing to the originator and pays no upfront fees or points. Originators can, however, continue to be compensated on the volume of loans closed. The intent of these restrictions is to limit the incentive of originators to place borrowers in higher-cost loans.

A recurring theme in Dodd–Frank's mortgage reforms is the assumption that many borrowers were simply in the wrong loan. Along this line of thinking, mortgage originators are prohibited from steering borrowers toward loans under which the borrower lacks a reasonable ability to pay or that have certain features (see Agarwal and Evanoff 2013). Originators are also prohibited from mischaracterizing either the credit history of the borrower or their loan options. The intent here reflects a belief that many prime borrowers were steered into subprime products. In general, originators placing borrowers into qualified mortgages (QM) will be protected from enforcement and liability.

On January 10, 2013, the Consumer Financial Protection Bureau (CFPB) issued final rules implementing Dodd–Frank's Title XIV, subtitle B, Minimum Standards for Mortgages (more commonly known as the Qualified Mortgage Rule) (table 11.1). Because the QM Rule amends the Truth in Lending Act, violations of the QM Rule that fall outside its safe harbor subject lenders to significant liability. Delinquent borrowers can also use violations of the QM Rule as a defense to foreclosure proceedings.

Table 11.1
Nine qualified mortgage (QM) criteria specified in the Dodd–Frank Act

1. Regular periodic payments do not result in an increase in the principal balance or result in a deferral of the repayment of principal (that is, the mortgage cannot have a negative amortization feature or interest-only period).

2. The loan term does not exceed thirty years. Rule makers may extend loan terms beyond thirty years for certain locales, such as high-cost areas.

3. Except for balloon loans under specified circumstances, the mortgage does not include balloon payments.

4. Borrower income and financial resources are verified and documented.

5. The loans comply with guidelines or regulations established by the Federal Reserve Board relating to ratios of total monthly debt to monthly income or alternative measures of ability to pay regular expenses after paying monthly debt.

6. A fixed-rate loan is underwritten based on a fully amortizing payment schedule that takes into account applicable taxes, insurance, and assessments.

7. An adjustable-rate mortgage is underwritten based on the maximum rate permitted during the first five years and on a fully amortizing payment schedule that takes into account applicable taxes, insurance, and assessments.

8. Total points and fees payable in connection with loan do not exceed 3 percent of the total loan amount.

9. A reverse mortgage meets qualified mortgage standards as set by the Federal Reserve Board.

Source: Dodd–Frank Wall Street Reform and Consumer Protection Act of 2010, Title XIV, Mortgage Reform and Anti-Predatory Lending Act, subtitle B, Minimum Standards for Mortgages.

The heart of the QM standards are found in section 1411's "ability to repay" requirements. Section 1411 prohibits lenders from a making residential mortgage unless the lender makes a good-faith determination that the borrower has a reasonable ability to repay the loan. Although section 1411 does provide some guidance on what constitutes a good-faith determination and what is reasonable, most details are left to the CFPB. Even under the currently proposed ability-to-repay rule, considerable discretion remains in interpreting these terms. Due to concerns over the lack of clarity in the ability-to-repay standard, Dodd–Frank's section 1412 allows for the creation of a safe harbor from liability if lenders meet the definition of a qualified mortgage. It is in minimizing liability risk that lenders will attempt to meet the standards for a qualified mortgage.

Lender compliance with the ability-to-repay requirements is likely to be both costly and extensive. What data are to be collected? How are that data audited? How long are they stored? How does the originator create a clear audit trail that can be shared and verified by both servicers and investors? These are difficult and subjective questions where the cost of being wrong will be significant. Ultimately, these compliance costs will be passed along to borrowers, mostly likely in the form of higher rate spreads.

Similar to the QRM, the statutory restrictions on QM ban certain mortgage features, such as interest only, balloon payments, and negative amortization. Section 1412 also limits points and fees to no more than 3 percent of the loan amount. For adjustable-rate mortgages (ARMs), section 1412 requires loans to be underwritten at the maximum possible rate during the first five years of the loan. Loan terms may not exceed thirty years. Income and financial resources must be fully documented. The CFPB is to establish maximum debt-to-income ratios for qualified mortgages as well.

Dodd–Frank's Title XIV contains additional prohibitions that go beyond its ability-to-repay requirements. Section 1414 severely limits the use of prepayment penalties, prohibiting them for non-QM loans and capping their amount and duration for QM loans. Despite the increased liability from Title XIV or perhaps because of it, lenders are prohibited from requiring mandatory arbitration for all residential mortgages. Even if such did not increase liability costs, it is likely to increase the variance of liability costs (see Hurwitz 2011). Section 1414 also requires lenders to make borrowers aware of their ability to "walk away" in antideficiency states. Section 1417 increases civil money penalties under the Truth in Lending Act, of which both QM and HOEPA are part.

Title X of Dodd–Frank creates the Consumer Financial Protection Bureau (CFPB). Enforcement and implementation of most preexisting mortgage regulation (including that under the Truth in Lending Act, the SAFE Act, and the Real Estate Settlement Procedures Act) transfers to the CFPB. This new agency is given considerable authority to rewrite existing rules and to police unfair and deceptive practices in the mortgage market. Dodd–Frank also adds a new category of abusive practices, yet to be defined by the CFPB. HUD and the Federal Reserve once were the primary federal regulators in the area of mortgage finance, but CFPB will now take their place. There is a strong expectation that CFPB will be a more aggressive regulator than was either HUD or the Federal Reserve.

Impact of Dodd–Frank on Mortgage Availability

A goal of the Dodd–Frank Act is to eliminate certain products and practices from the mortgage market. So at a basic level, the choices facing mortgage borrowers will be reduced. The difficult question is in gauging how much.

At least three independent attempts have been made to estimate the effects of QRM and QM on mortgage availability. These three analyses were performed by the U.S. Government Accountability Office (GAO) (U.S. Government Accountability Office 2011), the Federal Housing Finance Agency (FHFA) (U.S. Federal Housing Finance Agency 2011), and the private firm CoreLogic (Khater 2013). The GAO's analysis is based mostly on CoreLogic data, so (unsurprisingly) their conclusions are similar. The FHFA's analysis is based on its collection of Fannie Mae and Freddie Mac mortgage data. None of these studies attempts to incorporate behavioral changes, and they therefore are likely to overestimate the effect of the QRM/QM rules. These studies also do not incorporate the effect of house-price changes. If, for instance, the QRM/ QM reduces the demand for housing, then housing prices should fall, which would offset the reduced demand. The effects of the QRM/QM, in theory, are ambiguous as to net effect on homeownership rates.

The three studies yield similar conclusions about the effects of QRM. The most restrictive provision of the proposed QRM rule would be the ceiling on allowable debt-to-income ratios. The initial proposal included a cap of debt to income of 28 percent for the front-end ratio and 36 percent for the back-end ratio. At the time of this writing, press reports indicate a loosening of this standard. The final QRM rule is likely to have a back-end ratio of either 41 or 42 percent, which is consistent with the requirements under FHA.

Figure 11.1, reproduced from GAO's analysis, shows the proportion of prime, near-prime, and government-insured mortgages by over or under a 41 percent debt-to-income ratio. At one extreme, almost 40 percent of these mortgages displayed debt-to-income ratios above 41 percent in 2007 and 2008. In a more "normal" market environment of, say, 2004, the percentage was just under 30 percent. Many borrowers, however, are likely to have reported only sufficient income to meet the loan requirements, and other borrowers might have overreported income. Either would change the magnitude of this effect. A reasonable approximation is somewhere around 25 percent of mortgages will be

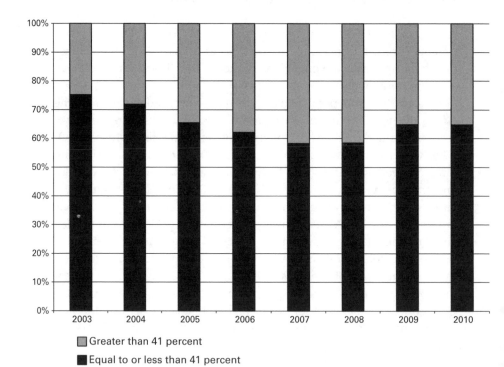

☐ Greater than 41 percent

■ Equal to or less than 41 percent

Figure 11.1
Percentage of subprime loans with debt-to-income ratios above 41 percent.
Source: U.S. Government Accountability Office analysis of CoreLogic data (GAO 2011).

non-QRM compliant due to the debt-to-income restrictions. Dodd–Frank's section 941 does not require a specific debt-to-income ratio, but it does require a debt-to-income test, leaving regulators little room to ignore this constraint.

Previous GAO analysis has indicated that the percentage of subprime loans with a debt-to-income ratio in excess of 41 ranged between 47.1 percent in 2000 to 59.3 percent in 2007. This will likely be the most significant effect of the final QRM rule—a large reduction in the percentage of subprime loans that are QRM eligible due to limitations on debt-to-income ratios. These loans can still be placed into a mortgage-backed security (MBS) as long as there is sufficient risk retention. Non-QRM loans can also be held on portfolio.

Several QRM restrictions are likely to have modest effects because their prevalence in the mortgage market was generally low. Both the proposed QM and QRM rules ban negative amortization features, yet according to GAO's analysis "almost 100 percent of [subprime] mortgage originations from 2001 to 2007 did not have negative amortization features." Within the prime market, the percentage with negative amortization features peaked in 2005 at 9 percent. The average between 2001 and 2010 was closer to 1 percent. The disappearance of negative amortization mortgages will not be noticed by the vast majority of participants in the mortgage market. To the extent that a small number of borrowers used negative amortization products to smooth income volatility, these households will be left worse off under Dodd–Frank's restrictions on negative amortization. If we return to the high levels of inflation that were witnessed in the 1970s, certain products (such as negative amortization) that gained acceptance as a reaction to high levels of inflation may return. QRM could pose an obstacle to the return of products geared toward managing high levels of inflation.

Dodd–Frank also places limitations on mortgages with terms in excess of thirty years. In the prime and near-prime markets, essentially 100 percent of mortgages were under a thirty-year term until about 2005, where longer than thirty-year mortgages grew slowly to 4 percent of the market in 2007 before disappearing by 2009. Subprime followed a more unusual situation, with nearly 100 percent of subprime being under thirty years until 2005 and 2006, when the share over thirty years peaked at 15 percent of the subprime market. Because longer loan terms allow borrowers to make higher house-price bids while maintaining a constant monthly payment, the growth in this market segment likely reflected a last-ditch attempt by some subprime borrowers to purchase before the boom was over. Some amount of these loans may have reflected an attempt to refinance into lower monthly payments. Given the relatively small share of mortgages with durations over thirty years, this Dodd–Frank restriction will also likely be minor. It may also signal the end of or at least a long pause in the decades-long push to extend maturity as an avenue for increasing affordability. There is some irony that the federal government historically has led the charge to extend maturity and now is taking the position that mortgage maturities should be no more than thirty years.

Another loan feature that is restricted by Dodd–Frank is the use of balloon payments, where the mortgage does not fully amortize over its term but leaves a balance due on maturity. Final balloon payments are multiples of the monthly payment. Despite the prevalence of balloon loans before the New Deal mortgage reforms of the 1930s, these products were rare, even during the height of the recent boom. GAO reports that almost 100 percent of prime, near-prime, and government-insured mortgages lacked any balloon features between 2001 and 2010. Among subprime loans, balloon features were also rare, close to zero until 2005 and growing to about 10 percent of subprime loans in 2007, after which they largely disappeared from the subprime market. As with long-maturity mortgages, balloon payments appeared as last-ditch efforts to get into the booming housing market. Their disappearance could constrain affordability during a boom, which is not necessarily a bad thing, but Dodd–Frank balloon restrictions are likely to have an insignificant effect on the mortgage market.

Both the QM and QRM place restrictions on borrower documentation, particularly in the area of income. A common concern is that no- or low-documentation loans lead to greater levels of fraud and higher losses in the mortgage market than would have occurred otherwise. Whereas the QRM is an obstacle for securitization, the QM standards come with substantial and uncertain liability, so although there is likely to be a market for non-QRM loans, non-QM loans will become rare. Accordingly, the option of simply holding no- or low-documentation loans on portfolio is not likely to be an attractive option for lenders. By the GAO's estimates, the percentage of subprime loans lacking full documentation ranged from 40 percent in 2006 to 20 percent in 2001. A similar but smaller trend was witnessed among prime loans, where those lacking full documentation ranged from around 20 percent in 2006 to almost zero in the early 2000s. The documentation requirements under QM/QRM are likely to affect most self-employed borrowers. Because there are over 15 million self-employed individuals in the

United States, these restrictions could be significant. Most lenders have significant experience documenting loans for the self-employed, so the extent to which these requirements reduce mortgage availability remains open. Most lenders are likely to reduce their risk on self-employed mortgages by requiring higher downpayments and credit scores. Self-employed borrowers with subprime credit are likely to see the greatest reduction in mortgage availability under Dodd–Frank's documentation requirements.

The most controversial element of the proposed QRM rule is the minimum downpayment requirement. As proposed, for a mortgage to be QRM compliant would require a minimum downpayment of 20 percent for home purchase, 25 percent for a standard refinance, and 30 percent for a cash-out refinance. There are no downpayment requirements for the proposed QM rule, and the downpayment requirements proposed under QRM are within the discretion of regulators and not required by the statutory language of Dodd–Frank.

The effect of a minimum downpayment requirement is perhaps the hardest to measure of the Dodd–Frank restrictions. The GAO estimates that 22 percent of mortgages originated in 2006 had a loan-to-value (LTV) ratio in excess of 80 percent. For the same cohort, 11 percent had a LTV in excess of 90 percent. These figures tell us only how much of a downpayment borrowers made, not how much they could have made. Without extensive data on borrower wealth, it is hard to gauge if borrowers could have afforded increased downpayment requirements. Ellen Wilson and Robert Callis (2013), using the Survey of Income and Program Participation, estimate that moving from a zero to 5 percent downpayment would eliminate 1.3 percent of renters from being able to purchase a "modestly priced" home. A 20 percent downpayment would have a larger effect. Given the FHA's exemption from the QRM rule, borrowers should still seek a low-downpayment alternative via FHA, and lenders could either hold low-downpayment loans on portfolio or meet the required risk-retention levels of the QRM rule. Increased downpayment requirements could also be offset with house-price declines. Juan Carlos Hatchondo, Leonardo Martinez, and Juan Sanchez (2011) estimate that in the absence of house-price declines, a 15 percent downpayment requirement would reduce homeownership rates by only 0.2 percentage points and that a house-price reduction of 0.7 percent would result in no decline in homeownership rates.

Loans that do not meet the QRM requirements can still be securitized, with the caveat that the issuers must retain not less than 5 percent of the credit risk of the securitized asset pool. Issuers are also prohibited from hedging or otherwise transferring this risk. The proposed QRM rule, which was reissued for comment on August 28, 2013, offers a number of options for determining the 5 percent retention. The most obvious would be a 5 percent "first loss," where the issuer bears the first 5 percent of loss. Other options include a 5 percent prorated share of total losses, in which issuers retained 5 percent of each class of ABS under the transaction, or a so-called vertical risk retention. Only in cases of 100 percent loss would such equal the 5 percent first-loss framework. Questions have also been raised as to whether risk retention should be calculated on a fair-value basis. Although regulators could ultimately go above 5 percent retention, such appears unlikely. Ultimately, the greater risk from the QRM is likely to be liability under the securities laws rather than the retention of a sliver of credit risk.

Press reports at the time of the August 2013 reissue indicate that regulators may abandon any downpayment requirement for the QRM and harmonize the QRM rule to mirror the QM. Dodd–Frank requires regulators to establish a QRM standard that is "no broader" than the QM standard. There is some question as to whether "broader" means that the set of QRM complaint loans is greater or smaller than the set of QM-compliant loans. At least one legal expert (Natter 2012) has argued that "broader" eliminates the ability of regulators "to have a more inclusive definition of QRM" than of QM. In all likelihood, regulators will solve this issue by having a QRM rule and a QM rule that are largely mirrors in terms of loans eligible. Such would result in having no minimum downpayment requirements.

Effect of Dodd–Frank on Mortgage Default

The Dodd–Frank Act is a response to the theory that bad mortgage lending and lenders drove borrowers into default, which ultimately drove the housing market into decline, leading to a fall in the value of mortgage-backed securities, resulting in a panic among the holders of mortgage-backed securities. Setting aside that national house prices reached an inflection point almost a year before the inflection point in defaults, one measure of the effectiveness of Dodd–Frank's mortgage rules will be the extent that it reduces mortgage defaults.

Table 11.2 reproduces select estimates from GAO's analysis of the marginal effect on default probabilities of a standard deviation increase in the variable in question. In most cases, the measure is a dummy variable, yielding the effect on default probabilities of change in the dummy. Effects are presented for fixed-rate, long-term ARM and hybrid ARM, all estimates for non-prime purchase loans. Similar effects (not reported) are found for refinancings.

Despite having the largest effect on the number of loans, the proposed QM/QRM restrictions on debt-to-income ratios appear to have modest effects on projected defaults. The presence of a debt-to-income ratio in excess of 41 percent increases the probability of default by 0.25, 0.08, and 0.59 for fixed-rate mortgages, long-term ARMs, and hybrid ARMs, respectively. According to GAO's analysis, reducing the prevalence of mortgages with a debt-to-income ratio in excess of 41 will have barely noticeable effects (although statistically significant in all cases).

Restrictions on low- or no-documentation loans do appear to have noticeable effects on defaults in the subprime market. If all but full-documentation loans were used, default probabilities (according to GAO's analysis) would fall by -1.08, -1.17, and -1.24 percentage points for fixed-rate mortgages, long-term ARMs, and hybrid ARMs, respectively.

Although the finality of the QRM's downpayment requirements is in question, GAO's default analysis predicts substantial declines in

Table 11.2
Marginal effect on default probability

	Nonprime purchase mortgage		
	Fixed	Long-term ARM	Hybrid ARM
Loan amount	1.82	1.59	5.11
HPA: first year	-2.05	-2.35	-8.51
HPA: second year	1.05	1.26	3.45
Difference:			
DTI > 41%	0.25	0.08	0.59
Full documentation	-1.08	-1.17	-1.24
CLTV < 80	-0.21	-0.92	-2.42
CLTV 80 to 90	-0.09	-0.39	-1.36
CLTV 90 to 100	0.56	0.56	-0.37
CLTV ≥ 100	1.64	1.18	1.88

Notes: Marginal effect from one standard deviation increase in mean. HPA: House price appreciation. DTI: Debt to income. CLTV: Combined loan to value.

Source: U.S. Government Accountability Office (2010).

defaults from reductions in loan-to-value ratios. For fixed-rate nonprime purchase loans, moving from a loan-to-value ratio of 100 to under 80 percent reduces projected default probabilities by over 3 percentage points. For hybrid nonprime ARMs, the reduction in projected default probabilities is just over 6 percentage points. Coupled with full documentation and a loan-to-value ratio of under 80 percent, one could eliminate over 70 percent of the standardized default risk among hybrid nonprime ARMs. CoreLogic estimates that the proposed QM and QRM rules would "remove 60 percent of loans [and] more than 90 percent of the risk." Again, CoreLogic does not incorporate behavioral changes and does not calculate the effect on portfolio-held loans.

Patrick Bajari, Sean Chu, and Minjung Park (2010) arrive at similar conclusions when examining the drivers of default among subprime mortgages, with the exception of finding a larger effect from debt-to-income ratios than does GAO.

The approach of Dodd–Frank's mortgage provisions is to focus on loan characteristics, largely ignoring borrower characteristics or housing-market effects. For instance, QM/QRM places no restrictions on borrower credit, other than verification. Bajari, Chu, and Park (2010) find that the largest effects on subprime defaults come from borrower credit, as measured by FICO credit score. Increasing borrower FICO by one standard deviation (or about 74 points) decreases default probability by around seven times as much as switching from an ARM to fixed rate. A 74 point increase in FICO also has over twice the effect of moving from a no- or low-documentation to a full-documentation loan. Both GAO and Bajari, Chu, and Park (2010) also find that the effect of house-price changes to be magnitudes higher than the provisions of the QM/QRM rule.

If the downpayment requirements of the proposed QRM rule are abandoned, the remaining changes are likely to have modest effects on default probabilities. The biggest effect would be from the full-documentation requirements and the cap on debt to income. These two changes combined, however, are projected to lower default probabilities by around 1 percentage point.

Morris M. Kleiner and Richard M. Todd (2009) find that states with more stringent licensing requirements for mortgage brokers witnessed higher levels of mortgage default. The hypothesis is that increased barriers to entry reduce underwriting efforts to such an extent that offsets any improvements in broker quality that result from the licensing scheme. Kleiner and Todd's results raise the possibility that Dodd–Frank's section 1401 originator requirements, coupled with the SAFE Act, increase mortgage defaults rather than reduce them, as the statute intends.

The barely noticeable reduction in projected defaults could be more than offset by Dodd–Frank's effect on the foreclosure process. As noted, Dodd–Frank's section 1413 allows borrowers an additional delay to the foreclosure process. A longer foreclosure process increases the borrower's incentive to default. The CFPB has also issued new regulations relating to mortgage servicing that are likely to extend the ultimate time to foreclosure. Benjamin Keys, Tomasz Piskorski, Amit Seru, and Vikrant Vig (2013) document the increase in "strategic default" during the recent crisis. Dodd–Frank's section 1414(g) notice on antideficiency and the increased delays to foreclosure may well increase strategic defaults more than an amount to offset reductions resulting from the QM/QRM provisions. As Kristopher Gerardi, Lauren Lambie-Hanson, and Paul S. Willen (2011) have demonstrated, delays in the foreclosure process largely extend the process, raising the overall level of loans in foreclosure at any one time without significantly improving final outcomes for the borrower. Dodd–Frank could very well result in an increase in the level of mortgage defaults during the next housing bust.

Sins of Omission

Dodd–Frank contains the most sweeping changes to mortgage regulation since at least the slate of congressional activity in the aftermath of the savings and loan crisis. With various sections and as many as forty-nine separate rule makings, it would be easy to assume that everything worth covering in the mortgage market is covered. Yet Dodd–Frank leaves the basic structure of our mortgage finance system in place. The failures of Fannie Mae and Freddie Mac are addressed by Dodd–Frank in the form of a study that has subsequently been released by the Treasury Department.

The various forms of moral hazard in the mortgage market that result from various government guarantees remain and, if anything, are stronger than before the crisis. The various federal efforts to extend credit, such as the Community Reinvestment Act (CRA) and Home Mortgage Disclosure Act (HMDA), have not been reformed. Jevgenijs Steinbuks and Gregory Elliehausen (2013) suggest that the effect of

Dodd–Frank's mortgage restrictions will be to reduce subprime credit significantly. After the enactment of North Carolina's predatory lending law, Steinbuks and Elliehausen estimate that subprime originations declined over 20 percent. Yet federal regulators and politicians are unlikely to sit and watch this restriction of credit, particularly if this reduction is not felt evenly across racial groups. An open question will be to what extent regulators will leverage CRA and HMDA to pressure banks to continue making loans to borrowers with subprime credit. A possible outcome of Dodd–Frank's mortgage reforms is a reduction in the use of risk-based pricing. The only certainty appears to be continued uncertainty and tension in the federal regulation of mortgage finance.

Conclusions

The Dodd–Frank Act institutes the most significant changes to the federal oversight of mortgages in at least twenty years. Many of the details, however, have been left up to financial regulators, with the new Consumer Financial Protection Bureau playing a leading role. Although the proposed qualified mortgage rules and qualified residential mortgage rules will likely increase the cost of mortgage credit (particularly due to increase litigation, compliance, and foreclosure costs), their effects on reducing foreclosures during the next housing bust are likely to be modest and may even increase foreclosures. Despite the significant changes in Dodd–Frank to the mortgage market, those features of the American mortgage market that are most relevant to the financial crisis, such as lack of market discipline, remain unaddressed and in many cases have been made worse.

References

Agarwal, Sumit, and Douglas Evanoff. 2013. Loan Product Steering in Mortgage Markets. Working Paper, Federal Reserve Bank of Chicago. January.

Bajari, Patrick, Sean Chu, and Minjung Park. 2010. An Empirical Model of Subprime Mortgage Default from 2000 to 2007. Working Paper, Federal Reserve Board of Governors.

Gerardi, Kristopher, Lauren Lambie-Hanson, and Paul S. Willen. 2011. Do Borrower Rights Improve Borrower Outcomes? Evidence from the Foreclosure Process. Paper No. 11-9. Public Policy Discussion Paper Series. Federal Reserve Bank of Boston.

Hatchondo, Juan Carlos, Leonardo Martinez, and Juan Sanchez. 2011. Mortgage Defaults. Working Paper 2011-019A. Federal Reserve Bank of St. Louis.

Hurwitz, Eric. 2011. Litigation Risk for the Residential Mortgage Industry in the Wake of the Dodd-Frank Act. *The Review of Banking and Financial Services* 27(1) (January).

Keys, Benjamin, Tomasz Piskorski, Amit Seru, and Vikrant Vig. 2013. Mortgage Financing in the Housing Boom and Bust. In *Housing and the Financial Crisis*, ed. Edward L. Glaeser and Todd Sinai, chap 4. Chicago: University of Chicago Press.

Khater, Sam. 2013. The Mortgage Market Impact of Qualified Mortgage Regulation. *The MarketPulse* 2(2). CoreLogic.

Kleiner, Morris M., and Richard M. Todd. 2009. Mortgage Broker Regulations That Matter: Analyzing Earnings, Employment, and Outcomes for Consumers. In *Studies of Labor Market Intermediation*, ed. David Autor, 183–231. Chicago: University of Chicago Press and National Bureau of Research.

Natter, Raymond. 2012. Congressional Intent Regarding the Qualified Mortgage Provision. Bloomberg-BNA Banking Report.

Steinbuks, Jevgenijs, and Gregory Elliehausen. 2013. The Economic Effects of Legal Restrictions on High-Cost Mortgages. *Journal of Real Estate Finance and Economics*.

U.S. Federal Housing Finance Agency (FHFA). 2011. Qualified Residential Mortgages. Mortgage Market Note 11-01.

U.S. Government Accountability Office (GAO). 2011. Mortgage Reform: Potential Impacts of Provisions in the Dodd–Frank Act on Homebuyers and the Mortgage Market. Report to Congress. GAO-11-656.

U.S. Government Accountability Office (GAO). 2010. Nonprime Mortgages: Analysis of Loan Performance, Factors Associated with Defaults, and Data Sources. Report to Congress. GAO-10-805.

U.S. Government Accountability Office (GAO). 2009. Characteristics and Performance of Nonprime Mortgages. Report to Congress. GAO-09-848R.

Wilson, Ellen, and Robert Callis. 2013. Who Could Afford to Buy a Home in 2009? Affordability of Buying a Home in the United States. United States Census. Current Housing Reports. H121/13-02.

12 The Dodd–Frank Act and the Regulation of Risk Retention in Mortgage-Backed Securities

Cem Demiroglu and Christopher M. James

In contrast to traditional lending (in which vertically integrated lenders own and service the loans that they originate), securitization involves a number of different agents who perform different services often for fees that may be unrelated to the performance of the securitized pool of loans.[1] A potential problem with securitization is that loan originators might retain too little skin in securitized loans and have limited incentives to screen the mortgages that they originate with the intent to securitize. Critics of securitization contend that an important contributor to the collapse of the real estate and mortgage markets that began in 2007 was a decline in originators' screening standards that was fostered by the originate-to-distribute model of securitization.

The Dodd–Frank Wall Street Reform and Consumer Protection Act of 2010 was enacted, in part, to address concerns over misaligned incentives in the securitization process. The act attempts to address agency problems associated with originators' or sponsors' incentives to collect and use information. It does not address potential inefficiencies in ex post renegotiations of securitized loans that may arise due to distortions in the incentives of loan servicers.[2]

The Dodd–Frank Act attempts to address incentive conflicts associated with securitization in five ways. First, it requires sponsors to retain a significant credit-risk exposure to the securitized pool of loans (or skin in the game) to provide them an incentive to originate and securitize better-quality mortgages and thereby align their interests with those of investors in residential mortgage-backed securities (RMBSs).[3] The act requires sponsors to retain not less than 5 percent of the aggregate credit risk of the assets that they transfer through a securitization, subject to exception for securitizations backed by qualified residential mortgages (QRMs). Also, it limits sponsors from directly or indirectly hedging or otherwise transferring the credit risk that they are required to retain with respect to an asset for specified periods after the RMBS are issued (see section 941 of the act). Second, the act requires sponsors to disclose to investors standardized information on the characteristics of loans underlying each class of RMBS (on an ongoing basis) as well as information on the identity, compensation, and risk retention of originators or mortgage brokers (see section 942). Third, the act requires sponsors to disclose to investors representations and warranties given to rating agencies as well as fulfilled and unfulfilled repurchase requests aggregated by the originator to allow investors to identify originators with underwriting deficiencies (see section 943). Fourth, the act requires sponsors whose offerings are registered under the Securities Act of 1933 to conduct a review of the assets underlying those securities and make certain disclosures about those reviews (see section 945). Finally, the act prohibits RMBS sponsors and underwriters from engaging in any transaction that would involve or result in any material conflict of interest with respect to the RMBS investors for a period of one year after the closing date of the RMBS transaction (see section 621).[4]

In this chapter, we discuss the economic rationale for the regulation of risk retention in RMBSs as well as insights that empirical and theoretical studies provide about how best to regulate skin in the game. We argue that empirical evidence strongly supports the view that skin in the game increases originators' incentives to collect and incorporate so-called soft information in their lending decisions. The empirical evidence also indicates, however, that investors were aware of the effects that securitization has on originators' underwriting decisions and that the pricing and structure of RMBSs reflected differences in originators' incentives to collect soft information. We also argue that risk retention is multifaceted and that simple measures of risk retention (such as the size of the equity or residual tranche retained by the sponsor) do not provide an accurate measure of the extent to which the originator or sponsor has skin in the game. Finally, we argue that the empirical evidence suggests that the amount of risk retention required to align the incentives of the various participants in the securitization process is likely to vary across segments of the RMBS market based on differences in informational frictions, reputational concerns, and the nature of the underlying collateral. We conclude with a summary of the implications that the empirical and theoretical studies have for regulating risk retention.

Two permissible forms of sponsor risk retention have been proposed by the federal regulatory agencies that are responsible for formulating the Dodd–Frank Act's risk-retention rules (final rules have not yet been promulgated or adopted as of this writing).[5] These include vertical risk retention (whereby the sponsor retains at least 5 percent of the fair value of each cash-flow tranche issued in the transaction) and horizontal risk retention (whereby the sponsor retains a first-loss interest in the issuing entity, such as the equity tranche, that bears losses on the mortgages before any other classes of interests and amounts to at least 5 percent of the fair value of all RMBS interests). Sponsors are also allowed to utilize any combination of the vertical and horizontal risk-retention options as long as the total retained amount is no less than 5 percent of the fair value of all RMBS interests issued as part of the securitization transaction. We discuss issues that may arise with each of these forms of risk retention later in this chapter.

Securitization and the Growth of Nonprime Mortgage Lending
Proponents of risk-retention regulation argue that the originate-to-distribute model of securitization led to a decline in underwriting standards as evidenced by the growth of subprime mortgages and the growth of mortgage products whose value depended primarily on continued house-price appreciation (most of which were securitized).[6] For example, the dollar value of subprime and Alternative A-paper (Alt-A) mortgage originations increased fourfold from $250 billion in 2001 to $1 trillion in 2006 (Inside Mortgage Finance data, 2008). During the same period, the fraction of securitized subprime mortgages rose from 39.5 percent to 81.4 percent, suggesting that roughly 95 percent of the $750 billion increase in subprime originations was ultimately funded in the market for private securitizations. Confirming the role that securitization played in the growth of subprime loans, A. Mian and A. Sufi (2009) find that from 2002 to 2005, high securitization activity in subprime ZIP codes was associated with increased availability of residential mortgages.

Greater securitization activity was also associated with the origination of mortgage products with riskier features. For example, hybrid adjustable-rate mortgages (ARMs) (such as ARMs with lower initial teaser rates that reset to a higher level after two or three years) and negative amortization loans (such as option ARMs and interest-only Alt-A loans without any principal payments for a predetermined period of time) with prepayment penalties became commonplace (see B. J. Keys, T. Piskorski, A. Seru, and V. Vig 2013 and C. Mayer, K. Pence, and S. M. Sherlund 2009). These products increased affordability of mortgages for low-income borrowers (by increasing leverage and reducing initial monthly payments) but also increased the sensitivity of loan repayments to continued house-price appreciation. According to U. Rajan, A. Seru, and V. Vig (forthcoming), investors increasingly relied on borrower FICO credit scores and loan-to-value (LTV) ratios as sufficient statistics to predict loan default, which reduced demand for documentation or other credit-relevant information.

Several events are cited as factors that contributed to the expansion of the nonprime mortgage market—agency and adverse selection problems among various players in the securitization market, placement of the mezzanine RMBSs into collateralized debt obligations (CDOs), the global liquidity glut in the precrisis period that increased demand for high-yielding but safe assets (such as high-rated RMBS tranches), competitive pressures on originators and issuers, and political pressure on financial institutions to increase the supply of mortgage credit to low-income neighborhoods to promote homeownership (through, for example, the Community Reinvestment Act). Identifying the causal contribution of each of these potential factors is difficult. However, recent empirical studies provide persuasive evidence on three narrower and important issues that arise in the debate over regulations mandated by Dodd–Frank. These are how much securitization led to a reduction in the use of soft information by originators that were active in securitizing their loans, whether investors recognized these incentive effects and priced RMBSs accordingly, and whether differences in the amount of skin in the game affected performance.

Evidence of the Incentive Effects of Securitization

Theory predicts that securitization will reduce originators' incentives to collect credit-relevant soft information—information that is costly to verify and transfer from one agent to another, such as the loan underwriter's subjective judgment of the character of the borrower. Hard information is information that is verifiable and easy to summarize and transfer among agents. FICO scores and LTV ratios are examples of hard information. Given that soft information cannot be verified or easily transferred, its quality cannot be reflected in the price that a deal sponsor or loan investor will pay for a loan. As a result, lenders have less of an incentive to collect soft information on loans that they plan to securitize or sell (see J. C. Stein 2002). Note that incentives to collect soft information in securitization transactions may not be very different from the incentives to collect soft information in large lending institutions that follow an originate-to-hold strategy because soft information that is collected by individual loan officers cannot be passed up the organizational hierarchy.[7]

Consistent with the predictions above, several recent papers find that securitization is associated with reduced incentives to produce soft information (that is, less diligent screening). For example, B. J. Keys, T. K. Mukherjee, A. Seru, and V. Vig (2010) compare ex post default rates of loans with a high versus low ex ante probability of securitization. Using discontinuities in the ease of securitization around the FICO score threshold of 620, they find that, in the segment of the subprime market where originators' screening effort matters the most (that is, low-documentation loans), loans with a higher ex ante probability of securitization were 10 to 25 percent more likely to default than loans with similar risk characteristics but a lower probability of sale (see also W. Jiang, A. A. Nelson, and E. Vytlacil 2014). U. Rajan, A. Seru, and V. Vig (forthcoming) examine the relation between securitization and screening by examining whether securitization is associated with an increased reliance on hard information and a decreased reliance on soft information in lending decisions. They find that, consistent with less soft information being produced as securitization increases, the interest rate on loans depends more on hard information reported to investors (primarily borrower FICO score and LTV ratio), dispersion of interest rates conditional on hard information falls, and mortgage interest rates become poorer predictors of default.

The likelihood of securitization also appears to vary with mortgage loan features and the channel through which the loan was originated. Among nonconforming loans that generally are not eligible for purchase by the government-sponsored enterprises (GSEs) and therefore could potentially serve as collateral for private-label securitizations, subprime and Alt-A loans were much more likely to be securitized than jumbo prime loans. For example, according to Inside Mortgage Finance, in 2007, 93 percent of subprime and Alt-A loans originations were securitized. In contrast, only 51 percent of jumbo prime loans were securitized in 2007. In addition, there is some evidence that loans originated through mortgage brokers as well as negative amortization and adjustable-rate loans were more likely to be securitized by originators.[8]

Why were riskier loans more likely to be securitized instead of being held on portfolio? One explanation is that investors in RMBSs had broader diversification opportunities than originators and thus were in a better position to bear the higher credit risks that were associated with subprime and Alt-A mortgages. Another explanation is that investors were unaware of or misunderstood the quality of securitized loans, which created an incentive for originators and deal sponsors to place risky, mispriced loans into securitized pools. However, RMBS investors are predominantly large institutional investors, and the offering prospectuses for RMBS provide detailed information (at least since 2005, when Regulation AB, which governs registration, disclosure, and reporting requirements for asset-backed securities, became effective) on the characteristics of the underlying loan collateral as well as the identity of the primary originators and the channel through which the loans were originated.[9] Moreover, this explanation is at odds with the academic literature on loan sales that predicts that rational investors will anticipate the potential for opportunistic behavior and discount purchase prices accordingly.[10] This discount provides originators and sponsors an incentive to structure securitizations to minimize the discount or focus on securitizing loans for which soft information is least important.

Another explanation for the securitization of riskier loans is that investors understood the incentive effects of securitization but, given their expectations concerning future house-price changes, underestimated the effects that more relaxed underwriting standards would have on loan performance. As G. B. Gorton (2009) explains, a defining feature of the subprime/Alt-A design is that the borrower and investors can benefit from house-price appreciation over a short horizon. Features such as low or no documentation of borrower income or assets, low initial rates on ARMs, negative amortization, and high LTV ratios make mortgage repayments for subprime and Alt-A mortgages more dependent on the value of the underlying collateral than for prime fixed-rate mortgages.[11] Given the importance of house-price appreciation for the performance of subprime and Alt-A mortgages, RMBS investors may have believed that the information loss would have less effect on the expected performance of these types of mortgages leading to higher securitization rates than prime mortgages.[12]

Did Investors Recognize Incentive Effects of Securitization When Pricing and Structuring RMBSs?

Whether investors priced the incentive effects of securitizations is important for understanding the need for regulation and the form it should take. It could be argued that regulation is needed even if RMBS investors were fully informed and acted rationally, due to the social cost associated with securitization that induces risky mortgage lending. But evidence that RMBS investors failed to recognize the agency costs of securitization would suggest more far-reaching regulation is needed. Such a finding would suggest that originators who retain skin in the game will not be properly compensated by investors for their risk bearing.

The empirical evidence suggests that investors carefully screened the loans that they purchased and incorporated new information relatively quickly into their purchase decision. For example, similar to B. J. Keys, T. K. Mukherjee, A. Seru, and V. Vig (2010), W. Jiang, A. A. Nelson, and E. Vytlacil (2014) find that, controlling for observable risk factors, loans with a higher ex ante probability of being sold have a higher delinquency rate. This finding is consistent with less rigorous screening of securitized loans. However, they also find that adverse selection works against the originator after the loan is originated. They find that investors selected relatively higher-quality loans for purchase by exploiting information revealed between the time that the loan was originated and the time that the loan was sold (typically only a couple of months), including specific information about the performance of individual loans, general information about the recent performance of loan products, and neighborhood effects (such as house-price changes) in the area where the mortgaged property resides.

Direct evidence of the relationship between the amount of originator or sponsor risk retention and the performance of RMBSs is difficult to obtain because risk can be retained in a number of ways. For example, accounting rules and bank capital regulation require securitized loans to be sold without recourse, but originators retain credit-risk exposure through representations and warranties, warehousing risk (the risk that originated loans cannot be sold due to, for example, market disruptions), and the retention of the residual or equity tranches of the securitizations that they are involved in.

Accurate measurement of the size of the equity tranche and thus the credit-risk potential retained by the sponsor is also difficult because of differences in how RMBS deals are structured. There are basically two types of RMBS structures: the six-pack structure is used in prime and most Alt-A deals, and the OC/XS (or overcollateralization/excess-spread) structure is used in some Alt-A and most subprime deals (see G. B. Gorton 2009). In six-pack structures, the residual interest is at its thickest at issuance. In the early years of the deal, there is sequential amortization, which means that the senior bonds are paid first. In an OC/XS structure, the residual trance is likely to be thinest at issuance.

Excess spread (the difference between the contract rate on the underlying mortgages and coupon rate on the tranches issued) net of losses is added to the OC account until an OC target is met. When the target is reached, conditional on performance tests concerning the collateral, excess spread is paid to residual tranche holder. Thus, the amount of risk retained will vary with RMBS structure, the timing of cash flows, as well as deal-specific performance targets, sequential pay rules, and OC targets. The risk retained by holding a particular tranche will also vary by the extent to which individual loans are covered by mortgage insurance.

Further complicating things is the fact that even if the thickness of the equity tranche is measured accurately, it might not be a good proxy for the size of sponsor's exposure because during the precrisis period, sponsors routinely executed net interest margin (NIM) transactions alongside their RMBS transactions to securitize and thus transfer their retained residual interests.[13] Moreover, although the financial statements of many originators and sponsors reveal that they held in aggregate significant positions in the RMBSs that they sponsored, to our knowledge, information on specific tranche holdings is generally not available. The difficulty in accurately measuring originator or sponsor risk retention in past securitizations suggests that disclosure requirements and limits on the sale or hedging of residual interests by sponsors may improve investors' ability to assess the amount of skin the game that participants in the securitization process have.

Despite the difficulties in measuring the equity tranche, two recent studies find evidence that investors recognized and accounted for agency conflicts when investing in RMBSs. We conducted the first of these studies (see C. Demiroglu and C. M. James 2012). We argue that affiliation with the sponsor of the RMBS deal or the servicer of securitized loans strengthens the originator's screening incentives and results in production of better-quality loans both in terms of observable and unobservable characteristics. For example, because the sponsor often retains first loss exposure (and the potential for upside profits) by holding the equity tranche of the securitization, when the originator is also the sponsor, greater loss exposure (skin in the game) is retained by the originating entity than when the originator is unaffiliated with the sponsor of the RMBS. Also, originators that expect to retain servicing responsibilities are expected to have more skin in the game because the value of mortgage-servicing rights is increasing in the expected duration of the mortgage. Finally, for affiliated deals the originator is likely to internalize the warehousing risk and any adverse effects of poor loan quality on the reputation of the sponsor. Overall, consistent with the importance of skin in the game, we find that ex post default rates are significantly lower for securitizations in which the originator is affiliated with the sponsor or servicer. Consistent with investors' expectations that performance will vary with affiliation, we find that the initial yields on RMBSs are lower and the percentage of AAA-rated securities issued against the securitized pool of loans is higher when the originator is affiliated with either the sponsor or servicer. Finally, skin in the game appears to matter only for deals that consist primarily of low-documentation mortgages in which soft information that is generated by the originator would matter most.

The differences that we observe in performance appear to arise from reduced incentives to collect soft information and not from originators that collect information and then cherry-pick better-quality loans to put into affiliated deals. We suspect that there is no cherry-picking because we find no difference in the average performance of unaffiliated loans that are originated by institutions capable of sponsoring their own RMBS deals and those originated by institutions that do not sponsor RMBS (that is, mortgage brokers).

Despite the challenges associated with measuring the size and ownership of the equity tranche, a recent paper by T. Begley and A. Purnanandam (2013) examines how the thickness of an RMBS deal's equity tranche at issuance (which they assume is retained by the sponsor and is similar to the horizontal first-loss piece in the new regulation) is associated with ex post performance of securitized loans and ex ante pricing of securities issued in the deal, using a sample of prime and subprime RMBS deals from vintages 2001, 2002, and 2005. They find that the size of the equity tranche is positively related to ex post performance (conditional on the risk of underlying mortgages) and negatively related to initial RMBS yields (conditional on RMBS rating) in deals that include mainly low-documentation loans (deals in which information problems between investors and sponsors are most severe).

Overall, the evidence suggests that skin in the game affects originator incentives to collect information and that investors recognized and priced the incentive effects of having skin in the game. Whether investors correctly priced the incentive effects ex ante is far more difficult to determine.

Implications for the Regulation

If the primary motive for regulating risk retention is to provide incentives for the collection and use of soft information in lending decisions, the primary focus should be on requiring originators to retain some skin in the game. However, the Dodd–Frank Act does not require mortgage originators to retain any risk exposure to securitized loans (although it allows sponsors to allocate at least a portion of the credit-risk retention to them). This is a bit surprising given that existing research finds that originators' screening incentives have a significant effect on loan performance (see, for example, B. J. Keys, T. K. Mukherjee, A. Seru, and V. Vig 2010). One reason for not requiring originators to invest in the collateral pools that they sell loans into may be that free-rider problems associated with a large number of originators may diminish any incentive effects associated with originator risk retention.[14] However, concerns with free-rider problems would argue in favor of basing the requirement for risk retention on the number of originators involved and not a blanket exemption for originators.[15]

Existing research suggests that although skin in the game matters, the importance of skin in the game varies with the nature of the underlying collateral. One consistent finding is that skin in the game matters most, if not only, for low-documentation loans. The Dodd–Frank Act recognizes, at least in part, that the importance of the risk retention varies with the type of collateral. However, the proposed risk-retention rules have limited granularity. The proposed rules exempt from risk-retention requirements only RMBSs with collateral that consists entirely of QRMs. The proposed rules require the definition of QRM to be "no broader" than the Consumer Financial Protection Bureau's (CFPB) definition of a qualified mortgage (QM), which is based on ability-to-repay rules.[16] Based on those rules, low-documentation loans, interest-only loans, loans with negative amortization, and loans to a borrower with a debt-to-income ratio greater than 43 percent will not be considered QRMs. The lack of granularity is concerning because it implies potentially large differerences in risk retention for RMBS with similar types of collateral (such as collateral pools with only a few non-QRMs versus pools with no QRMs) and no difference in required risk-retention requirements for pools backed by very different types of collateral. Such a one-size-fits-all approach is likely to lead to significant distortions in the mortgage market.

There is also a concern that the definition of QRM may be too conservative. For example, according to CoreLogic, despite significantly tighter mortgage lending standards in 2010, 60 percent of the 2.2 million mortgages originated in that year do not satisfy the QRM requirements that were originally proposed in 2011.[17] This implies that the rule may significantly increase the cost of mortgage finance for a broad cross-section of the population. The short-term effects of implementing the rule may be limited, however, because according to Moody's, 90 percent of recent residential mortgages are underwritten by the Federal Housing Administration (FHA), Federal National Mortgaghe Association (Fannie Mae), and Federal Home Loan Mortgage Corporation (Freddie Mac) entities that are are exempt from the risk-retention rule. The exemption of the agencies may have an unintended consequence of proving that the new regulation is largely ineffective by channeling securitization of high-risk mortgages from the private market to the agency market.

One potential way to create more granularity while maintaining transparency and simplicity would be to establish a QRM blend exception to the standard 5 percent risk-retention requirement. The idea would be to scale risk-retention requirements based on the proportion of non-QRMs in the pool or base risk-retention requirements based on average pool characteristics.

Requiring either 0 percent or 5 percent risk retention is unlikely to be optimal. The average sizes of the equity tranche (excluding excess spread) for subprime and Alt-A RMBSs in 2006 were 1.9 percent and 0.8 percent, respectively, well below what is mandated under the Dodd Frank Act.[18] The act also does not permit an offset or a reduction in the 5 percent requirement for other forms of risk retention. For example, a 5 percent requirement applies to non-QRM pools regardless of how seasoned the loans are at the time of securitization and thus the amount of credit risk that the originator retained initially.

The proposed rules concerning risk retention quantify retained risk as a percentage of fair value instead of par value. This mitigates the ability of a sponsor to evade the risk-retention requirement through the use of deal structures. For example, a sponsor could structure a first loss tranche that amounts to 5 percent of par value of all issued RMBS interests but with a fair value of only a few cents. Also, one common practice by RMBS sponsors prior to the financial crisis was to monetize the excess spread at the inception of a securitization transaction by selling premium or interest-only tranches to investors. By monetizing the excess spread before the performance of the securitized assets could be observed and losses realized, sponsors were able to reduce the sensitivity of their economic interest in the transaction to the credit quality of the assets they securitized.

In terms of whether horizontal or vertical risk retention is optimal, theoretical work by B. Hartman-Glaser, T. Piskorski, and A. Tchistyi (2011) suggests that the timing of the cash flows to the residual tranche has important incentive effects. They derive the optimal mortgage-backed security contract in a dynamic model in which a mortgage underwriter with limited liability can engage in costly hidden effort to screen borrowers and can sell loans to investors. They find that bundling mortgages is more efficient than individual loan sales because the former allows investors to learn about originator effort more quickly due to an information-enhancement effect. In terms of the optimal form of risk retention, they find that the timing of payments to the originator rather than the type of asset that the originator retains is the key incentive mechanism. By making the payment contingent on a period of no default, the investors may provide originators incentives to underwrite low-risk mortgages. Although this may be difficult to implement in practice, the authors also demonstrate that requiring the underwriter to retain the first-loss piece can closely approximate the optimal contract. In terms of the duration of the optimal contract, they show that because delaying payments to the originator (or requiring the originator to hold the first-loss piece for an extended period of time) will increases costs and the relation between originator screening and loan performance decreases as time passes, the maturity of the optimal contract can be shorter than the maturity of the underlying mortgages. They estimate that a period of 2.25 years may be the optimal duration for sponsor risk retention (conditional on compliance with performance standards).

One advantage, however, of vertical risk retention is that by giving the sponsor proportional exposure to each class of security issued in the transactions, it effectively aligns the interests of the sponsor and investors. A potential issue that may arise when the sponsor holds the first-loss piece (in addition to the concerns raised in I. Fender and J. Mitchell 2009) is that servicers that are affiliated with the sponsor may take actions to maximize the value of the first-loss piece at the expense of the holders of other classes of securities (see Y. H. Gan and C. Mayer 2006). This might be less of a concern if regulators implement rules that standardize servicing of securitized mortgages (such as loss and default mitigation procedures).

The final proposed rules require sponsors to retain risk exposure for a specified period after the securitizations (based on various sunset provisions). As proposed, the restrictions on transfer and hedging would expire on the date that is the later of five years after closing or the date on which the unpaid balance of the pool balance is reduced to 25 percent of the original pool balance. If the goal of regulation is to increase incentives for originators to collect soft information while minimizing distortions in the mortgage market, then it makes sense not to require risk retention over the entire life of the securitization. The reasoning is that any serious problems in underwriting are likely to manifest themselves within the first year or two after origination. Moreover, default rates typically level out as loans season (that is, the hazard rate decreases over time), in part because borrower equity increases as the mortgage loan amortizes and housing prices increase (in normal times). Thus, the relevance of soft information collected at origination is likely to diminish over time. The rate at which the relevance of soft information decays will vary with the charcteristics of the underlying mortgage and conditions in the housing market.

Conclusions

Empirical studies on the performance of nonprime mortgages indicate that skin in the game affects originators' incentives to collect and use soft information in their lending decisions. However, empirical evidence also suggests that market participants were aware of the incentive effects of skin in the game and priced residential mortgage-backed securities accordingly. Thus, the economic argument for regulating retained interest has to rest on the argument that the market mispriced the risks arising from reduced screening, either because of behavioral biases (for example, due to overly optimistic forecasts of future house-price appreciation) or because of significant social costs associated with risky mortgage lending. The evidence on the structure and pricing of residential mortgage-backed securities also suggests that one-size-fits-all rules concerning risk retention are unlikely to be optimal because the importance of skin in the game is likely to vary with mortgage and borrower characteristics, affiliation between the deal sponsor and the originator and mortgage servicer, and the form in which risk is retained.

Notes

1. See A. B. Ashcraft and T. Schuermann (2008) for a detailed description of the securitization process and a discussion of frictions between various agents that participate in securitization transactions.

2. Several recent papers find that the likelihood and efficiency of loan modifications are lower for securitized mortgages than comparable bank-held loans (see T. Piskorski, A. Seru, and V. Vig 2010; S. Agarwal, G. Amromin, I. Ben-David, S. Chomsisengphet, and D. D. Evanoff 2011). One potential reason for this finding is that servicer fees are generally paid as a percentage of the principal amount of serviced loans, so servicers may have an incentive not to do principal writedowns, even if that would be in the best interest of RMBS investors.

3. The Dodd–Frank Act requires several entities—the Federal Deposit Insurance Corporation, Office of the Comptroller of the Currency, Federal Reserve Board, Securities and Exchange Comission, Federal Housing Finance Agency, and Department of Housing and Urban Development—to formulate and implement rules outlined in the act.

4. Final rules implementing sections 943 and 945 were adopted in January 2011. For details on implementation on these and other rules related to asset-backed securities, see http://www.sec.gov/spotlight/dodd-frank/assetbackedsecurities.shtml.

5. The most recent versions of proposed risk-retention rules are available at http://www.federalreserve.gov/newsevents/press/bcreg/bcreg20130828a1.pdf.

6. See, for example, the Financial Stability Oversight Council's "Macroeconomic Effects of Risk Retention Requirements" (January 2011) at http://www.treasury.gov/initiatives/wsr/Documents/Section%20946%20Risk%20Retention%20Study%20%20(FINAL).pdf.

7. A. Berger, N. Miller, M. Petersen, R. Rajan, and J. C. Stein (2005) provide evidence that small banks are better able than large banks to collect and act on soft information.

8. See, for example, W. Jiang, A. A. Nelson, and E. Vytlacil (2014).

9. See S. L. Schwarcz (2012) for a discussion of the investors in the residential mortgage-backed securities market and the need for regulation to protect these investors. In 2005, the SEC issued Regulation AB, which provides disclosure and reporting requirements for SEC filing involving asset-backed securities. Section (a) of item 1110 of the regulation requires the disclosure of the originators that originated 10 percent or more of the pool of assets.

10. See M. C. Jensen and W. H. Meckling (1976), G. B. Gorton and G. P. Pennacchi (1995), P. M. DeMarzo (2005), C. Downing, D. Jaffee, and N. Wallace (2009), and C. A. Parlour and G. Plantin (2008).

11. The offering prospectuses of many residential mortgage-backed securities that are backed by low-documentation loans pointed this out to investors. For example, the offering prospectus for Washington Mutual (WaMu) Series 2006-AR7 states, "Underwriting for limited or no documentation loans may be based primarily or entirely on an appraisal or other valuation of the mortgage property and the LTV or combined LTV ratio at the origination."

12. C. Demiroglu, E. Dudley, and C. James (forthcoming) find that house-price changes are a much more important determinant of delinquency for subprime and Alt-A

mortgage loans than for prime mortgage loans. There is evidence that investors understood ex ante the sensitivity of Alt-A and subprime products to house-price changes but held what turned out to be overly optimistic expectations concerning future house-price changes. For evidence of this, see K. Gerardi, A. Lehnert, S. M. Sherlund, and P. Willen (2008), who find that, in 2005 and 2006, analysts placed a low probability on a significant housing-price decline.

13. See Adelson & Jacob Consulting, Home Equity ABS Basics, http://www .adelsonandjacob.com/pubs/Home_Equity_ABS_Basics.pdf, 12–13.

14. Consistent with a free-rider effect, B. J. Keys, T. K. Mukherjee, A. Seru, and V. Vig (2009) find that default rates in RMBSs are inversely related to the number of originators who are involved in the deal.

15. Another reason may be regulatory concerns with placing small originators at a competitive disadvantage relative to originators that are affiliated with large financial services firms.

16. For information on QM standards, see http://www.consumerfinance.gov/ regulations/ability-to-repay-and-qualified-mortgage-standards-under-the -truth-in-lending-act-regulation-z.

17. See http://www.economy.com/mark-zandi/documents/Reworking-Risk-Retention -062011.pdf.

18. See A. B. Ashcraft and T. Schuermann (2008). T. Begley and A. Purnanandam (2013) report mean and median equity tranche thickness of 1.2 percent and 0.5 percent (excluding excess spread) for deals in their sample.

References

Agarwal, S., G. Amromin, I. Ben-David, S. Chomsisengphet, and D. Evanoff. 2011. The Role of Securitization in Mortgage Renegotiation. *Journal of Financial Economics* 102:559–578.

Ashcraft, A. B., and T. Schuermann. 2008. Understanding the Securitization of Subprime Mortgage Credit. *Foundations and Trends in Finance* 2:191–309.

Begley, T., and A. Purnanandam. 2013. Design of Financial Securities: Evidence from Private-Label RMBS Deals. University of Michigan Working Paper.

Berger, A., N. Miller, M. Petersen, R. Rajan, and J. C. Stein. 2005. Does Function Follow Form? Evidence from the Lending Practices of Large and Small Banks. *Journal of Financial Economics* 76:237–269.

DeMarzo, P. M. 2005. The Pooling and Tranching of Securities: A Model of Informed Intermediation. *Review of Financial Studies* 18:1–35.

Demiroglu, C., E. Dudley, and C. James. Forthcoming. State Foreclosure Laws and the Incidence of Mortgage Default. *Journal of Law & Economics*.

Demiroglu, C., and C. James. 2012. How Important Is Having "Skin in the Game"? Originator-Sponsor Affiliation and Losses on Mortgage-Backed Securities. *Review of Financial Studies* 25:3217–3258.

Downing, C., D. Jaffee, and N. Wallace. 2009. Is the Market for Mortgage-Backed Securities a Market for Lemons? *Review of Financial Studies* 22:2457–2494.

Fender, I., and J. Mitchell. 2009. Incentives and Tranche Retention in Securitization: A Screening Model. National Bank of Belgium Working Paper No. 177.

Gan, Y. H., and C. Mayer. 2006. Agency Conflicts, Asset Substitution, and Securitization. NBER Working Paper No. 12359.

Gerardi, K., A. Lehnert, S. M. Sherlund, and P. Willen. 2008. Making Sense of the Subprime Crisis. *Brookings Papers on Economc Activity* (Fall):69–159.

Gorton, G. B. 2009. The Subprime Panic. *European Financial Management* 15:10–46.

Gorton, G. B., and G. P. Pennacchi. 1995. Banks and Loan Sales: Marketing Non-Marketable Assets. *Journal of Monetary Economics* 3:389–411.

Hartman-Glaser, B., T. Piskorski, and A. Tchistyi. 2011. Optimal Securitization with Moral Hazard. *Journal of Financial Economics* 104:186–202.

Jensen, M. C., and W. H. Meckling. 1976. Theory of the Firm: Managerial Behavior, Agency Costs and Ownership Structure. *Journal of Financial Economics* 3:305–360.

Jiang, W., A. Nelson, and E. Vytlacil. 2014. Securitization and Loan Performance: A Contrast of ex ante and ex post Relations in the Mortgage Market. *Review of Financial Studies* 27:454–483.

Keys, B. J., T. K. Mukherjee, A. Seru, and V. Vig. 2009. Financial Regulation and Securitization: Evidence from Subprime Loans. *Journal of Monetary Economics* 56:700–720.

Keys, B. J., T. K. Mukherjee, A. Seru, and V. Vig. 2010. Did Securitization Lead to Lax Screening? Evidence from Subprime Loans. *Quarterly Journal of Economics* 125:307–362.

Keys, B. J., T. Piskorski, A. Seru, and V. Vig. 2013. Mortgage Financing in the Housing Boom and Bust. In *Housing and the Financial Crisis*, 143–204. Chicago: University of Chicago Press.

Mayer, C., K. Pence, and S. M. Sherlund. 2009. The Rise in Mortgage Defaults. *Journal of Economic Perspectives* 23:27–50.

Mian, A., and A. Sufi. 2009. The Consequences of Mortgage Credit Expansion: Evidence from the U.S. Mortgage Default Crisis. *Quarterly Journal of Economics* 124:1449–1496.

Parlour, C. A., and G. Plantin. 2008. Loan Sales and Relationship Banking. *Journal of Finance* 63:1291–1314.

Piskorski, T., A. Seru, and V. Vig. 2010. Securitization and Distressed Loan Renegotiation: Evidence from the Subprime Mortgage Crisis. *Journal of Financial Economics* 97:369–397.

Rajan, U., A. Seru, and V. Vig. Forthcoming. The Failure of Models That Predict Failure: Distance, Incentives, and Defaults. *Journal of Financial Economics*.

Schwarcz, S. L. 2012. Protecting Investors in Securitization Transactions: Does Dodd–Frank Help or Hurt? *Louisiana Law Review* 72:591–603.

Stein, J. C. 2002. Information Production and Capital Allocation: Decentralized versus Hierarchical Firms. *Journal of Finance* 57:1891–1921.

13 The Controversial New Disclosure Requirements in Dodd–Frank

Paul H. Schultz

The Dodd–Frank Wall Street Reform and Consumer Protection Act of 2010 touches on almost all areas of finance. Two of the lesser-known provisions—the internal pay equity rule and the conflict minerals rule—seem especially controversial. Each requires companies to disclose information that is unlikely to be material to investors.

Complying with the Conflict Minerals Rule

The Dodd–Frank Act's section 1502, Conflict Minerals, requires companies to report whether gold, tantalum, tin, and tungsten that are used in the companies' products originate in the Democratic Republic of the Congo (DRC) or surrounding countries and, if so, to report whether the mineral is "conflict free." As Karen Woody (2012) observes, the conflict minerals rule uses the Securities and Exchange Commission (SEC) to accomplish social goals that are outside of its normal sphere of activities. Establishing this precedent may be its real significance.

Compliance with section 1502 requires three steps. First, companies must determine whether any of these minerals are used in their products. If not, they are done. Second, if a company determines that its products use gold, tantalum, tin, or tungsten, it must trace the minerals that it uses back to the countries where they were mined. In many cases, this is not a trivial task. There may be a chain of several intervening refiners, producers, component manufacturers, and middlemen between the mine and the company that makes the final product. If the company can determine that the minerals used in its products do not come from the DRC or surrounding countries, it is done. It can disclose that its products are free of conflict minerals.

Third, if a firm cannot verify that the minerals do not come from the DRC, it must exercise due diligence on the source and chain of custody of the minerals to determine whether they came from a legitimate source in the DRC or whether they were used to fund the conflict. It also must hire an independent third party to audit the due diligence measures and report to the SEC on its findings.

Note that companies are not prohibited from using conflict minerals. They still can use them but must disclose that the minerals are not conflict free. The idea of section 1502 is to let shareholders and customers exert pressure on companies to stop using these minerals.

The objective of this rule is to remove a source of funding for a brutal, protracted conflict in the eastern part of the DRC. Over the last fifteen years or so, local warlords and militias have brutalized and murdered the civilian population. The number of deaths in the conflict is unknown, but estimates run into the millions. If armed groups in the DRC were unable to sell minerals, the thinking goes, their ability to finance the conflict would disappear.

The goal of the conflict minerals rule—to end a horrifying civil conflict in the Democratic Republic of the Congo—is laudable. Why, then, is it controversial?

Why the Conflict Minerals Rule Is Controversial

First, it appears that section 1502, the conflict minerals rule, will impose significant costs on many companies. These minerals are used in almost all electronic devices. Any company that makes something that is plugged in will be subject to this rule. The effect of the rule is not confined to the electronics industry, however. These minerals are also used in such diverse products as autos, ballpoint pens, jewelry, drill bits, and golf clubs. This rule will affect about six thousand companies that report to the SEC and now are required to disclose whether the minerals used in their products are conflict-free. The rule may affect as many as 275,000 private companies.

There are no de minimis exceptions for products that use minute quantities of the minerals, so companies may be surprised to learn that section 1502 applies to them. A financial company may need to consider whether chips in its credit cards contain these minerals. If one of these four minerals is needed for the functionality of the product, the conflict minerals rules applies, regardless of how little of the mineral is used.

It is not yet clear how much this will cost. A survey of almost nine hundred companies by PricewaterhouseCoopers (PwC) indicates that more than 25 percent have more than one thousand suppliers and 13 percent have more than five thousand (PricewaterhouseCoopers 2013). In each case, minerals must be traced back to the mine in which they were produced. It is difficult to estimate the cost of this exercise. When the rule was proposed, the SEC estimated compliance costs to be $71 million. It has since revised the total initial compliance costs to $3 billion to $4 billion and annual costs thereafter to $200 million to $600 million. Tracing minerals from the end user back to the mine is particularly expensive. After systems for tracking minerals from the mine to the user are established, compliance will be easier.

Others have placed a higher cost on compliance. A Tulane University study places the costs of compliance at $7.93 billion, most of which would be borne by suppliers to public companies (Bayer 2011). The National Association of Manufacturers estimates that the cost of implementation will be between $9 billion and $16 billion. We do not know how much it will cost.

A second reason that the conflict minerals rule is controversial is its unintended consequences. Many companies seem to be complying with the law by avoiding using any minerals from the DRC. A 2011 *New York Times* editorial says that the law has brought about a de facto embargo of minerals from the DRC.

This de facto boycott, although unintended, should not be surprising. A company that uses one of the four minerals can avoid the costs of tracing the minerals back to the mine and the costs of hiring an outside auditor simply by avoiding minerals from the DRC, and all four of these minerals are readily available from other sources. Tungsten can be obtained from Canada, China, Russia, and Bolivia, among other places. Brazil and Australia are prominent tantalum producers. Peru, Bolivia, and Brazil are major tin producers. Gold can be obtained from Australia, South Africa, and the United States. For many companies, it is easier and cheaper to avoid minerals from the DRC.

If this de facto boycott was stripping funding only from the warlords of the DRC, we could say that the conflict minerals rule was having its intended effect. But that is not what is happening. According to the Extractive Industries Transparency Initiative, as many as 12.5 million residents of the Congo make their living through mineral mining or trading. Artisanal miners, not soldiers or rebels, are the chief beneficiaries of the mining, and Laura Seay (2012) observes that section 1502 could have a devastating impact on them. A de facto boycott of conflict minerals from the DRC will further impoverish some of the poorest people on earth.

A third reason that the conflict minerals rule is controversial is that it uses the Securities and Exchange Commission in an entirely new way. Footnote 2 of a memorandum by the Monetary Policy and Trade Subcommittee of the U.S. House of Representatives notes that "The SEC's mission is to protect investors; maintain fair and orderly markets; and facilitate capital formation. The SEC has little or no experience in crafting trade sanctions or articulating and enforcing human rights policy, two areas which have not traditionally been within the purview of securities regulation" (U.S. House of Representatives, Committee on Financial Services 2013).

This may explain the SEC's delay in writing the conflict minerals rules. In his statement at the August 22, 2012, meeting to adopt the final rule, the SEC commissioner, Troy Paredes (2012), had the following comment:

Today the Commission is adopting its final rule pursuant to Section 1502 of Dodd-Frank. This rulemaking has proven to be especially difficult because the Commission has no expertise when it comes to the humanitarian goal of ending the atrocities that besiege the DRC. The agency is not even expert when it comes to supply chain management. More to the point, because the SEC's mission is to protect investors, maintain fair, orderly, and efficient markets, and facilitate capital formation, it is not clear that the SEC and the federal securities laws are the proper instruments for achieving the laudable social objective behind Section 1502.

The conflict minerals rule is an attempt to pursue social and foreign policy through the SEC, an institution that many consider ill-suited to the task. This precedent may be the most important outcome of the conflict minerals rule. Many other social goals also could be performed in this way. For instance, companies could be asked to certify that no components of their products were produced in sweatshops or in Cuba.

Implementation of the Conflict Minerals Rule

The U.S. Chamber of Commerce, the Business Roundtable, and the National Association of Manufacturers have challenged the conflict minerals rule in court (Hamilton 2013). A federal district judge upheld the law on July 23, 2013. The court emphasized that the SEC did not write the regulation on its own but did so in response to an explicit statutory directive from Congress. The court also ruled that the SEC could have pursued exceptions but that failing to do so did not make the commission's rules arbitrary or unreasonable. The court's ruling has been appealed.

The conflict minerals rule becomes effective at the end of May 2014. Some companies are making great efforts to ensure that their products are free of conflict minerals. Intel has a goal of manufacturing the first verified conflict-mineral-free microprocessor in 2013. Many firms that are subject to the rule, however, do not seem to be ready for it. Only 2.3 percent of the companies in the PwC survey had started due diligence as of spring 2013; 31.2 percent of companies said they did not have a conflict minerals policy and had not discussed one.

Of the companies in the PwC survey, 58 percent have not determined how deep they will go into their supply chain for due diligence. Almost 27 percent say that they will rely on information given by their immediate suppliers and not dig deeper into the supply chain. In some cases, confidentiality agreements may keep companies from gaining access to their supplier's suppliers even if they want to do so.

Section 953(b), Internal Pay Equity

Another controversial part of the Dodd–Frank Act is section 953, Executive Compensation Disclosures, (b), Additional Disclosure Requirements—the internal pay equity provision. This requires companies to report the median employee pay, the chief executive officer's (CEO) compensation, and the ratio of the two. CEO compensation is already reported. Reporting the median employee compensation and the ratio of employee to CEO pay is new. The SEC has received over 22,000 comment letters on section 953(b). The SEC has also received a petition on pay ratio disclosure with more than 84,000 signatures. The measure is controversial and is of interest to many people.

The benefits of this new rule are a subject of debate. Investors have not made the case that the ratio is useful for investment decisions. Proponents of the rule note that ratios of CEO to employee pay have been increasing, and suggest that the ratio of CEO to employee compensation will be useful in determining whether CEOs are overpaid.

Proponents of the rule claim that large differences in compensation can affect employee morale, productivity, and turnover. It is not immediately clear which way the causality goes, however. If a company's employees are not productive, they will not be paid well, and the ratio of employee to CEO pay will tend to be low. If employee turnover is high, it is likely that their compensation will be low and the compensation ratio will be low.

Costs and Complications of the Internal Pay Equity Rule

Critics of section 953(b) point to its cost. Companies have complained that calculating median employee compensation is not a trivial matter of just comparing W-2 forms. Base pay, bonuses, long-term incentives, options, and changes in the present value of accumulated benefits in a pension plan are included. The value of pension benefits is especially challenging. Choosing the right interest rate to discount the value of the pension plan benefits is a challenge, and the discount rate will change from year to year.

There are other complications. One is the treatment of foreign workers. In some cases, it may be difficult to obtain information on compensation of foreign employees, and in some cases, the inclusion of foreign workers may keep the ratio from being meaningful. It is also not clear how best to treat overtime or how to include part-time workers.

The rule does not impose any limits on the pay ratio, but its proponents seem to hope that companies will be shamed into raising the employee-to-CEO pay ratio. It is assumed that raising the ratio will be a desirable thing and will be accomplished either by reducing CEO pay or increasing employee pay.

For many large firms, CEO compensation is several hundred times the median employee compensation. To some, it might seem that this would embarrass the CEO and the board of directors, but experience to date suggests that shame has not been an effective tool for reining in executive pay. So it seems likely that companies will incur the costs of section 953(b) but not change either employee or CEO compensation.

On the other hand, suppose that companies are embarrassed by a high ratio of CEO to median worker pay. From the standpoint of proponents of the rule, the best outcome would be for companies to alter the ratio by increasing the compensation of rank-and-file employees. Perhaps they feel that the second-best outcome would be a decrease in CEO compensation. But there are ways to increase the ratio of employee to CEO compensation that are counterproductive. These are some of the potential unintended consequences of the rule.

The ratio of employee to CEO pay can be raised by shifting CEO pay into compensation that is not reported. This could include extra perks. The problem with this is that compensation in these forms is not efficient. A CEO would rather have cash than perks and so would demand higher total compensation if it was given in the form of perks.

The pay ratio also can be increased by reducing the number of low-paid workers. A company can do this by hiring fewer employees and outsourcing more jobs. Alternatively, the pay ratio can be increased by substituting machinery and equipment for unskilled workers. It is difficult to predict how companies will respond to section 953(b), but it is clear that publicizing the ratio of CEO pay to median worker pay will not increase demand for the labor of the least skilled workers.

Finally, companies can avoid the internal pay equity requirement by not going public. Section 953(b) adds one more cost to the costs of being a public company. Firms that are on the fence regarding an initial public offering may choose to delay going public. Foreign firms may choose not to list in the United States.

It does not appear that these pay ratios will be useful for comparing pay across firms. Suppose that firm A's CEO is paid three hundred times as much as its median employee and that firm B's CEO makes five hundred times as much as firm B's median employee. Firm A might outsource some of its low-paid work, and firm B might have employees doing the same tasks. Firm A's and firm B's employees may be from different locations, and there are differences in pay across countries and even across different parts of the United States. Even among firms within an industry, there may significant differences in skill and experience that will explain differences in relative pay. The temptation will be to compare ratios of employee to CEO pay across firms. These simplistic comparisons will be misleading.

In 2013, there was an attempt in Congress to repeal section 953(b). Those who were attempting to repeal the measure said that the internal equity pay provision is unworkable in practice because employee pay data are not standardized. This attempt failed, though, and the SEC has proposed rules for section 953(b) and asked for public comment.

The SEC has taken concerns about the costs of section 953(b) into account in writing the proposed rule. Rather than looking at the compensation of every employee, companies will be able to use statistical sampling to determine median compensation. They also will be permitted to use measures of compensation other than total compensation as long as they are consistently applied. They could, for example, use salaries and wages. Part-time, temporary, and seasonal employees are to be included. The compensation of a full-time employee who worked only part of the year can be annualized. The SEC will also allow companies to use annual periods other than their fiscal year to calculate compensation. This will allow them to use compensation data for calendar years that are assembled for tax purposes.

Sections 1502 and 953(b) call on companies to disclose information that is not material for investors to determine a company's profitability or financial health, so both provisions move the resource-strapped SEC away from its traditional mission of protecting investors. These precedents may prove to be among the most important legacies of Dodd–Frank.

References

Aronson, David. 2011. How Congress Devastated Congo. Editorial. *New York Times*, August 7, A19.

Bayer, Chris. 2011. A Critical Analysis of the SEC and NAM Economic Impact Models and the Proposal of a Third Model in View of Implementation of Section 1502 of the 2010 Dodd–Frank Wall Street Reform and Consumer Protection Act. Working Paper, Tulane University, Payson Center for International Development.

Hamilton, Jim. 2013. Business Groups Call SEC Conflict Minerals Regulations Arbitrary, Decry Lack of De Minimis Exception. *Securities Regulation Daily*, September 13.

Paredes, Troy. 2012. Statement at Open Meeting to Adopt a Final Rule Regarding Conflict Minerals Pursuant to Section 1502 of the Dodd–Frank Act. August 22. Available at http://www.sec.gov/News/Speech/Detail/Speech/1365171491022.

PricewaterhouseCoopers. 2013. Conflict Minerals Survey: How Companies Are Preparing. PricewaterhouseCoopers report, New York City.

Seay, Laura. 2012. What's Wrong with Dodd–Frank 1502? Conflict Minerals, Civilian Livelihoods, and the Unintended Consequences of Western Advocacy. Center for Global Development Working Paper No. 284, Washington, DC.

U.S. House of Representatives, Committee on Financial Services. 2013. Monetary Policy and Trade Subcommittee Hearing on the Unintended Consequences of Dodd–Frank's Conflict Minerals Provision.

Woody, Karen. 2012. Conflict Minerals Legislation: The SEC's New Role as Diplomatic and Humanitarian Watchdog. *Fordham Law Review* 81:1315–1351.

14 Conclusions

Paul H. Schultz

Implementation of the Act

It is now more than three years since the passage of the Dodd–Frank Wall Street Reform and Consumer Protection Act of 2010, but the law is far from being fully implemented (U.S. Government Accountability Office 2013). At the time of this writing (November 2013), 280 Dodd–Frank rulemaking deadlines have passed. Of the 280 deadlines, 170 (60.7 percent) have been missed, and 110 (39.3 percent) have been met with finalized rules. Regulators have not released proposals for 60 of the 170 missed rules (DavisPolk 2013).

There are an additional 118 rulemaking requirements without a deadline for a total of 398 rulemaking requirements. Of these, 162 (40.7 percent) have been met with finalized rules. Rules have not yet been proposed to meet 121 (30.4 percent) of the required rules. The reader can speculate as to whether the 40 percent of the rules that are finalized are the hardest 40 percent or the easiest 40 percent.

There are a number of reasons for the delay in implementing Dodd–Frank. One is that it attempts to create financial institutions and rules from scratch. The Securities and Exchange Commission (SEC), for example, is required to create five new offices. The Consumer Financial Protection Bureau (CFPB) hired over a thousand people in its first two years. But an organization with a thousand new employees and no experienced hands is an organization with no institutional memory, no precedents, and no established way of doing things. While it was hiring and training staff and establishing internal administrative procedures, the CFPB was conducting bank examinations and initiating enforcement actions. It is not surprising that it missed deadlines.

Even without the challenges of simultaneously creating an agency, it is difficult to write rules from scratch. Absent legislative action, financial practices and rules evolve over time. Things that do not work are discarded. When technology changes, financial practices change along with it. On the other hand, when regulators are trying, for example, to write rules for swap trading and clearing to meet the Dodd–Frank mandates, everything needs to be figured out in advance. That is hard to do. A thousand comment letters are no substitute for a month of experience.

A second reason that implementation is taking a long time is that it is difficult and in some cases almost impossible to write rules that do what Dodd–Frank requires. The original bill was 848 pages, and for every page of the bill, 16 pages of rules have been written—and the rulemaking is only 40 percent complete. The rules are much longer than the bill because they include needed definitions, clarifications, exceptions, and exemptions. If Dodd–Frank mandates were easy to put into practice, the rules would be shorter.

The Volcker Rule is a good example. In the Dodd–Frank Act, the rule was eleven pages long. In November 2011, four of the five agencies charged with writing the rule jointly put forth a 298-page proposal. The fifth agency followed with its own 489-page proposal in January 2012.

The Volcker Rule grew from an 11-page idea to a 298-page (or more) rule because it asks regulators to do something that is difficult in practice. The Volcker Rule prohibits banks from engaging in proprietary trading but permits bank holding companies to engage in market making and risk management and to execute trades for customers. In practice, it is difficult for regulators to differentiate between these activities. If a bank makes a market in a security, is it allowed to be more aggressive on the buy side when it is bullish on the security? Is that speculation or market making? Enforcing the Volcker Rule requires us to determine a bank's motives for trading, and that is difficult to do.

Consider the internal pay equity rule. It seems simple: calculate the ratio of the chief executive officer's compensation to the median employee's compensation. But what is to be included in compensation? How are employees of foreign subsidiaries to be treated? What about part-time employees or employees who worked only part of the year?

Another reason that the rulemaking is taking a long time is that it has global implications even though U.S. regulators do not have global authority. For example, non-U.S. firms may be required to register as major swap participants if they enter into enough swap contracts with "U.S. persons," so some foreign financial firms will try to avoid this designation by refusing to trade with U.S. firms. This may impede liquidity in the swaps market. Further complications arise in treatment of subsidiaries. For example, the Hong Kong subsidiary of Goldman Sachs would not be considered a U.S. person and could trade swaps freely in other countries.

A fourth reason for the long rule-writing period for Dodd–Frank is that more than a dozen regulatory agencies are involved in the rule-making. In many cases, their jurisdictions overlap, and in some cases they are jointly writing rules. These agencies include the SEC, Commodity Futures Trading Commission (CFTC), Federal Deposit Insurance Corporation (FDIC), and other familiar regulatory agencies but also include entities like Federal Energy Resources Commission and Department of Education that do not normally write rules for financial firms. As John Walsh observed, rulemaking is especially slow when agencies that seldom work together try to jointly produce rules.

Another factor that has delayed implementation is that in some cases, regulators had a lot to learn before they could write rules. For example, SEC staff had to learn about swaps and the swap market before they could effectively regulate them. To learn about swaps, they examined data on swap trading and met with industry participants and foreign regulators before writing rules.

Part of the learning process for regulators is soliciting and reading comment letters from the public on proposed rules. A notable example is, again, the Volcker Rule. In seeking comments on the Volcker Rule, regulators posed 750 questions to the public, and they received over 19,000 comment letters. Some of these letters were over 100 pages long.

There are complaints that in the long rulemaking process, financial institutions have succeeded in neutering much of Dodd–Frank. A large number of the comment letters to the SEC, CFTC, and other regulators have been written by financial institutions and trade organizations. Financial institutions will generally try to influence the regulations that will be applied to them, and for the most part, this can lead to better regulation. Institutions can point to unintended consequences of regulations and can suggest more efficient ways of meeting regulatory objectives. Nor is this lobbying of regulators one-sided. Some church groups, for example, have written comment letters requesting an early implementation and strict enforcement of the conflict minerals rule. Two grassroots organizations—Public Citizen and Americans for Financial Reform—were responsible for thousands of comment letters on the Volcker Rule.

Will Dodd–Frank Prevent Another Crisis?

With many rules yet to be written, we need to be cautious about the likely effects of Dodd–Frank. Even after the rules have been written, there will be court challenges. Congress may also seek to amend the law. On October 30, 2013, for example, the House of Representatives voted to roll back the swaps pushout rule. Finally, financial institutions and practices will evolve to circumvent Dodd–Frank regulations.

Nevertheless, at this point, it is appropriate to ask whether Dodd–Frank will accomplish its primary goals of preventing another financial crisis and creating a way to resolve troubled financial institutions without bailouts. The contributors to this book provide tentative answers to this question.

Dodd–Frank uses a many-pronged approach to accomplish its goal of preventing another financial crisis. The creation of the Financial Stability Oversight Council (FSOC), enhanced regulatory supervision, the Volcker Rule, new regulations for securitization of mortgages, more stringent consumer protection in mortgage lending, and central clearing of derivatives are some of the ways that Dodd–Frank tries to prevent another crisis. The good news is that contributors to this book agree that the financial system is on sounder footing than it was in 2008. Tom Hoenig, Anjan Thakor, and Larry White, among others, point out the dangers of the excessive leverage of financial institutions before the crisis. John Walsh and John Dearie note that capital and liquidity are now much greater than they were at the start of the 2008. Part of the credit for this goes to stress tests mandated by Dodd–Frank's section 165. Stricter regulatory enforcement and the realization by banks that they were overleveraged are also factors leading to higher capital levels.

The Financial Stability Oversight Council was created by Dodd–Frank to identify systemic risk and act to prevent future crises. The Office of Financial Research was created to assist the FSOC by providing data and research on risks to the financial system. It is not clear how effective the FSOC will be, however. Anjan Thakor observes that high leverage can create risk in subtle ways that may not show up in the data that the FSOC tracks. Jim Barth observes that the FSOC consists of the same regulatory agencies that were in charge before the financial crisis and failed to prevent it.

The Volcker Rule is intended to prevent financial institutions from taking too much risk and blundering into another crisis. But it cannot affect the likelihood of a financial crisis until regulators finalize the

Volcker Rule. Even if the rule proves to be well written, the contributors to this book disagree about whether it will be beneficial. Matt Richardson says that principal trading was a source of problems up to the crisis and that the Volcker Rule will play an important role in limiting risk. Priyank Gandhi, on the other hand, claims that principal or proprietary trading actually makes banks less risky. Charles Calomiris says that underwriting and market making are core activities of banks and that proprietary trading may be as well. In his view, we risk destroying U.S. global universal banking with this rule.

The failure of AIG in 2008 led to Dodd–Frank's mandating of centralized trading and clearing of swaps to reduce the likelihood of a crisis. Pat Fishe observes that centralized clearing will improve transparency in the swaps market, and that is likely to be a positive result for most participants. Bob McDonald notes that centralized clearing is likely to make it easier to "assess in advance the fallout from a failure." So the derivatives panel finds some clear benefits to Dodd–Frank's regulation of swaps. On the other hand, Craig Pirrong notes that relative to the over-the-counter market, clearinghouses operate on "metronomic time scale" and that the need to pay variation margin on this schedule can be destabilizing. Centralized clearing may also create new too-big-to-fail institutions in the clearinghouses. Amy Edwards observes, though, that the new clearinghouses will be required to be well capitalized.

Losses on mortgage-backed securities were behind the failures of a number of financial institutions in 2008, so it is to be expected that Dodd–Frank would try to reduce the risks from investing in these securities. One of the ways that Dodd–Frank does this is by requiring sponsors of mortgage-backed securities to have "skin in the game" by requiring them to retain 5 percent of the credit risk of the securities, subject to an exemption for qualified residential mortgages (QRMs). Cem Demiroglu and Chris James cite evidence that risk retention does provide incentives for mortgage originators to gather soft information—that is, information that cannot easily be verified or transmitted. It appears, though, that buyers of mortgage-backed securities (MBSs) were aware that securitization without risk retention reduced incentives to collect soft information and priced the MBSs accordingly. Mark Calabria cites General Accounting Office estimates of the effect of QRM rules on the number of foreclosures. He concludes that their effect on foreclosures is likely to be modest in another financial crisis.

Some observers believe that mortgage originators sold inappropriate mortgages to naïve homebuyers and that the subsequent defaults led to the 2008 financial crisis. The idea behind giving the Consumer

Financial Protection Bureau the power to regulate mortgages is to prevent another crisis by ensuring that homebuyers are not given mortgages that they are unable to repay. The idea that mortgage defaults occurred because naïve homebuyers were sold mortgages that they could not repay is rejected by Todd Zywicki. He believes that defaults occurred mainly because sophisticated homebuyers walked away from underwater mortgages. In his view, the CFPB will do nothing to prevent another financial crisis.

To summarize, the U.S. financial system is sounder and more stable than it was before the 2008 crisis. Enhanced supervision of systemically important financial institutions (SIFIs) and higher capital levels deserve much of the credit for this increase in safety. The Volcker Rule, regulations on securitization, and mandated clearing of derivatives are also attempts to reduce the likelihood of another financial crisis. Contributors are less convinced that these other provisions of Dodd–Frank will do much to strengthen the U.S. financial system.

Will Dodd–Frank Make It Easier to Resolve Failed Institutions?

An important part of the supervision of banks and other SIFIs is market supervision. Creditors of financial institutions monitor those institutions and withdraw funding or charge higher interest rates in response to higher levels of risk and leverage. Creditors' incentives to monitor financial institutions disappear if they expect failing institutions to be bailed out—which was the de facto U.S. policy from the bailout of Continental Illinois in 1984 until Lehman Brothers was allowed to fail in 2008. If Dodd–Frank provides a quick and orderly way to resolve troubled SIFIs, it will eliminate bailouts and end too big to fail. This is important in part because it restores incentives for creditors to monitor financial institutions.

Has Dodd–Frank succeeded in eliminating bailouts? Contributors to this book are skeptical. Larry White says that we will not know whether the large financial institutions in the United States are too big to fail until the next crisis. John Walsh believes that regulators will close the next failing bank but is not sure what will happen if there is a crisis and several institutions are in trouble. David Skeel also asks whether regulators "will ever pull this trigger" or whether they will just bail out SIFIs in another crisis. He suspects that if more than one institution is in trouble, they will be bailed out.

The participants in the conference generally agree on one point: we do not know what will happen the next time that a SIFI gets into trouble. The temptation to bail out one of these institutions is always present. If a number of SIFIs are in financial distress at the same time, the temptation to bail out failing financial institutions may be overwhelming.

There is a great deal of uncertainty about how Dodd–Frank will work in practice. Most of the rules have yet to be written. We do not know how financial markets and institutions will react to Dodd–Frank, and history suggests that financial institutions will find ways to evade parts of a law that they find onerous. We will be debating Dodd–Frank for a long time.

References

DavisPolk. 2013. Dodd–Frank Progress Report. Client Newsletter. November. http://www.davispolk.com.

U.S. Government Accountability Office. 2013. Financial Regulatory Reform: Regulators Have Faced Challenges Finalizing Key Reforms and Unaddressed Areas Pose Potential Risks.

About the Authors

James R. Barth is the Lowder Eminent Scholar in Finance at Auburn University and a senior finance fellow at the Milken Institute. His research has focused on financial institutions and capital markets, both domestic and global, with an emphasis on regulatory issues. Recently, he served as leader of an international team advising the People's Bank of China on banking reform.

Barth was an appointee of Presidents Ronald Reagan and George H. W. Bush as chief economist of the Office of Thrift Supervision until November 1989 and previously served as the chief economist of the Federal Home Loan Bank Board. He has also held the positions of professor of economics at George Washington University, associate director of the economics program at the National Science Foundation, and Shaw Foundation Professor of Banking and Finance at Nanyang Technological University. He has been a visiting scholar at the U.S. Congressional Budget Office, Federal Reserve Bank of Atlanta, Office of the Comptroller of the Currency, and World Bank. He was a member of the Advisory Council of George Washington University's Financial Services Research Program.

Barth's expertise in financial institution and capital market issues has led him to testify before the U.S. House and Senate banking committees on several occasions. He has authored more than two hundred articles in professional journals and has written and edited several books, including *The Great Savings and Loan Debacle* and *The Reform of Federal Deposit Insurance*. His most recent books are *Rethinking Bank Regulation: Till Angels Govern* (with Gerard Caprio Jr. and Ross Levine) and *Financial Restructuring and Reform in Post-WTO China* (with Zhong-fei Zhou, Douglas W. Arner, Berry F. C. Hsu, and Wei Wang).

Jeff Bloch is the associate general counsel of the Consumer Bankers Association. Bloch specializes in consumer and fair lending, various payments issues, issues with regard to government-sponsored enterprises, and deposit insurance. His background includes positions with the Federal Home Loan Bank Board, Federal Deposit Insurance Corporation, and Credit Union National Association. A graduate of Boston University and Duke University School of Law, Bloch is a member of the District of Columbia, Maryland, and the American Bar Associations.

Mark A. Calabria, Ph.D., is director of financial regulation studies at the Cato Institute. Before joining Cato in 2009, Dr. Calabria spent seven years as a member of the senior professional staff of the U.S. Senate Committee on Banking, Housing, and Urban Affairs. In that position, he handled issues related to monetary policy, housing, mortgage finance, economics, banking and insurance. During his service on Capitol Hill, Calabria drafted significant portions of the Housing and Economic Recovery Act of 2008, which established a new regulatory regime for the government sponsored enterprises (Fannie Mae and Freddie Mac). Prior to his service on Capitol Hill, Calabria served as deputy assistant secretary for regulatory affairs at the U.S. Department of Housing and Urban Development, where he oversaw HUD's enforcement of the Real Estate Settlement Procedures Act. Calabria has also held a variety of positions at Harvard University's Joint Center for Housing Studies, the National Association of Home Builders and the National Association of Realtors. Calabria has been a Research Associate with the U.S. Census Bureau's Center for Economic Studies. He holds a doctorate in economics from George Mason University

Charles W. Calomiris is Henry Kaufman Professor of Financial Institutions at Columbia Business School, a professor at Columbia's School of International and Public Affairs, and a research associate of the National Bureau of Economic Research. He has been a member of the Shadow Financial Regulatory Committee, Shadow Open Market Committee, Financial Economists Roundtable, and Task Force on Property Rights at the Hoover Institution. He has held other positions at the Council on Foreign Relations, American Enterprise Institute, and Pew Trusts. He also served on the International Financial Institution Advisory Commission, a U.S. congressional commission that advised the U.S. government on the reform of multilateral institutions in 1999 and 2000. In 2011, he was the Houblon-Norman Senior Fellow at the Bank of England. Calomiris received a B.A. in economics from Yale University in 1979 and a Ph.D. in economics from Stanford University in 1985. His research and teaching span the areas of banking, corporate finance, financial history, and monetary economics. He is the member of numerous editorial boards, has authored many books and scholarly articles, and is the recipient of research grants from the National Science Foundation and others.

Shane Corwin is an associate professor in the department of finance at the University of Notre Dame Mendoza College of Business. He received a Ph.D. in finance from The Ohio State University. Corwin's research focuses on security market design and investment banking. He has published articles in numerous finance journals, including the *Journal of Finance*, the *Journal of Financial Markets*, the *Journal of Financial Intermediation*, and *Financial Management*. In recent articles, he has studied the role of limited attention in securities trading, the measurement of transaction costs, and the effects of systematic liquidity in financial markets. Corwin has also served as a member of the NASDAQ Economic Advisory Board and has been awarded research grants from the Notre Dame Deloitte Center for Ethical Leadership, Morgan Stanley, and the Q Group.

Cem Demirgolu is an assistant professor of finance at Koç University in Turkey. He received his Ph.D. in finance from the University of Florida in 2008. He has published numerous papers in the *Journal of Financial Economics*, *Review of Financial Studies*, *Journal of Banking and Finance*, and *Journal of Money Credit and Banking*.

John Dearie is executive vice president for policy at the Financial Services Forum, which he joined in January 2001. The Financial Services Forum is an economic policy organization comprising the chief executive officers of eighteen of the largest and most diversified financial institutions with business operations in the United States.

Dearie spent nine years at the Federal Reserve Bank of New York, the central bank of the United States, where he held positions in the Banking Studies, Foreign Exchange, and Policy and Analysis areas. He was appointed an officer of the Bank in 1996. In addition to his regular duties, Dearie also served as a speechwriter for New York Federal Reserve presidents E. Gerald Corrigan and William J. McDonough.

Dearie was educated at the University of Notre Dame and Columbia University's School of International and Public Affairs. He is the author of two novels and is coauthor of "Where the Jobs Are: Entrepreneurship and the Soul of the American Economy," released in September of 2013.

Amy K. Edwards is assistant director of the Office of Markets of the Division of Economic and Risk Analysis (formerly the Division of Risk, Strategy, and Financial Innovation) at the Securities and Exchange Commission, which she joined June 1997. She earned her Ph.D. in finance from The Ohio State University. Edwards provides economic advice and conducts empirical studies of current SEC policy and recent market events. She is primarily interested in the area of market microstructure and has conducted research on issues related to decimalization, fragmentation, short sale rules, limit order display, specialist participation, and transparency. She has published articles in the *Journal of Finance*, the *Journal of Financial Economics*, *Financial Management*, and the *Journal of Financial Markets*. Her research results have been discussed in the *Wall Street Journal*, the *Financial Times*, and *The Economist*.

Raymond P. H. Fishe has been a consultant with the Commodity Futures Trading Commission since 2009. He holds the Patricia A. and George W. Wellde, Jr. Distinguished Chair in Finance at the University of Richmond. Prior to consulting for the CFTC, he was a visiting academic scholar at the Securities and Exchange Commission. He provides economic advice on the SEC's rulemaking, supports enforcement investigations, and conducts quantitative analysis on the structure of derivatives markets and the strategic behavior of market participants. He has written extensively in the area of futures, options, and market microstructure, especially in economics journals such as the *Journal of Finance*, the *Journal of Financial Economics*, the *Journal of Financial Markets*, the *American Economic Review*, the *Journal of Econometrics*, and *Financial Management*. He received a Ph.D. in economics from the University of Florida in 1979.

Priyank Gandhi is currently an assistant professor at the University of Notre Dame's Mendoza College of Business. From 2001 to 2004, Priyank was a manager at the Hong Kong and Shanghai Banking Corporation (HSBC) in India. He has also been a consultant to investment banks and real estate firms. His current research interests include financial intermediaries, credit risk, computational finance, liquidity and its effects on asset prices, and contagion risk. His most recent research explores the impact of implicit government guarantees to large U.S. financial institutions on their equity returns. His research has been presented in seminars at University of Chicago, NYU, Harvard, Emory University, Ohio State University, University of Rochester, and other leading schools. Priyank's research has appeared in leading academic journals including the Journal of Financial Economics. His work has been quoted in the *Wall Street Journal* and Germany's leading newspaper, *Handelsblatt*.

Thomas M. Hoenig is the vice chair of the Federal Deposit Insurance Corporation, receiving confirmation from the Senate on November 15, 2012. He joined the agency on April 16, 2012, as a member of the FDIC board of directors for a six-year term. Prior to serving on the FDIC board, Hoenig was the president of the Federal Reserve Bank of Kansas City and a member of the Federal Reserve System's Federal Open Market Committee from 1991 to 2011. Hoenig was with the Federal Reserve for thirty-eight years, beginning as an economist and then as a senior officer in banking supervision during the U.S. banking crisis of the 1980s. In 1986, he led the Kansas City Federal Reserve Bank's Division of Bank Supervision and Structure, directing the oversight of more than a thousand banks and bank holding companies with assets ranging from less than $100 million to $20 billion. He became president of the Kansas City Federal Reserve Bank on October 1, 1991. A native of Fort Madison, Iowa, Hoenig received a doctorate in economics from Iowa State University.

Christopher M. James is the William H. Dial/SunBank Eminent Scholar in Finance and Economics at the University of Florida. James is also a senior adviser to Cornerstone Research. Prior to joining the faculty at the University of Florida, he taught at the University of Michigan and the University of Oregon. He received a Ph.D. in economics from the University of Michigan in 1978 and an M.B.A. in finance from the University of Michigan in 1977. His research has been published extensively in academic and professional journals in the areas of banking, corporate finance, and applied econometrics. He has served as an editor or associate editor of several journals, including the *Journal of Finance, Journal of Financial Economics, Journal of Financial Intermediation, Journal of Banking and Finance, Journal of Financial and Quantitative Analysis*, and *Journal of Financial Services Research*. James's current research focuses on the role played by financial intermediaries in the corporate capital acquisition process and on the valuation of mortgage-backed securities.

Anil K Kashyap is the Edward Eagle Brown Professor of Economics and Finance and Richard N. Rosett Faculty Fellow at the University of Chicago Booth School of Business. He is one of the faculty directors of the Chicago Booth Initiative on Global Markets. He has authored and edited five books and over forty scholarly articles on banking, business cycles, the Japanese economy, and monetary policy.

Kashyap currently works as a consultant for the Federal Reserve Bank of Chicago, serves as a member of the Economic Advisory Panel of the Federal Reserve Bank of New York, and is a research associate for the National Bureau of Economic Research. He is an international adviser to the Economic and Social Research Institute of the Cabinet Office of the Japanese government, is on the Congressional Budget Office's Panel of Economic Advisers, and serves on the board of directors of the Bank of Italy's Einuadi Institute of Economics and Finance. He is a member of the Squam Lake Group, the Bellagio Group of academics and economic officials, and the International Monetary Fund's Advisory Group on the development of a macroprudential policy framework.

Robert McDonald is Erwin P. Nemmers Professor of Finance at Northwestern University's Kellogg School of Management. He received a B.A. in economics from the University of North Carolina and a Ph.D. in economics from the Massachusetts Institute of Technology. A faculty member since 1984, he has also served as department chair. He has taught courses in derivatives, corporate finance, and taxation. His research interests include corporate finance, taxation, derivatives, and applications of option pricing theory to corporate investments. In 2010, he was elected a director of the American Finance Association.

James Overdahl is currently a partner at Delta Strategy Group. Prior to joining Delta, he was a vice president of NERA in its Securities and Finance Practice. He previously served as a chief economist for the Securities and Exchange Commission, chief economist for the Commodity Futures Trading Commission, and a senior financial economist for the Risk Analysis Division of the Office of the Comptroller of the Currency and has taught as an adjunct professor of finance at George Washington University, the University of Maryland, Johns Hopkins University, Georgetown University, Virginia Tech, and George Mason University. He also served as assistant professor of finance at the University of Texas at Dallas School of Management. He has a Ph.D. in economics from Iowa State University.

Craig Pirrong is a professor of finance and the energy markets director for Global Energy Management Institute at the Bauer College of Business at the University of Houston. Pirrong previously was the Watson Family Professor of Commodity and Financial Risk Management and associate professor of finance at Oklahoma State University. He has also served on the faculty of the University of Michigan Business School, Graduate School of Business of the University of Chicago, and Olin School of Business of Washington University in St. Louis. He holds a Ph.D. in business economics from the University of Chicago.

Pirrong's research focuses on the economics of commodity markets, the relation between market fundamentals and commodity price dynamics, and the implications of this relation for the pricing of commodity derivatives. His recent research is concentrated on the power markets. He has created a power derivatives pricing model that links observable fundamentals (such as temperature and loads) to power derivatives prices. Pirrong also has published extensively on the economics of financial exchanges. He has published thirty articles in professional publications and is the author of three books. Pirrong has consulted widely, and his clients have included electric utilities, major commodity processors and consumers, and commodity exchanges around the world.

Matthew Richardson is the Charles E. Simon Professor of Applied Economics in the finance department at the Leonard N. Stern School of Business at New York University. He currently holds the position of the Sidney Homer Director of the Salomon Center for the Study of Financial Institutions, which is a leading financial research center. Prior to being at NYU, Richardson was an assistant professor of finance at the Wharton School of the University of Pennsylvania. In addition, he is a research associate of the National Bureau of Economic Research.

Richardson has done research in many areas of finance, including both theoretical and empirical work. His research has been published in the *American Economic Review, Journal of Finance, Review of Financial Studies*, and *Journal of Financial Economics*, among other places. He was an associate editor of the *Journal of Finance, Review of Financial Studies*, and *Journal of Financial and Quantitative Analysis*. He recently coedited two books on the financial crisis—*Restoring Stability: How to Repair a Failed System* and *Regulating Wall Street: The Dodd-Frank Act and the New Architecture of Global Finance*—and is a coauthor of *Guaranteed to Fail: Fannie Mae, Freddie Mac and the Debacle of Mortgage Finance*.

Paul H. Schultz is the John W. and Maude Clark Professor of Finance at the University of Notre Dame and the director of the Center for the Study of Financial Regulation. He received his B.A. from Macalester College and his M.B.A. and Ph.D. in finance and economics from the

University of Chicago. He has published numerous papers in leading finance journals. Schultz's paper "Options and the Bubble" (coauthored with Robert H. Battalio) was named as one of eight finalists for the 2006 Smith Breeden Award, given by the *Journal of Finance*. He had previously won the Smith Breeden Award for his paper "Why Do NASDAQ Market Makers Avoid Odd-Eighth Quotes?" (coauthored with William G. Christie). He is currently an associate editor of the *Journal of Financial and Quantitative Analysis* and an advisory editor of the *Financial Review*. He has served as an associate editor of the *Journal of Finance*.

David Skeel is the S. Samuel Arsht Professor at the University of Pennsylvania Law School. He is the author of *The New Financial Deal: Understanding the Dodd-Frank Act and Its (Unintended) Consequences, Icarus in the Boardroom*, and *Debt's Dominion: A History of Bankruptcy Law in America*, as well as numerous articles and other publications. He has been interviewed on *The News Hour, Nightline, Chris Matthews' Hardball, National Public Radio*, and *Marketplace*, among other programs, and has been quoted in the *New York Times, Wall Street Journal, Washington Post*, and other newspapers and magazines. Skeel has received the Harvey Levin award three times for outstanding teaching as selected by a vote of the graduating class, the Robert A. Gorman award for excellence in upper-level course teaching, and the university's Lindback Award for distinguished teaching. In addition to bankruptcy and corporate law, Skeel also writes on sovereign debt, Christianity and law, and poetry and the law and is an elder at Tenth Presbyterian Church in Philadelphia.

Chester Spatt, PhD, is the Pamela R. and Kenneth B. Dunn Professor of Finance at the Tepper School of Business at Carnegie Mellon University, where he has taught since 1979. He served as Chief Economist of the U.S. Securities and Exchange Commission and Director of its Office of Economic Analysis from July 2004 through July 2007.

Professor Spatt is a well-known scholar in the field of financial economics, with broad interests in financial markets. He has analyzed extensively market structure, pricing and valuation, and the impact of information in the marketplace. For example, he has been a leading expert on the design of security markets in various settings, mortgage valuation, financial regulation and taxation and investment strategy. Professor Spatt's coauthored 2004 paper in the *Journal of Finance* on optimal asset location and allocation won TIAA-CREF's Paul Samuelson Award for the Best Publication on Lifelong Financial Security.

Professor Spatt has served as executive editor and one of the founding editors of the *Review of Financial Studies*; president and a member of the Founding Committee of the Society for Financial Studies; president of the Western Finance Association; treasurer of the Foundation for the Advancement of Research in Financial Economics; and is currently an associate editor of several finance journals. He also is currently a research associate of the National Bureau of Economic Research; senior economic adviser to Kalorama Partners; a member of the Federal Reserve's Model Validation Council, the Systemic Risk Council, the Shadow Financial Regulatory Committee as well as the Financial Economists Roundtable; and a fellow of the TIAA-CREF Institute.

Professor Spatt earned his Ph.D. in Economics from the University of Pennsylvania and received his undergraduate degree from Princeton University.

Anjan Thakor is the John E. Simon Professor of Finance, Director of Doctoral programs, and Director of the WFA Center for Finance and Accounting at the Olin Business School at Washington University. Prior to joining the Olin Business School, Thakor was the Edward J. Frey Professor of Banking and Finance at the Ross School of Business, University of Michigan, where he also served as chair of the finance area. He has served on the faculties of Indiana University, Northwestern University, and the University of California at Los Angeles. He has worked with many companies, including Allision Engine Co., Anheuser-Busch, AT&T, Borg-Warner Automotive, Bunge, CH2M Hill, CIGNA, Citigroup, Dana Corporation, RR Donnelley, Landscape Structures, Inc., The Limited, Lincoln National Corporation, JPMorgan Chase, Reuters, Ryder Integrated Logistics, Spartech, Takata Corporation, Tyson Foods, Waxman Industries, Whirlpool Corporation, and Zenith Corporation. He also has served as an expert witness in many federal cases involving banking litigation.

John Walsh leads the Financial Regulation Practice at McKinsey and Company. Prior to joining McKinsey, he was appointed acting comptroller of the currency by Treasury Secretary Timothy Geithner and served in that capacity from 2010 to 2012. In this position, he served as director of the Federal Deposit Insurance Corporation and chief executive of the Office of Comptroller of the Currency, overseeing about two-thirds of commercial banking assets in the United States. He also served as chief of staff to the previous comptroller from 2005 to 2010. Walsh served as an international economist for the U.S. Department of the Treasury from 1984 to 1986 and on the Senate Banking Committee from 1986 to 1992. In 1992, he joined the international economic think tank the Group of Thirty and became its executive director in 1995.

Lawrence J. White has been with New York University Leonard N. Stern School of Business for more than thirty-five years. His primary research areas of interest include financial regulation, antitrust, network industries, international banking, and applied microeconomics. White has published numerous articles in the *Journal of Business, Journal of Economic Perspectives, Journal of Economic Literature, Journal of Political Economy, American Economic Review, Review of Economics and Statistics, Quarterly Journal of Economics,* and other leading journals in economics, finance, and law. He is the author of *The S&L Debacle: Public Policy Lessons for Bank and Thrift Regulation,* among other books, and he is the coeditor (with John E. Kwoka Jr.) of the sixth edition of *The Antitrust Revolution: Economics, Competition, and Policy.* He contributed chapters to both of the NYU Stern books on the financial crisis—*Restoring Financial Stability* and *Regulating Wall Street.* He is the coauthor (with Stern's Viral V. Acharya, Matthew Richardson, and Stijn Van Nieuwerburgh) of *Guaranteed to Fail: Fannie Mae, Freddie Mac, and the Debacle of Mortgage Finance.*

Arthur Wilmarth joined the faculty of the George Washington University Law School in 1986, following eleven years in private law practice. Prior to joining the Law School, he was a partner in the Washington, DC, office of Jones Day. Wilmarth is the author of more than thirty articles and book chapters in the fields of banking law and American constitutional history, and he is coauthor of a book on corporate law. In 2005, the American College of Consumer Financial Services Lawyers awarded him its prize for the best law review article published in the field of consumer financial services law during the previous year. Wilmarth has testified before committees of the U.S. Congress, the California legislature, and the District of Columbia Council on bank regulatory issues. In 2010, he was a consultant to the Financial Crisis Inquiry Commission, the body established by Congress to report on the causes of the financial crisis. In 2008 and 2009, he served as chair of the section on financial institutions and consumer financial services of the Association of American Law Schools, after serving as the section's chair-elect and annual program chair in 2007 and 2008. Wilmarth is a member of the editorial board of the *Journal of Banking Regulation.* He is also a member of the advisory board of the American Antitrust Institute.

Todd J. Zywicki is George Mason University Foundation Professor of Law at George Mason University School of Law, senior scholar of the Mercatus Center at George Mason University, and senior fellow at the F. A. Hayek Program for Advanced Study in Philosophy, Politics, and Economics. In 2009, Zywicki was the recipient of the Institute for Humane Studies 2009 Charles G. Koch Outstanding IHS Alum Award. In 2012, he was awarded the Society for the Development of Austrian Economics prize for best article in Austrian economics for his article "Hayekian Anarchism" (coauthored with Edward Peter Stringham). He has served as coeditor of the *Supreme Court Economic Review* since 2006. In 2003 and 2004, Zywicki served as the director of the Office of Policy Planning at the Federal Trade Commission. He teaches in the areas of bankruptcy, contracts, commercial law, business associations, law and economics, and public choice and the law. He has also taught at Vanderbilt University Law School, Georgetown University Law Center, Boston College Law School, and Mississippi College School of Law.

Index